A Geography
of Production

By the same author

FRONTIERS OF GEOGRAPHY

Oswald Hull is Head of the Department of Social Studies, J.F.S. Comprehensive School (formerly Jews' Free School), London

Oswald A Geography
Hull of Production

1968 London
Macmillan Melbourne Toronto
St Martin's Press New York

© *Oswald Hull 1968*

Published by
MACMILLAN & CO LTD
Little Essex Street London WC2
and also at Bombay Calcutta and Madras
Macmillan South Africa (Publishers) Pty Ltd Johannesburg
The Macmillan Company of Australia Pty Ltd Melbourne
The Macmillan Company of Canada Ltd Toronto
St Martin's Press Inc New York

Library of Congress catalog card no. 67-16866

Printed in Great Britain by
ROBERT MACLEHOSE AND CO LTD
The University Press, Glasgow

Contents

Contents

List of Plates

List of Figures

Preface

The purpose of this book is to examine, geographically, the elements of production. The approach is by way of: (i) food and raw-material output; (ii) the organization of production on the land, in mining, and in manufacturing; (iii) selected industries, including some of the more recent developments in fields such as electronics and chemicals; (iv) the varied economic scene, as represented by large regions: the United States, the Soviet Union, India, East and West Africa, and Brazil.

There are sections on planning and on government intervention and the author has sought to examine recent trends in production and organization. Major themes are the roles of energy and transport. In agriculture, emphasis is laid upon the impact of technology; in industry, on British problems and solutions, but against a background of competing and developing industrial Powers. The intention is to picture Britain's situation in the world economy — in a world of producers.

This book is directed to economic geography and Scholarship courses in Sixth Forms, to Colleges of Education and to business geography courses in Polytechnics and Technical Colleges.

O. H.

Statistics

The ton of 2,240 lb. is used throughout, except where otherwise stated.

Conversion Factors

1 long ton (2,240 lb.) = 1·106 metric tons.
1 short ton (2,000 lb.) = 0·907 metric ton.
1 acre   = 0·405 hectare.

Acknowledgements

I am greatly indebted to Norman Wallace, Esq., who gave much time to the reading of the whole of the manuscript and made many valuable criticisms and suggestions for improvement; also to Elaine Thwaites, for help with the compilation of chapter notes.

I have made use of a large number of official and other sources, including the Commodity Series and other publications of the Commonwealth Economic Committee, *Anuario de Pesca*, of Lima, Peru, *The Statesman's Year-Book* (Macmillan & Co. Ltd.), the *Statistical Abstract of the United States* and many publications of the United Nations, especially its *Monthly Bulletin of Statistics* and the F.A.O.'s *Monthly Bulletin of Agricultural Economics and Statistics*.

I have received help from a great number of official bodies, institutions and companies, including: the Agent-General for Ontario; the Automobile Association; the Bank of London and South America; and Barclays Bank; the British Non-Ferrous Metals Research Association; the Forestry Commission; the Gas Council; the High Commissioners for India, Kenya and Zambia; Metallgesellschaft Ltd. of Frankfurt-am-Main; the Ministry of Power; the National Farmers' Union; the U.S. Bureau of Mines; Cotton Board; Courtaulds Ltd.; International Wool Secretariat; Tennessee Valley Authority; National Coal Board and Jewish National Fund.

Permission to make use of copyright material has been given by the following: Alberta Society of Petroleum Geologists (*Oilfields of Alberta*) (Fig. 14.5); Associated Book Publishers Ltd. (*An Atlas of Soviet Affairs*) (Fig. 12.1); British Iron and Steel Federation (Figs. 7.4, 7.5, 7.6); British Petroleum Ltd. (Figs. 14.4, 14.14, 16.2); British Railways Board (Fig. 20.3); British Trawlers' Federation (Fig. 3.2); Clarendon Press, Oxford (*Oxford Regional Economic Atlas of the U.S.S.R. and Eastern Europe*) (Fig. 16.3); Crosfield (Joseph) Ltd. (Fig. 14.3); J. C. Crossley, Esq. (Fig. 19.2); *Financial Times* (21 July, 1966) (Fig. 1.4); Food and Agricultural Organization of the United Nations (*Monthly Bulletin of Agricultural Economics and*

Acknow-ledgements

Statistics and *Yearbook of Forest Products and Statistics*) (Figs. 1.5, 3.1); French Railways (Fig. 20.4); Gas Council (Fig. 14.15); Geographical Association (Fig. 18.4); Her Majesty's Stationery Office (*Traffic in Towns*) (Fig. 20.5); Iliffe Electrical Publications Ltd. (Fig. 14.12); Office Nationale de la Navigation, Paris (Fig. 20.1); Ontario Department of Mines (Fig. 8.4); Penguin Books, Ltd. (*The Geography of African Affairs*) (Fig. 18.3); George Philip & Son (Fig. 18.1); Postmaster General (Fig. 11.6); Prentice-Hall Inc. (*Soviet Power — Energy, Resources, Production and Potentials*) (p. 226); Progress Publishers, Moscow (Figs. 16.1, 16.4); Sampson Low Ltd. (*Jane's World Railways*) (pp. 233, 235, 236, 283); San Francisco Bay Area Rapid Transit District (Fig. 20.7); Scientific American Inc. (Figs. 1.1, 5.1, 5.2, 18.3); Shipbuilding Conference (Fig. 19.1); Society for Cultural Relations with the U.S.S.R. (Figs. 6.2, 16.5); Steel Company of Wales Ltd. (Fig. 7.3); *Sunday Times* (Fig. 14.13); *Times* (Figs. 11.2, 14.8, 14.9, 14.16); Unilever Ltd. (Fig. 2.3); Union Minière (Figs. 8.2, 8.3); U.S. National Academy of Sciences and National Research Council, Washington, D.C. (Publications No. 1000-D and 1000-E, *Energy Resources and Mineral Resources*, 1962, Hubbert and Frasché) (Figs. 14.1, 14.6, 14.7); John Wiley Inc. (*A Geography of the U.S.S.R.*) (p. 126); *World Crops* (Figs. 1.1, 18.2).

Introduction

The most primitive form of economic activity involves the collection of nature's wealth. Once, hunting and accumulation for personal use occupied all of man's time; today, the activities of most economic communities entail the processing and alteration of the original materials. There are exceptions, of greater or lesser importance: some items of food from forest and sea are received in the home unchanged from their natural environment. But even fish and fruit require preservation, and often they are changed from their primary state.

Production may involve the cultivation, with or without improvement, of the soil, or manufacture on a large or small scale, using few or many processes. It will certainly require the transport and assembly of a considerable variety of raw materials and commodities, demanding both industrial and supporting organizations. The results of modern industry are seen in vast and complicated exchanges between producers, as well as between producers and consumers.

Wealth is created by agriculture, whether it is pastoral or arable and whether the crop is for use or for sale. It is created also in the course of mining, just as in the course of all forms of manufacture.

Forms of production can be classified in a number of ways: agriculture lends itself to functional separation between hunter, pastoralist, and tiller of the soil; and economic activity can be divided, according to its motive, into subsistence and market operations. It is possible to make a division into communal and free enterprise, or into social and individual production.

The distinction that has often been made between primary, secondary, and tertiary activities suggests that the transformation involved in manufacture implies a higher secondary stage of production, and that the highest stage contains a considerable intensity of trade and other 'service' industries.

It is difficult to produce a convincing world division of production forms. A political map does not correspond with economic reality, since even inside a single country such as Italy for example, there

Introduction are opposing trends. But there do exist real differences of regional emphasis: between the United States, well established as the country of economic abundance, and the Soviet Union, only recently recruited to the ranks of the advanced economies; between the largely primary producers of the tropics and their industrial customers; between the comparatively affluent regions of temperate cereal production and the crisis-ridden lands of South-East Asia.

Surveying the world scene, one cannot but be struck by the enormous variety of the resources available to man and, perhaps, still more by the genius with which he has utilized them. But the uneven distribution of the world's wealth and the widening gap between rich and poor, between the affluent and the under-nourished, present ever more serious problems to national governments and international associations.

Food Production   Chapter 1

For most of the world's population, production means farming. The **POPULA-** overwhelming economic problem is to produce enough for them- **TION** selves and their families to consume until the next harvest — to find enough to eat. For many, the task is to survive.

The size of the world's population is not exactly known, but the United Nations' estimate for 1965 was 3,400 million, China and India together containing 35 per cent of the total. More important for the immediate future than the existing level of population is its rate of increase. This has been accelerating since the eighteenth century, and the curve of growth has become steeper. The result is that whereas, at the start of this century, the world was doubling its population about every eighty-five years, this now happens in only half that time. It seems that by the year 2000 the world's people will be increasing at 3 per cent per annum, as compared with the rate of 1·8 per cent today. Population would then be doubling every twenty-three years (Fig. 1.1). In Asia, at the present time, the rate of annual increase is 1·8 per cent.[1] In southern Asia, including India, Pakistan, and Indonesia, the annual rate of increase for 1960–63 was 2·4 per cent.[2]

The rate of growth in some of the poorer countries is shown in the figures given by Kingsley Davis for the natural increase (excess of births over deaths) per thousand population. During the period 1950–60, the average figure for Costa Rica was 37·3, for Mexico 31·8, and for Taiwan (Formosa) 31·4.[3] The corresponding increase for Britain a century ago was less than half of Taiwan's figure now.

There is little doubt that population growth will continue to accelerate. The 'natural' enemies of growth — famine and disease — are now, in fact, treated as unnatural. They are combated with every resource by governments that daily become more powerful and there are now very few people who would really tolerate epidemics for the control they exercise on population. The historical background to the present situation is well summarized in the *Oxford Economic Atlas of the World*.

Food Production

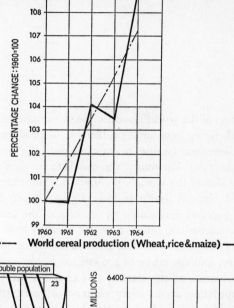

World population — · — World cereal production (Wheat, rice & maize) ———

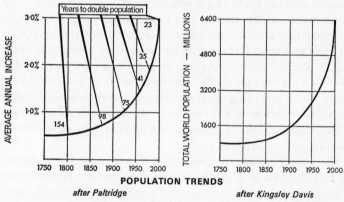

POPULATION TRENDS

after Paltridge   after Kingsley Davis

FIG. 1.1 Population growth and food production

The world's population growth continues to accelerate at an alarming rate and opinions vary as to our ability to feed the additional numbers, but there is a large measure of agreement between the views of Paltridge and Kingsley Davis.

There exists, in the hands of governments, a remedy for this pressure of population upon resources: this lies in the official propagation of and support for measures of family limitation. But it is far from certain that such remedies as exist will be pushed sufficiently hard to have a significant effect upon the population during this

2

century. The inconclusive debates inside China as to the desirability of population control, and the methods that might be acceptable, have been well outlined by H. Yuan Tien. China's growth rate of about 2·5 per cent has pushed her population up to 'some 740 million'.[5]

Population

Figures for national diets conflict, but most of them demonstrate that the best-fed nations (Amos puts New Zealand above the U.S.A. and England)[6] are nearly twice as well nourished as the worst-fed. Some authorities have disputed the actual figures of the millions threatened by starvation; but the seriousness of a situation can hardly be disputed where, over wide areas, population growth is exceeding the development of resources. The crisis period cannot be far off in some areas. When this occurs, massive crash-programmes of aid will be needed from the more affluent nations.

FOOD SUPPLY National Diets

Meanwhile, population increases fast and governments strive, often energetically, sometimes desperately, to stave off disaster. Some countries would be in a far more serious condition today were it not for the efforts of the United Nations Special Agencies. Many people have deplored the lack of purposeful government support for deliberate family planning; but the reservations felt by those in authority in the poorer countries are partly attributable to religious objections.

National and International Efforts

The international campaigns led by public and private bodies to succour the needy cover only a fraction of the real problem. The solution to the dire needs of these people lies largely in the hands of their rulers and the educated minorities staffing their administration and professions. The acquisition of an incorruptible Civil Service would be worth a great deal. The ultimate test will lie in the ability of each separate State to meet the challenge of hunger within its own confines.

An appraisal of world resources shows that about 65 per cent of the farming population of the world is to be found in the Far East. It is in Asia that there occur the main problems of relating production to population. Some assessments, while stressing the seriousness of the present and potential situations, insist that adequate solutions are possible, whereby food production 'could even easily outstrip population growth'.[7]

3

Food Production

The world's food output is achieved under a variety of production systems. In Britain and the 'advanced' regions — these include North America and Australasia, Western Europe, the Soviet Union, and the temperate grasslands of South America and South Africa — farm activity is generally characterized by its direction towards the wholesale market. One standard of comparison of farming systems lies in the amounts of capital and labour required, per unit of area. The steppes and prairies, and the pampas of Argentina and the wheatlands of Australia illustrate 'extensive' types of land exploitation, where farm workers may be few but the degree of mechanization high. Production on a Soviet collective, as well as on a South Dakota farm, is very largely dependent upon the availability of tractor spares and fuel. In Western Europe, on the other hand, the nature of farms and the extent of mechanization may vary greatly, even inside a single country. An example is France, where animal power is still normal in the south, but the tractor is supreme in the northern part of the Paris Basin. In Italy nearly half of all farms are of less than 25 acres. But on a world scale, there is a contrast between the sophisticated farm scenes of our civilization — the 'European cultural heritage', as Thoman calls it — and the intensive methods of the tropics; and there is a vital difference between the production/population ratios of the two systems.

Production in the crucial tropical and subtropical areas of South-East Asia is marked by intensity of human effort — by the enormous amounts of labour-power that are devoted to maintaining yields. Population pressure on the tiny plots is ever-increasing. The actual farm organization varies in detail of course. In China a very determined effort has been made to outshine the Russian Soviets in Communist achievements. The size of the commune is huge, but it is based upon exact applications of human muscle-power to a fraction of the total land surface. The primary purpose of this toil, in a rice-growing environment, is the attainment of subsistence conditions. In such 'intensive-subsistence' regions (Thoman), accounting for nearly a third of the world's total cultivated area, production is normally for local use. Contrast this with the position of the grain-grower in the temperate wheatlands, where the market may lie across a continent and an ocean.

In much of central Africa and the outlying islands of Indonesia, where population densities are moderately high, as well as in the interior selvas of South America, where densities are low, production is organized on a more primitive, hand-to-mouth basis, with a less concentrated application of effort.

Subsistence farming in these regions may include shifting agriculture — slash-and-burn methods — wasteful of land of limited resources, but producing crops similar to those of intensive-subsistence farming.

Ample natural resources are squandered by the practice of a 'robber economy', which takes out but does not replace or provide for the future. Some regions are a prey to shifting cultivation; in the Philippines, this has been responsible, under what is known locally as the *kaingin* system, for the spoliation of the native forest and its replacement by scrub. Grasslands, often man-made, occupy $17\frac{1}{2}$ per cent of the land area of the islands, but cultivated land only $12\frac{1}{2}$ per cent.[8] On the grasslands, soil erosion and destruction by flood proceed, in conditions where a policy of conservation could have enriched the hardwood forest wealth.

For food production to prosper and increase, minimum physical requirements for plant growth must be met. In particular, water supply must be adequate and the choice of crop needs to be related to the chemical conditions present in the soil. But the desperate position with regard to soil science in many parts of the unindustrialized world is illustrated by the following, from Iran: 'Unfortunately, we the agriculturalists of this region, have no information whatsoever about the conditions of the soil of our fields, and no soil laboratory exists here. Therefore we do not know what types of chemical fertilizers are needed for our soil . . . it is quite possible that the fertilizers we are using may have the effects opposite to those intended.'[9]

Wheat is well ahead of maize and rice as a world cereal, but rice is the chief cereal in areas critical to the world's population problem. The world's leading rice-producers are all to be found in Asia (Fig. 1.2). India, in a good year, produces a third of all the rice grown outside China. In 1962–63 the Indian harvest was disappointing, owing to bad weather, but production was still 30 per cent of all the non-Chinese output. Production in Japan, the second-largest non-Communist grower, has steadily increased, and is now greater than that of Pakistan, although there are now more Pakistani than Japanese mouths to feed.

Thailand and Burma still lead in world exports of rice, as they have done for many years. Burma no longer has the position that

Food Production

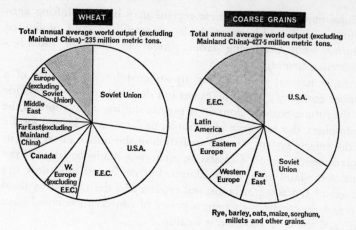

WHEAT

Total annual average world output (excluding Mainland China)-235 million metric tons.

E. Europe (excluding Soviet Union)
Middle East
Far East (excluding Mainland China)
Canada
W. Europe (excluding E.E.C.)
E.E.C.
U.S.A.
Soviet Union

COARSE GRAINS

Total annual average world output (excluding Mainland China)-427·5 million metric tons.

E.E.C.
Latin America
Eastern Europe
Western Europe
Far East
Soviet Union
U.S.A.

Rye, barley, oats, maize, sorghum, millets and other grains.

4-year average : 1962/63 to1965/66

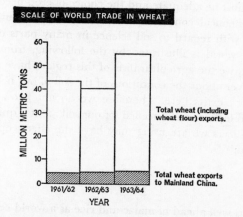

SCALE OF WORLD TRADE IN WHEAT

MILLION METRIC TONS

Total wheat (including wheat flour) exports.

Total wheat exports to Mainland China.

1961/62   1962/63   1963/64

YEAR

FIG. 1.2   Food grains — world production

The production situation shows the commanding lead of the Soviet Union in wheat, and of the United States in coarse grains. The world trade in wheat includes significant exports to China.

she held in the pre-war years: in 1937–39 the Burmese provided 39 per cent of total world exports; in 1964, barely 20 per cent. Since before the war, world output of rice has increased by 50 per cent — by more than this, if one includes China — but international trade in rice has decreased. One notable feature of very recent years has been the emergence of the United States as the third-largest exporter in the world after Thailand (first in 1964) and Burma (first in 1963).

In the case of the largest producer of all, mainland China, there have often been statistical difficulties. Hemy produced a notable compilation of Communist Chinese statistics and of leading opinions on them; the conflicting figures for 1952 that he instanced were:

		(*'ooo tons*)
1.	Communist Chinese source . .	67,000
2.	W. Rostow	55,000
3.	F.A.O.	47,000

but he expressed the view that Peking figures of production over the period 1952–55 were 'broadly true'.[10]

Since that date, the Commonwealth Economic Committee[11] has issued figures indicating a peak in Chinese production in the season 1958–59, after which a considerable setback is estimated to have resulted in a 1963–64 output of 51,000 tons; but Peking's Ministry of Agriculture has claimed a production figure more than 50 per cent higher than this.

Wheat is a sufficiently hardy crop to be introduced into the fringes of marginal regions. The areas of wheat cultivation have advanced in Canada, in Australia, and in northern Europe. Elsewhere, diminishing areas of production can furnish increasing yields.

TEMPERATE CEREAL PRODUCTION
Wheat

The United States has one of the biggest latitudinal ranges of wheat cultivation. The harvest commences in Texas and continues north to the Spring Wheat Belt in the Dakotas. Over large areas, wheat and maize are grown alongside each other: this is done in Missouri, in eastern Kansas, and in southern Illinois. Hardy winter wheat is grown in most of Kansas, in western Oklahoma, and in northern Texas. Wheat farming used to be the dominant activity of Kansas, though in the east it gave way to maize. Today there are new industries in Wichita, just as there are in Kansas City (Missouri) and in Omaha. The rainfall has not altered; in the western part of the Great Plains there is no more than 15 inches on the average, and droughts may occur lasting effectually for years. In the wheatlands, more than anywhere else, farms may be 1,500 acres in extent. A smaller acreage may permit only relative poverty. Yields have risen, so that a much smaller farm population is able to exceed by far the production of pre-war years. Put another way, fewer farms are required to feed a larger urban population. It has been said that 'one American farmer can now support 24 people whereas a dozen years ago, he could only support 15'.[12] It has even been suggested that, in order to produce really efficient agriculture, the farm community should be reduced by another 2 million.[13] There has been a considerable variation from year to year in American wheat production.

Over-cropping of land has on many occasions, and in many areas, produced a crisis in agriculture. In most areas crop rotation is important in rejuvenating and conserving soil nutrients in cereal areas. It is possible, in dust-bowl conditions, for land to revert to waste or to poor ranching country.

Even under the best climatic conditions, wheat yields have been less in the Soviet Union than in the U.S.A., and they have been less in the U.S.A. — though here the margin is smaller — than in Western Europe generally. Average British yields are more than twice those of North America. The biggest concentrations of British wheat are in the Fenlands and north-east of London.

Climatic conditions can produce great variations in wheat output. The abnormal conditions of 1961–62 in the Canadian Middle West halved the wheat yield as compared with 1960–61. By 1964, Canadian production had fully recovered, enabling massive exports to be made to the Soviet Union.

Maize

The necessary conditions of moderate-to-high rainfall and high summer temperatures are found over wide areas of the world. Generally speaking, they prevail on the equatorial side of the Wheat Belts. The climatic control over cereal distribution brings about a concentration on maize in a wide belt stretching across the Middle West of the United States, embracing much of the states of Iowa, Illinois, Indiana, and Ohio.

The world distribution of maize depends upon the type of local demand as well as upon the possibilities of trade. Maize is a subsistence crop over large areas of Africa: in Kenya, before independence, it was overwhelmingly the most important food crop in African areas.

There is a tremendous production in the United States for local and regional consumption. Here maize is not made into bread or used directly in cooking as it is by the Negro in Africa, but is used primarily as animal and especially cattle feed. The result is that the producers in Illinois and Iowa provide a base for the meat-packing plants of Chicago. The Ohio farmer supports the factories of Cincinnati; the Missouri farmer those of St. Louis.

The climatic conditions of the American Middle West are paralleled in eastern Argentina and in Uruguay. Maize production there supports the plants on either side of the Plate estuary. In contrast to the U.S.A., the region provides a big export of coarse grains to Western Europe.

The promotion of agriculture under Khruschev was marked by a notable increase in the acreage sown with maize. Before the Second World War, the Soviet Union had only about the same maize acreage as Argentina, and little more than that of Roumania. By 1962–63 Soviet maize acreage was five times that of Argentina, with a similar margin in output.

Barley

Barley is a profitable crop over a very wide range of regions — Norfolk, the Nile Valley, Algeria, and some of the most northerly cereal areas of Scandinavia, as well as Finland, Japan, and Ethiopia. Most of the barley grown in Europe and North America goes to feed livestock, with an important secondary use for malting and brewing beer. In Japan and other Asiatic countries, the chief use of barley is as a food grain. In recent years the production of barley in Britain has easily exceeded that of wheat (Fig. 1.3). The gap increased fast after 1957. British yields are second to those of specialist Denmark, ahead of West Germany, and well in advance of France. In Belgium, the story of cereal production since the 1930s has been one of a steep rise in barley acreage and of an even greater drop in rye. In France, there was an increase in barley acreage from 2·5 million acres in 1952 to 5·6 million acres in 1955. Since that time the proportion of arable land in France under barley has fallen and again risen, so that barley acreage in 1965–66 was more than half that of wheat.

Oats

Oats, which are much more important as animal feed than as an element in human diet, are produced in large quantities in the cooler and damper regions that lie adjacent to the wheatlands. In Britain, oats are important in the north and in the west: in eastern

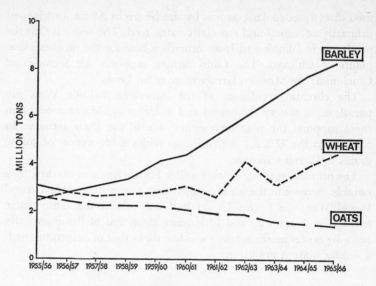

FIG. 1.3   U.K. cereal production
Recent developments underline the great increase in barley
output and the relative decline in wheat.

Scotland and Northern Ireland they may be grown on the same
farm and in the same region as wheat and barley. Especially in
Europe, there is no hard-and-fast regional demarcation of cool-
climate cereals. Oats are not important north of the September
isotherm for 48° F. (9° C.). In the United States there is a southern
limit, since excessive summer heat is harmful, and little is grown
south of the May isotherm for 59° F. (15° C.). The most important
oats-producing areas are to be found, of course, in the temperate
grasslands — in Soviet Russia, in the U.S.A., and in Canada. The
chief markets in the New World are Chicago and Winnipeg. In some
years Canadian oats production has exceeded that of wheat, but
none of the three leaders has a high production efficiency. The
Danish yield is almost as great as those of the United States, Russia,
and Canada combined.

Rye   Rye also is a significant cereal in the grasslands of continental
Europe, from Belgium eastwards across Germany and Poland to the
Ukraine, and in Canada and the American Middle West. It is an
exceedingly important source of bread grain on the North European

Plain, although production in Belgium and France has fallen from pre-war figures. The French growers were producing an average of 638,000 tons in the 1930s, but this had fallen to 380,000 tons by 1965–66. The versatility of rye stems from its tolerance of low-grade and acid soils. Rye is essentially a north European crop, and the Soviet Union and Poland are the major producers. The third world producer is West Germany; East Germany is fourth.

Britain's present-day cereal farming is most remarkable if compared with pre-war achievements, showing an improvement in average wheat yields of 66 per cent, in the period 1960–61 to 1962–63, as compared with the late 1930s.[14] In 1965, Britain was self-sufficient to the extent of 48 per cent in wheat and flour supplies, being considerably less dependent in these items than in butter and sugar. Outside Britain, one of the most striking contrasts in cereal achievements is provided by the United States and the Soviet Union. The American maize crop, in 1962–63, yielded nearly 34 cwt. per acre; the Russian, only 12.[15]

Comparison of Wheat Yields
(cwt./acre)[16]

	1960–61	1961–62	1962–63	1963–64
Denmark .	31·0	32·8	33·4	29·2
Netherlands.	36·7	31·3	36·8	33·5
U.K. . .	28·5	28·2	34·7	31·1

The picture of Danish barley production is similar to that of wheat. A high yield, applied to a much bigger acreage than that allotted to wheat, enables Denmark to be in the first ten barley producers in the world. With an acreage under barley not much more than a third of France's, production in Denmark is at least half that of France.

Comparison of Barley Acreages, Yields, and Production in Denmark, France, and the U.K.[17]
(1963–64)

	'000 acres	cwt./acre	'000 tons
France . .	6,273	23·2	7,267
U.K. . .	4,713	28·0	6,599
Denmark .	2,319	28·8	3,345

Food Production

In Poland, though, even the application of more machines and more fertilizer has not succeeded in producing the expected improvement in cereal output, which in 1958 was only 10 per cent higher than the pre-war figure.

THE CATTLE INDUSTRY

Most of the world's people would eat meat if they could afford it. Most of us drink milk, and many of us use leather. Beef cattle are reared under a number of different climatic circumstances; dairy cattle can do well only in plentifully watered lands. Where rainfall is deficient, irrigation can supply what is required. In dry Nevada, 49 per cent of all farms are cattle and sheep ranches, only 9 per cent being dairy farms. The average Nevada ranch covers over 2,800 acres; but, in numbers of cattle, the states in the lee of the Rockies are much more important. Nebraska has over 5 million cattle, ten times as many as Nevada; Texas over 9 million, exclusive of milch cows.

Dairy cattle must have good-quality pasture, but meat-producing animals can manage on moderate to inferior grass. So it is usual for beef cattle to be dispersed extremely widely. They can be supported on the savannah tropical grasslands. There they may be subject to such pests as the tsetse fly, and there are likely to be difficulties of transport to markets, arising from inadequate railroads, dry-weather tracks instead of roads, and the need for overlanding to populated centres or to the coast.

Where the local demand is sufficient, beef cattle may be the chosen speciality of European farmers. We find them being reared in Eire and from there being dispatched to English ports for fattening and slaughter. Beef and dairy farming are often compatible, and both kinds of cows can be milked regularly. Beef calves may be sold to continue as 'feeders', or be kept for slaughtering as yearlings or two-year-olds. On better land, where cash crops are important, there may be no breeding herd and the grass is probably rotation pasture. Either climatic or economic circumstances may decree that cattle be stall-fed for at least a large part of the year. Well-diversified farming areas, such as southern Ontario, may have a great variety of farm programmes, and very large seasonal movements in proportion to total farm effort.

Cattle breeding has been vastly improved. The bigger the farming organization, the more it can afford to spend on costly bulls or techniques, but wherever there is specialisation in beef production,

12

it is quite likely that the emphasis in breeding will be on Aberdeen-
Angus, Hereford, and Scottish Shorthorns. Some of the greatest
weaknesses — and the biggest fields of opportunity — in breeding
are to be found in the savannah and monsoon regions, with their
enormous numerical strength in cattle. In Brazil, local stock has
been crossed with Zebu, a strain of Indian hump-backed cattle,
with good results. Similar crossings — of British with Zebu stock —
have succeeded in Australia and in Texas. In other parts of the south
and south-west of the U.S.A., the Brahman, a variety of the Indian
Zebu, has been found to thrive. On the campas of inland Guyana
is the Longhorn, introduced four centuries ago from Spain. India,
with twice the number of cattle of any other country, has too many
poor animals, but they have been protected by religious scruples.

Australia provides the best example of cattle rearing in great
numbers in a thinly settled area. There are a total of over a million
head in the herds — very largely beef — of the Northern Territory,
where there live less than 30,000 people. If it were not for the
aborigines, the cattle industry could not be carried on there in its
present form.

Cattle rearing in the Southern Hemisphere is dependent upon the
supply of coarse-grain feeding-stuffs from the grasslands, and on
export through the tropical zone to markets north of the Equator.
The volume of beef exports from the Plate region is due to methods
of processing the slaughtered meat in the local *frigorífico* and subsequently transporting it, chilled, to Europe, and especially to
Britain. The climate of Argentina's pampas region and the skill of
her farmers has enabled her to lead the world in beef exports. In
numbers of cattle, Argentina is only fifth in the world, but one
should note the tremendous concentration (17·8 million head of
cattle in 1961) in Buenos Aires province alone. In 1965, Uruguay,
with 2,715,000 people, had 8,142,000 cattle, a ratio of more than
3 : 1.

The growing population of the world is consuming more meat, and
in the United States the numbers of cattle (other than dairy) more
than doubled between 1930 and 1962–63.

The dairy farmer may produce for a market that is near or distant
— sometimes on the other side of the world — but in the case of
milk production the journey from producer to consumer is likely to
be much shorter. The milk-producer in Britain delivers to a market
that is usually in a city. London's supply may come from as far away
as the West Country, Glasgow's from the Southern Dales. These

distances are not great compared with the journey covered by the processed products of the dairy industry, such as butter and cheese.

United Kingdom output of farm products is on a small scale compared with that of the super-Powers, and it is less specialized than is the agriculture of the leading exporters. Home-produced butter, in 1961, was only 8 per cent of total requirements. Nevertheless, output had doubled during the 1950s. Cheese production in the U.K. increased by 57 per cent in the period 1950–59, to 45 per cent self-sufficiency,[18] but between 1960 and 1964 domestic consumption increased faster than production, leading to record imports of 150,000 tons in 1965.

Britain's dairy import trade has long been notable for the status of her traditional suppliers — New Zealand, Denmark, Australia, and Canada. Britain needs these countries' produce, and they her custom. In 1965 Britain took 100,000 tons[19] of butter from Denmark, about 90 per cent of that country's total butter exports. The Danish industry has been founded upon co-operation, efficient breeding, and receptiveness to new technology. Milk yields have increased greatly, while the farm population has fallen. Only about a fifth of the working population is now in farming, but exports of cheese have risen, and Denmark is now the third world exporter, after New Zealand and the Netherlands.

In the United States, dairy production is notably concentrated in the southern regions of both Wisconsin and Minnesota, areas in which beef cattle are conspicuously few. Dairy cattle are also numerous in Iowa, one of the zones of concentration of beef herds. Few dairy cattle are found west of longitude 102° W. The 20-inch isohyet is critical.

The spur of competition and the declining productivity of some areas have prompted a closer analysis of basic physical controls, particularly those concerning soil. This has been done in New Zealand. An intensive survey of soil conditions there has brought ameliorative action, for instance on the yellow-brown clay soils of North Auckland, which tend to acidity, and on the pumice-derived soils of central North Island. In New Zealand dairy output has been stabilized, though exports of butter have shown a decline.

New Zealand Butter and Cheese Production
('ooo tons) [20]

	1960	1961	1962	1963	1964
Butter .	213	211	217	232	245
Cheese .	99	101	98	95	105

New Zealand Exports of Dairy Produce
('000 tons)[21]

	1960	1961	1962	1963	1964
Butter	155	163	165	171	188
Cheese	79	88	92	87	96

Generalizations concerning yield can be dangerous. Thus a
'national yield' for milk may have little local meaning. Milk yield
in the U.S.A. is much higher in the specialist Dairy Belt (extending
from Rhode Island and central Maryland to southern Minnesota)
than it is in the southern states. It is higher in comparatively mild
Jaeren (southern Norway) than it is in the north of that country.
The differences in yield may be produced by one or more of various
factors: (i) physical conditions exert a direct and immediate control;
(ii) specialization, organization, and planning can produce remarkable results — the highest national milk yields in Europe are to be
found in the Netherlands; (iii) the effects of agro-science and farm
technology can be achieved through fertilizer application, as New
Zealand has shown.

Cane sugar is a subtropical commodity that is usually grown on or   **SUGAR**
near to the actual tropics, on the eastern side of the great land-
masses. Its cultivation is characterized especially by a short,
extremely intensive picking-season. Climate and work alike make
heavy demands on the plantation labourers. The Imperial Powers
of the present and past — Spaniards and Portuguese, French,
Dutch, and British — established plantations on or near the tropics.
The labourers were Negroes or *mestizos* in the New World, Tamils
and Javanese in Asia, and Negroes again in Africa.

As in the case of the other tropical products, sugar is today often
produced by newly independent States, so that labour relations on
the plantations are differently ordered. Occasionally the change has
been dramatic: in Cuba, a Communist-type government has expropriated the sugar estates with profound consequences both for the
sugar-consuming and owning companies and for the consuming
nations. The chief market for Cuban sugar is now not the U.S.A.
but Soviet Russia, with secondary markets in Eastern Europe; but
events in Cuba are still decisive in affecting market conditions. The
price of sugar on the London market, which had been £19 15s. per

ton in January 1962, rose steeply to £105 in October 1963 — the result of the hurricane disaster. Subsequently the price fell, in June 1965, to a new critical low of £19. World production reached a peak of 55 million tons in 1960–61. (This figure included beet supplies.) During the next year there was a fall in world production of 4 million tons, and a further decline in 1962–63 to a total of 49·9 million tons. By November 1963 sugar prices had leapt ahead; but they were to fall with equal speed as world production increased again during the seasons 1963–64 and 1964–65.

Hurricane Clara was a particular disaster to Cuban production since it struck and then re-struck the eastern provinces where most of the island's crop is grown. The figures of percentage production for these provinces in the season 1959–60, as given by the International Sugar Council, were: Oriente, 27; Camagüey, 25; Las Villas, 23 per cent.[22] Cuba provides, in normal years, almost a quarter of the world's supply from sources outside China. The Soviet Union produces over a third of the world's beet.

The effect of two world wars has been to increase the output of beet in favourable areas such as north Germany and the British Fenlands. In West Germany, a comparison of 1938 and 1958 is significant. An increase in the area planted of 78 per cent led to a rise in output of 115 per cent. The period 1956–59 may perhaps be taken as portraying the normal pattern of world sugar production and trade, before the imposition of American sanctions on Cuba. A third of the world's trade in sugar originates in Cuba, most of whose exports now go to Communist countries. Before 1960, most of Cuba's sugar exports went to the United States.

The specific optimum rainfall requirements for tea, as given by Van Royen — '100 to 150 inches [of rain] well distributed throughout the year, with frequent dews and fogs '[23] — are not easy to find. They preclude maximum growth in areas such as south-central China, where tea is actually a major crop.

The world's leading tea-producer is India; Ceylon is second; Communist China (according to F.A.O. estimates) third, followed, in order, by Japan and Indonesia. Production in India and Ceylon has been high for many years. A peak in Indian output was reached in 1957 and again in 1961. The Indian Third Five-Year Plan called for a 24 per cent increase in production over the 1960 output.

Production of Tea[24]
1960–62 average ('000 metric tons)

India	340
Ceylon	205
Japan	79
Indonesia	45
Pakistan	23
World total (excluding U.S.S.R. and mainland China) . . .	803

The size and type of tea-growing organizations can vary greatly. For the Indian tea-gardens, Thoman gives an average of around 500 acres.[25] The waiting-period for tea cultivation can be as much as eight years. Great quantities of labour are required in picking: in Assam this occurs every nine days or so during the season. Planting, weeding, and pruning are also demanding of labour.

Coffee

Coffee is a competitor with tea over large areas of the tropics. It shares some of tea's climatic demands, cultivation being possible in many of the lands around the Indian Ocean, as well as in eastern South America. However, the areas of optimum climate are smaller than in the case of tea. It is a less hardy crop. Frost is an implacable enemy and disease can be fatal, as was shown in nineteenth-century Ceylon. Some high-quality producers, such as the Yemen,[26] supplement seasonably inadequate precipitation with irrigation.

Today, world coffee cultivation is overwhelmingly concentrated in a relatively small section of Brazil lying to the north of São Paulo, where the red soil on the hills sloping away from the coast provides ideal conditions. The vast Brazilian effort in coffee dates from the surreptitious removal of beans from the Guianas. In Africa, the chief plantations are in Angola, but there is an important output from the small-holdings in the former French territories of the Ivory Coast, Cameroun, and Malagasy. Large-scale coffee production is universally associated with the *arabicas* grown in Brazil. Since the middle of the nineteenth century there has been a steady increase in output from the hills between Santos and São Paulo. The *terra roxa* (red-earth) soils behind Santos are ideal for the coffee, which was often grown with the help of Italian immigrant labour. The flowers

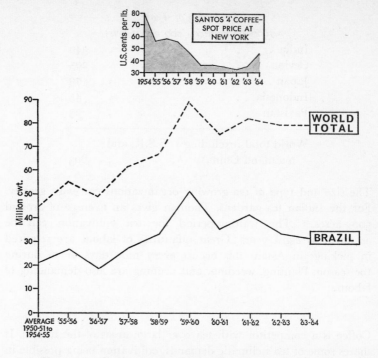

FIG. 1.4   Coffee production — Brazil and the world
Production is still dominated by events in Brazil, but to a less
extent than a decade ago.

are vulnerable to very heavy rain or frost, and the killing frosts of
1902 and 1918 were national disasters.[27]

Coffee is a crop that has proved, economically, difficult to manage.
The record output occurred in 1933–34 (nearly 30 million bags).
But this bountiful crop came, disastrously, in the middle of the
greatest economic slump that had ever hit the world. The primary
producers suffered, along with industrialized nations (Fig. 1.4). The
Brazilian Government bought the coffee, most of which could not
be sold, and burned the surplus. In the decade of the 1930s, 80
million bags of coffee were destroyed in this manner.[28] In 1963
Brazil exported 1,150,000 tons of coffee, though, by 1965, this had
fallen to 715,000 tons; the U.S.A. buys about a half of the normal
Brazilian crop. It was estimated in 1963 that Brazil, as a result of
the high yields in 1961–62, had accumulated stocks of 30
million bags, but natural disasters came to the help of harassed

18

administrators.[29] Exceptionally abnormal climatic conditions are Beverages
capable of influencing production over a long period.

The long-term results of difficulties encountered in marketing
coffee have been met by international action. An International
Coffee Agreement was reached in 1962 and an International Coffee
Council established; this despite the reluctance of the U.S.A. to
ratify the undertaking. But American ratification was secured, in
December 1963, and the Agreement began to operate. Its primary
objectives were:

(i) to achieve a reasonable balance between supply and demand
for coffee which will ensure adequate supplies to consumers
and markets to producers at equitable prices;

(ii) to alleviate the serious hardship caused by burdensome surpluses and excessive fluctuations in the price of coffee.[30]

The cacao tree can grow well under the wet conditions obtaining in Cocoa
much of West Africa. It is the staple farming product of southern
Ghana, which for two generations has been the world's chief producer, despite the fact that the cacao tree is native to the New
World. The Ghana industry is notable for its well-established and
close connections with the chocolate trade in Britain.

Minimum temperature requirements of cacao are much more
exacting than those of tea. Also, the swollen-shoot disease has
wreaked havoc in Ghana, most recently during the 1950s. Another
pest is the capsid fly, which has been combated by spraying
programmes.

Production forecast for Ghana in 1965–66 was 415,000; for
Nigeria, 185,000 tons. Until 1960 Brazil had been second in
world production and Nigeria third. Most Nigerian cocoa goes to
Britain; on the other hand, Britain, in 1960, took only 18 per cent
of Ghana's cocoa exports. More than half of these went to other
countries in Western Europe; even the U.S.A., in both 1959 and
1960, bought more cocoa from Ghana than did Britain, and throughout this century has been the leading world consumer (Fig. 1.5).

The cacao plant's susceptibility to fungoid and other ailments
increases the relative advantages of the plantation system. The large
concerns can afford expensive organization and precautions to avoid
the disasters that find a small man helpless. The tsetse fly precludes
the large-scale use of animal transport, and large labour gangs are
needed to move the Ghanaian crop to river, road, or railhead.

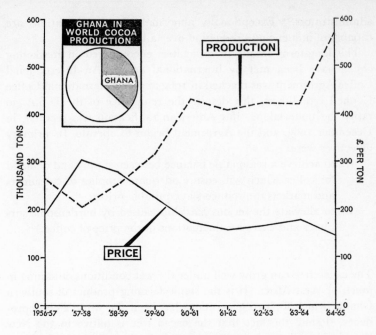

FIG. I.5   Cocoa in Ghana — movement of production
and price

As with coffee, the market is dominated by a single producer; the
graph shows the steep rise in output in Ghana and the direct
relation between production and price.

The years between 1951 and 1958 saw serious damage occasioned
by disease to the plantations of West Africa. During the period
1954–58, average annual world production was 840,000 tons; during
the period 1959–63, the average annual crop was 1,145,000 tons.
The resulting situation illuminated a conflict of interest between
producer and consumer nations. This showed itself in the failure of
the United Nations Cocoa Conference held in Geneva during
September–October 1963. The breakdown was perhaps the result
of its *ad hoc* organization, which embraced both ends of the supply-
demand process — producers and consumers. The subsequent
meeting of the Cocoa Producers' Alliance initially promised success.
This body contained only growers — Ghana, Nigeria, Brazil, the
Ivory Coast, Cameroun, and Togo — who between them accounted
for 82 per cent of world output in 1964. The Alliance aimed to
control prices by the limitation of exports[31] where this was necessary

to protect the producer countries. But the lack of success of an essentially voluntary association was demonstrated in 1964–65. Following on a large crop, the Alliance failed to agree upon a plan to halt sales when the price fell below £160 per ton. The result, in 1965, was a disastrous collapse to £87 10s. per ton. In the mid-1950s the price had been as high as £437.

1. See T. B. Paltridge 'World Population and the World Food Supply', **NOTES** *World Crops*, vol. 15 (Sept. 1963), p. 287.
2. *The Times*, 19 Aug. 1965.
3. Kingsley Davis, 'Population', *Scientific American*, vol. 209, no. 3 (Sept. 1963), p. 63.
4. H. Yuan Tien, 'Population Control in China', *Population Studies*, vol. 18, no. 3 (March 1965).
5. Financial Times, 16 Nov. 1965.
6. A. J. Amos, 'Science and Food: Feeding the World's Millions', *Financial Times*, 19 Sept. 1962.
7. The Director-General of F.A.O., quoted in *Agriculture in the World Economy* (F.A.O., Rome, 1962), p. 9.
8. B. Legarda, *The Philippine Economy* (Manila, 1958), pp. 11–13.
9. P. Collins, 'Soil Fertility in Iran', *World Crops*, vol. 17, no. 3 (Sept. 1965), p. 60. (Letter to the Soil Fertility Dept. of Iran, signed by some forty farmers of the Khui region.)
10. G. W. Hemy, *Production Statistics of Communist China* (Joseph Crosfield, Warrington, 1956), p. C.3-1.
11. Estimates of the Commonwealth Economic Committee for 1963–64 season: *Grain Crops* (H.M.S.O., 1966), pp. 136–7.
12. 'The North American Scene: Signs of Decay on the Great Plains', *Financial Times*, 19 Sept. 1962.
13. Ibid.
14. Commonwealth Economic Committee, *Grain Crops*, p. 75.
15. Ibid.
16. Ibid., p. 39 (provisional).
17. Ibid., pp. 91, 94, 95.
18. *Financial Times*, 16 Nov. 1962.
19. Commonwealth Economic Committee, *Dairy Produce* (H.M.S.O., 1966), p. 44.
20. Ibid., pp. 37, 54.
21. Ibid., pp. 42, 57.
22. *The World Sugar Economy, Structure and Policies* (International Sugar Council, London, 1963), vol. i, p. 124.
23. W. Van Royen, *Agricultural Resources of the World* (Prentice-Hall, 1954), p. 115.
24. F.A.O., *Monthly Bulletin of Agricultural Economics and Statistics*, vol. 14, no. 5 (May 1965), p. 11.

Food Production

25. Richard S. Thoman, *The Geography of Economic Activity: An Introductory World Survey* (McGraw-Hill, 1962), p. 333.
26. Van Royen, *Agricultural Resources of the World*, p. 110.
27. C. F. Jones and G. C. Darkenwald, *Economic Geography*, 3rd ed. (Macmillan, New York, 1965), p. 176.
28. Celso Furtado, 'The Development of Brazil', *Scientific American*, vol. 209, no. 3 (Sept. 1963), p. 214.
29. *The Times*, 20 Dec. 1963.
30. Commonwealth Economic Committee, *Plantation Crops* (H.M.S.O., 1964), p. 206.
31. *The Times*, 4 July 1964

Raw Materials Chapter 2

The industries of a country such as Britain would very soon grind to a halt if they were deprived of the hundreds of millions of pounds worth of raw materials that are imported every year. Nearly all of our purchases of cereals come from cool temperate lands. One of the most important of these — Canada — experiences winter temperatures in its wheatlands far more severe than Britain's. But many raw materials — the rubber for the British car and electrical industries, the vegetable oils for the making of soap and margarine — come very largely from the equatorial zone. Fibre imports, on the other hand, are derived from a very large latitudinal range of areas.

These raw materials are 'market products'. They are often exported in an unprocessed state, destined for factories that will probably transform them entirely. Where these raw materials are produced, there is a local superabundance. Where they are consumed — mostly by wealthier nations — there is a sustained industrial demand. The producing areas may be highly localized and subject to intense organization and large-scale applications of capital from abroad. Their markets may be truly world-wide.

Hevea rubber is a native of Brazil, whence the seeds were taken first **RUBBER** to Kew Gardens in London and thence to Malaya and the East Indies — areas having a similar equatorial climate to that of the point of origin. Primary rubber production is highly organized, but mechanization has little place in it.

Tapping is a laborious but also a quite skilled operation, and has been said to account for a third of the entire cost of producing marketable rubber.[1]

Capital requirements are very considerable, both because of the initial outlay involved, and also because of the time it takes for the rubber tree to mature. Cumulative financial problems may occur in plantation areas after the peak of production is reached. In Malaya

Raw Materials   the World Bank investigators found that two-thirds of the small-holdings in rubber consisted of trees of over twenty-five years. Half were over thirty-three years old. Their conclusion was that 'mainly because of advanced age, the yield from existing trees on small-holdings is expected to decline steadily'.[2] The smallholding can rely on a remarkable variety of tropical crops being available as 'intercrops', to be planted between the rows of rubber.[3]

All production is very sensitive to price. If industrial consumers pay less, the native farmers may go out of production, though this may be only temporary: they can revert to subsistence farming and then return to rubber. Efficient native production can prosper: in the Malayan natural rubber industry, during the period 1963–65, smallholding increased faster than estate production; this was contrary to the experience of Indonesia.[4]

There is a logical contrast between the size of foreign-owned (European) holdings and indigenous plantations. However, 'indigenous', in Malaya, may be Malayan or, almost as often, Chinese. About half the Malayan rubber smallholdings are owned by Malays; 30 to 40 per cent are owned by Chinese.[5]

Rubber Consumers   The modern demand for rubber has arisen chiefly through the needs of the transport industry, in both its automobile and aircraft sections. By far the greatest producer of automobiles is the U.S.A., which is also the largest consumer of rubber. In Britain, the tyre industry in 1961 took 47 per cent of total consumption of natural rubber.[6]

Natural Rubber Production
('ooo metric tons)

	1963	1964
Malaya .	799·3	837·4
Indonesia	582·3	648·7
Thailand	198·0	223·2
Ceylon .	104·8	111·6
World total .	2,110	2,270

The percentages of national consumption attributed by Thoman to the American motor industry are: natural rubber, 65; synthetic, 63; and reclaimed rubber, 39 per cent.[7] The macintosh and clothing industries generally take only a small part of total rubber consumption today.

In certain years the combined demand from the Soviet Union and the East European Communist countries may exceed purchases by the United States, and the demand from individual countries may vary greatly from year to year. The Eastern (Soviet) bloc consumed 60 per cent more rubber in 1961 than in 1960. In 1961 also the Eastern bloc bought as much, in Singapore and the other rubber markets, as Britain, France, and West Germany. In 1962, the Soviet Union imported 50 per cent more natural rubber than Britain.

There have been a number of attempts to find a reliable alternative to natural rubber. These have been successful enough to form a serious threat to the primary producers in the tropical world. Before the Second World War, Du Pont in the U.S.A. and I.G. Farbenindustrie in Germany were jointly concerned in the promotion of the synthetic rubbers, buna and butyl. Since then, experiment and development have been renewed in Europe — both East and West — and in America. In 1961 world synthetic overtook natural rubber production for the first time, since when it has gone further ahead. In 1965, synthetic rubber production in the United States was twice the natural rubber combined production of Malaysia and Singapore.

In the interest of the balance of payments of the Commonwealth, the American Government instituted control of synthetic output inside the U.S.A., so that the natural producers should not be swamped and driven out of business. Nevertheless, the United States manufactures and consumes most of the world's synthetic rubber.

Because the sheep is tolerant of a variety of climatic conditions, it can live on land that is inadequate for other types of farming. This most useful animal, having been pushed on to poorer land, has nevertheless often thrived there, sometimes in adverse climatic conditions. **FIBRES Wool**

Sheep farming is an activity with a wide geographic and economic scope. The volume of output is due to the relative ease of production and breadth of consumption, as sheep rearing does not demand a large amount of capital for its basic organization. The small farmer is still able to survive today, whereas the small industrialist is subject to heavier pressure. Wool is purchased and sold over most of the

RAW WOOL - Production and Consumption

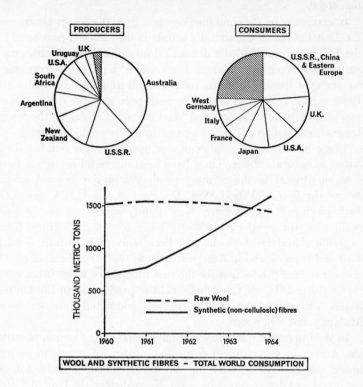

FIG. 2.1   Wool in the world

Production is predominantly from the temperate regions; the main consumers are the industrialized countries and China. Wool is being challenged by synthetic fibres in the more advanced countries.

globe. It happens that the largest populated area where wool is not required is the equatorial zone where the climate does not suit the sheep. Apart from wool, the sheep provides man with meat: the two products are vital to the export trade of Australia, which contains over a fifth of the world's sheep. In wool statistics, one is struck by the evenness of production as compared with some of the other major world commodities. The largest buyers of wool are the U.S.A., Britain, the E.E.C., and the Soviet Union (Fig. 2.1).

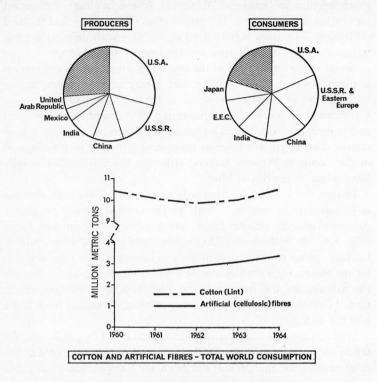

COTTON (LINT) Production and Consumption

Fibres

FIG. 2.2   Cotton in the world

The U.S.A. is still outstanding as both producer and consumer. Cotton consumption is still growing overall, despite the challenge of artificial fibres.

Cotton

Cotton is a subtropical crop with a greater climatic range than is possessed by most of the tropical plantation commodities. In the United States, cotton cultivation is associated with the early development of what was basically a one-crop economy. Today, other crops have prospered and industry — some of it large-scale — has come to the southern states. Methods too have changed. Fertilizers are regarded as essential, and in fact the Cotton Belt uses more than half of all the fertilizer produced in the U.S.A.[8]

The Negro labourer has, at least in part, become a town worker, and the technology of cotton production has changed, with machines entering more and more into primary production. But the degree of

27

Raw Materials   mechanization in the cotton lands of the Atlantic seaboard is very much less than in Texas and Oklahoma, where, in places, the market for machines — at least in the preparation of the soil — has reached saturation. The most mechanized of all American districts are the irrigated valleys of California and the interior south-west.[9]

Soviet writers are proud of the degree to which cotton cultivation is mechanized in their country, but Hemy says: 'it seems highly unlikely that as much as one-third (in the most mechanized area — Uzbekistan) is mechanically harvested'.[10] A number of countries and regions have developed an unhealthy dependence on the sale of cotton. The Egyptians have at times had difficulty in the disposal of their crop to Western buyers, although the surplus has usually been taken by the Soviet bloc.

In 1965 the U.S.A. provided only 16 per cent of world production of cotton lint, as compared with 31 per cent in 1959. The largest Asiatic producers outside China are the Soviet Union and India (Fig. 2.2). As with much of her agricultural and industrial output, Chinese cotton statistics are difficult to interpret. The official claim for the season 1959–60 was almost 2·5 million metric tons, although the average for the four previous years had been 868,000 metric tons.[11] Certainly, there have been big increases in output from India and the U.S.A.

Seen against this background of increased effort by producers, the fall in consumption since 1961–62 becomes more serious. One of the chief reasons for the decline has been the competition from man-made fibres. Britain, for instance, is now less important as a cotton consumer than Pakistan or Brazil.

Jute   Expanding economies demand packaging and covering materials of many kinds. Almost all of the world's jute comes from the deltas of the Brahmaputra and the Eastern Ganges. It demands a great amount of heat and moisture during the growing-period. Unlike many of the important items in world trade, Pakistani production stems from a multitude — millions, in fact — of small producers. It is not surprising that their earnings are extremely low. The creation of Pakistan separated many of the growing areas from the jute mills of Calcutta, but the Indian Third Five-Year Plan provided for a 53 per cent increase in jute acreage in West Bengal between 1961 and 1965–66. By 1963–64, Indian production had overtaken that of Pakistan, although Pakistan went ahead again in 1965–66.

There is a small jute-growing area in the Paraíba Valley of south- **Fibres**
east Brazil, but its production is of quite negligible proportions
compared with the vast output of the Brahmaputra delta region.
The main trade in jute is between Calcutta on the one side and
London and Dundee on the other. Jute can yield up to 1,200 lb. to
the acre and is cheaper than the other fibres. However, the almost
complete dependence of Dundee upon the jute industry has been
economically unhealthy for that city. The familiar underpriced
competition from the East has affected both Dundee and Kirkcaldy.

Tanzania, Kenya, and Uganda produce about half of the world's **Sisal and**
sisal, the plant having been originally introduced into East Africa **Kindred**
in 1893 by the Germans, who brought it from Florida.[12] Sisal is **Fibres**
grown principally in the area between the East African coast and
the Central Plateau, where every month has a mean maximum
temperature of 80° F. (27° C.) and heavy rainfall — 9 or 10 inches
— falls in both April and May. There is a much smaller production
in Kenya. Brazil is now the second producer in the world.

Producers of natural fibre are now faced with competition from
artificial and synthetic textile fibres and from plastics. Sisal is the
principal hard fibre and, despite competition from the new materials,
demand for it and for the other important natural fibres remains
firm. Of the hard fibres, sisal makes up nearly 70 per cent; henequén
(over 90 per cent from Mexico) and abaca (almost entirely from the
Philippines) most of the rest.

In view of the increasing demand for fibres, and bearing in mind
the climatically exacting requirements of jute, efforts have been made,
especially since the end of British rule in India and Pakistan, to
develop natural jute substitutes. One of the most successful of these
has been Urena Lobata, developed in south central Ghana. There
is a very large demand by the cocoa industry for sacking, and provided that yields continue to be satisfactory (drought reduced
production in some areas by almost 50 per cent in 1956), the future
for Urena could be bright.

Silk is an ancient product, one of the items of trade between the **Silk**
Orient and the West before a sea route to China and Japan was
discovered. The mulberry leaf, on which the silkworm feeds, is not
confined to the Far East. It can be cultivated in warm-summer

29

Raw Materials

climates such as those to be found in the middle Rhône Valley and in the Plain of Lombardy.

Like other natural fibres, silk has been greatly affected by the development of artificial and synthetic products. Factors important in the resulting competition include cost and quality. It may be that the texture and feel of natural silk can create a sufficiently large luxury market to justify what would otherwise be an uneconomic product. The demand of fashion is important but erratic. The first result of the introduction, in the 1930s, of the large-scale production of rayon in Japan and in the other principal world textile markets was to reduce the sale of natural silk, and rayon was popularly called 'artificial silk'. The production of raw silk ('sericulture') in Japan reached an all-time peak in 1934, and Japan is still the chief world producer.

Flax

Flax is still important industrially, although it has lost ground to man-made fibres in this, as it did to cotton in the last century.[13] Eighty per cent of total world supply comes from the Soviet Union and most of the remainder from the other East European countries and from the Common Market. Total E.E.C. output is about equal to that of Poland, the second world producer.

VEGETABLE OILS

Industry and the home demand more and more vegetable oils, especially in the form of margarine and soap. By far the most important vegetable source, today, is the soya bean. So far as sources of commercial supply are concerned, as a Unilever report has pointedly demonstrated: 'It is not in the developing tropical countries but in the rich developed countries that the bulk of the world's supplies of oils and fats originates'.[14]

Soya-Bean Oil

The soya bean has a great variety of uses, and since the links with the former sources of supply in Asia were severed during the Second World War, it has been grown more and more extensively in the northern part of the United States and in Canada. Major areas of production are now found in the southern two-thirds of Illinois and in western Indiana. The old concentrations, however, still remain in the lowland provinces of China, north of the Yangtze and south

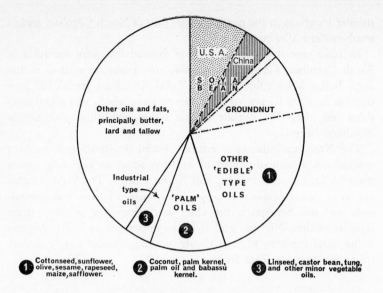

FIG. 2.3   Soya — distribution of world production
The soya bean is the most important vegetable source of oil; as a
soya producer the U.S.A. is now well ahead of China.

of the Hwang Ho, with Honan being the most important. The bean
has a short growing-season — in optimum areas this can be less than
three months, although normally it is around four months.
Manchuria, in the central plains and in the Sungari Valley, is famous
for its soya crop, and the return of Manchuria to China in 1945 gave
a fillip to production (Fig. 2.3).

Soya is important enough to have accounted for two-fifths of the
growth in world exports of vegetable oils over the period 1955–56
and nearly all world soya exports come from the U.S.A.[15]

Groundnuts flourish in dry-season tropical climates, especially on
well-drained soils. Rainfall can be excessive for this crop, but prolonged drought is disastrous. There was a famous occasion of this
kind at the time of the groundnut failure in Tanganyika in the years
after 1947. Twenty inches of rainfall during the growing-season of
three to five months is sufficient.[16] There is a remarkable concentration of production in the United States in south-western Georgia
and the adjacent counties of south-east Alabama, and important

Groundnuts

Raw Materials smaller locations in the north-eastern part of North Carolina and in south-eastern Virginia.

In 1960 record yields per acre of groundnuts were recorded in South Carolina, Florida, Oklahoma, and Texas, as well as in the areas better known for this crop. Total American groundnut production in 1963–64 was 917,000 metric tons, which was about one-third less than the output of the older-established industry of Northern Nigeria.

The Nigerian industry is entirely based on small-scale peasant production. About one-third of world production normally comes from India; China is second, and Nigeria, third. The West African are far more important than any other countries for trade in groundnuts and oil. Senegal is the chief world exporter of oil — more significant than Nigeria, and twice as important as India. Nigeria is the chief exporter of groundnuts, sending abroad nearly twenty times the quantity from India.

Palm Oil The oil palm grows in tropical areas having a moderate to high, well-distributed rainfall, so that it is found along the West African littoral from Senegal to the Congo Republic. Palm oil is obtained from the flesh of the palm tree's fruit; palm-kernel oil from the fruit's black centre. Thirty per cent of the world's trade in palm oil originates in Nigeria, but local consumption of this rich oil, so valuable in cooking, is not far short of the export figure.

Sunflower Oil Sunflower oil is an alternative to peanut (groundnut) oil for cooking, and is important in both the United States and the South American pampas. In Argentina it is the chief edible oil. In the Soviet Union sunflower plots are a characteristic feature of farms in the Ukraine and the Kuban.

Coconut Oil and Copra Coconut oil is obtained from copra, the dried flesh of the coconut, which is found especially in the coastlands of South-East Asia, in the Philippine Islands, and in the islands of the South Pacific. The potential of copra is shown by the fact that in its dried form it contains from 60 to 68 per cent oil.[17]

A generation ago, cotton seed was twice as important as any other vegetable source of oil. There is a correlation between the statistics of production for cotton lint and oil. For both commodities, the outstanding producer is the United States, followed by China, the Soviet Union, and India. Since 1960 Chinese output has tended to decline.

Vegetable Oils

Cotton-Seed Oil

Linseed, like the soya bean, is at home in the temperate grasslands — in prairies, pampas, and steppes. In Argentina production is concentrated along both sides of the Paraná River north of latitude 35° S., with an area of lower-density production south of this line and north-east of Bahía Blanca. During the inter-war period, linseed (obtained from the flax plant) was by far the largest source of vegetable oil, the largest supply coming from Argentina. Exports of linseed from Argentina have now been resumed, but barely a third of production enters the world market.

Linseed Oil

The olive, which has remained important in the Mediterranean lands throughout historical times, yields a cooking-oil that is still a significant element in production in Italy, Spain, and Greece, these three countries together producing about two-thirds of the total world output of olive oil. During the period 1960–64, world olive-oil production increased by 50 per cent, which was much greater than the advances in the other vegetable oils. This was despite the fact that olive oil was much more expensive than its competitors.

Olive Oil

Production of rapeseed in India has declined in recent years by 30 per cent, but in Canada there has been a most notable increase in the crop, from an average of 7,000 tons in 1950–55, to over 500,000 tons in 1965–66.[18]

Rapeseed

Sesame is almost exclusively a peasant crop, two-thirds of world production coming from China and India.

Sesame Seed

The tung-oil tree is a native of central and western China, providing an important export from that country, being used, along with linseed and soya oil, in the manufacture of paints and varnishes.

Tung Oil

Raw Materials   The climatic demands of the tung-oil tree are quite exacting: a cooler winter is required than is found in the equatorial zone — temperatures, in fact, 'at or below 45° F. (7° C.) for at least 470 hours'.[19] Some oil has been produced in the coastlands from north Florida through Mississippi to eastern Texas, American planters having been encouraged by the severance of supply routes from China in 1941–45, but for this commodity China remains supreme. In 1960 she produced four times as much tung oil as the next largest producer — Argentina.

NOTES   1. G. A. Watson, 'Cover Plants in Malayan Plantations', *World Crops*, vol. 15, no. 2 (Feb. 1963), p. 49.

2. World Bank, *The Economic Development of Malaya* (Singapore, 1955), p. 250.

3. Ooi Jin-Bee, *Land, People and Economy in Malaya* (Longmans, 1963), p. 210. See also Loren G. Polhamus, *Rubber* (Leonard Hill, 1962), p. 187.

4. F.A.O., *Monthly Bulletin of Agricultural Economics and Statistics*, vol. 15, no. 5 (May 1966), p. 25.

5. Ooi Jin-Bee, *Land, People and Economy in Malaya*, p. 215.

6. F.A.O., *Monthly Bulletin of Agricultural Economics and Statistics*, vol. 15, no. 5 (May 1966), p. 25.

7. Thoman, *The Geography of Economic Activity*, p. 491.

8. Jones and Darkenwald, *Economic Geography*, p. 194.

9. H. B. Brown and J. O. Ware, *Cotton* (McGraw-Hill, 1958), p. 313.

10. G. W. Hemy, *Cotton Growing in the Soviet Union* (Joseph Crosfield, Warrington, 1958), pp. 42, 44.

11. F.A.O., *Production Yearbook*, vol. 19, p. 149.

12. G. W. Lock, 'Factors Affecting Sisal Growing', *World Crops*, vol. 15, no. 4 (April 1963), p. 142.

13. Commonwealth Economic Committee, *Industrial Fibres* (H.M.S.O., 1964), p. 133.

14. Unilever Ltd., *Annual Report*, 27 April 1966.

15. Ibid.

16. Van Royen, *Agricultural Resources of the World*, p. 152.

17. Ibid., p. 165.

18. F.A.O., 'Soft Oil: Current Situation and Outlook', *Monthly Bulletin of Agricultural Economics and Statistics*, vol. 13, no. 11 (Nov. 1964), p. 2.

19. L. J. Foster, 'The Tung Oil Trees', *World Crops*, vol. 15, no. 6 (June 1963), p. 220.

Forest and Sea Chapter 3

More than a quarter of the land surface of the world is occupied by forest — a larger proportion than is given up to agricultural land. Where man has multiplied in the mid-latitudes, he has often destroyed their forest resources. The valuable trees of the tropics, as well as the more numerous stands of the sub-Arctic lands — only relatively recently, in the Earth's history, vacated by glaciers — have also been seriously depleted. The forest is a primary resource that lends itself to wasteful exploitation — to a robber economy. But there remains a vast total of wealth, especially in the Soviet Union and in North America: these areas contain over 40 per cent of total world reserves of accessible forests. Timber — raw, processed, or through its by-products — is vital to industrialized, underdeveloped, and primitive regions (Fig. 3.1).

THE WORLD'S FORESTS

Most of the world's timber consumption is from the coniferous forests that almost encircle the Northern Hemisphere. The distribution of the land-masses is such that the southern half of the world contains comparatively few such forests. In the north, the pine, spruce, fir, and larch trees provide a major part of the wealth of Canada, of Scandinavia, of the Soviet Union, and of the United States. There are also very important elements in northern Japan and in central Europe. The latitudinal effect is paralleled by the operation of altitude, so that coniferous trees appear elsewhere in the highlands of the Mediterranean and the tropics.

The northern forests are the foundation for a number of important industries, chief of which are wood pulp and its derivatives, paper and rayon. Building also requires large quantities of timber, and the cellulose from wood is a source of explosives for industry and for war, and also for artificial fibres other than rayon.

Coniferous Forests North America

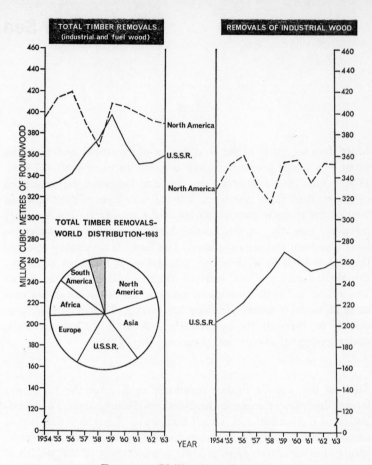

FIG. 3.1   Utilization of timber

The Soviet Union is rapidly increasing its timber consumption,
but Asia has a notable share of total timber removals.

Paper and rayon consumption have increased steeply with the
spread of civilization, technology, and prosperity. It happens that
the large resources of Canada are near to the huge newsprint market
of the United States, but Newfoundland and Labrador also serve
British industry through commercial organizations that cover both
ends of the industrial process — the forests and the mills — whether
in the New World or the Old.

The dimensions of some American softwoods are enormous. The
Californian redwood *Sequoia sempervivens* commonly grows to between

200 and 340 feet; the Sitka spruce to between 125 and 175 feet and occasionally to 250 feet.[1] These are West Coast timbers, the redwood being found in northern California and southern Oregon, the Sitka spruce southwards from Alaska, through British Columbia, Washington, and Oregon.

Canadian forests are vast enough to sustain a huge demand from the United States and Europe as well as from domestic industry, and also to endure periodic disastrous ravages by fire. Productive forest covers nearly one million square miles of Canada, and cutting of lumber, although regulated, amounted nevertheless to nearly 3,000 million cubic feet in 1963. The productive forest of British Columbia alone covers more than three times the total area of England. In this province in 1961 the percentage distribution of felled timber, according to species, was: Douglas fir, 31; hemlock, 22; spruce, 17; red cedar, 13; balsam, 9; other species, 8 per cent.

Pulp and newsprint must play an increasing part in world trade, as the world's literate population increases. In 1944 Canadian newsprint output was 3·6 million tons and capacity 4·3 million tons. In 1962 output was 6·7 million tons and capacity 7·7 million tons, on the basis of a six-day week.[2] One fact is clear: the United States will continue to rely, to a large extent, upon imports from Canada to feed her newspaper, magazine, and printing industries. In 1939, 63 per cent of the U.S.A.'s pulp and paper came from Canada. In 1944, under war conditions, 75 per cent of America's needs came from Canada. During the period 1944–60, over four-fifths of Canadian pulp and paper exports went to the United States. In 1965, Canada produced nearly four times as much newsprint as the United States.

Finland occupies a region in the same latitudes as the northernmost **Scandinavia** mining camps in Canada. But whereas much of Canada's wealth comes from her mines, most of Finland's natural resources belong to her forests. The characteristic farm forests, with holdings attached to individual farms, account for nearly two-thirds of the total Finnish forest area, and are especially significant in an environment where climatic and soil factors often militate against successful production.

Finland's most important trees are the pine and spruce, and to some extent the birch; they go to make sawn timber, rayon, and pulp (for paper). Pulp may be produced either mechanically —

mainly by grinding — or chemically — by solution. Finland, in
1965, produced almost as much newsprint as her two neighbours,
the Soviet Union and Sweden, combined.

There are giant concerns operating the timber and forest
industries and their derivatives. Some of the biggest units in British
industry are concerned with paper. In Sweden, the Swedish Pulp
Company (the Svenska Cellulosa A.B.) produces enough chemical
pulp to satisfy all the exports of that commodity to Britain, the
largest market for Swedish paper pulp. Sweden's output of pulp in
1900 was about 300,000 tons. By 1937 a peak of 3·5 million tons had
been reached, and this was surpassed only in the 1950s. In 1960
pulp production had reached 4·4 million metric tons. The industry
in Norway is different in its raw-material location from the Swedish
industry. In Sweden, timber resources are distributed throughout
the Northland, though there are also important producing areas in
the Southern Uplands, but in Norway the north and west are un-
forested compared to the east and the Trondelag. Chemical pulp in
Sweden is more important than mechanical; in Norway this position
is reversed. In neither country are the timber industries as pre-
eminent as they once were in the export markets. Norwegian pulp
and paper now take second place as exports to base metals and
manufactures from these metals; in Sweden the value of wood
products exported is almost equalled by that of machinery and
transport equipment.

The Soviet Union

The Soviet Union has a greater area than any other country and
occupies the entire range of latitude covered by the coniferous
forests. Her resources of timber, as of a number of other commodities, are the greatest in the world and, moreover, there is still a
very big reservoir of untapped riches in her forest land.

In general, it is necessary to conserve timber resources carefully
and to ration cutting. No country, not even Russia, can afford to be
wasteful. In the northern part of European Russia annual cutting
takes up about 85 per cent of the natural increase of exploitable
timber. In the Siberian area cutting is on a bigger scale, and
increased twelve times between 1913 and 1958, but represents only
a fragment of the resources there. The percentage distribution of
Soviet Russia's timber resources is as follows: larch, 40; pine, 10;
birch, 13; spruce, 11; cedar, 5 per cent.[2] Not only is there a very
wide longitudinal range produced by the enormous extent of

Russia from the Gulf of Finland to Kamchatka, but the circumstances of growth and consumption are such as to give the Soviet Union an annual rate of increase of 900,000–1,000,000 cubic yards of sawn timber. The major timber-collecting centres of the U.S.S.R. are Kotlas and Arkhangelsk, both on the North Dvina, Igarka and Dudinka on the Yenisei, and Yakutsk on the Lena.

In 1961 softwood stands constituted more than half of Britain's timber imports and, as Peter Meyer has pointed out, timber represents by far the most important item in our imports of basic materials — more important than metals, ores, or wool.[4]

Thoman reports that the Soviet Union, surprisingly, is only four-fifths self-sufficient in timber needs.[5] He sees an eastward movement of the timber industry in Siberia, comparable to the westward movement of cutting in the United States between 1900 and 1950.[6]

The tropics still hold huge untapped reserves of hardwoods that are valuable industrially as well as domestically. The disadvantage of the natural forest is that it contains few pure stands. Transport is an outstanding problem. Railways are a rare amenity, roads are almost non-existent, and a river highway is usually required to take away the wealth of the forest. In parts of South-East Asia, for instance in Burma, the elephant is still of the greatest importance as a forest draught animal. But here, as elsewhere, the ubiquitous bulldozer has effected some change in the scale of exploitation.

In South America the sheer cost of preparing a virgin forest for economic use may be prohibitive. The cost of tropical exploitation at '£ to £ per acre', and 'the cost of the improvement operations, at interest, becomes a millstone around the neck of the silviculturist mindful of economics'.[7]

South and Central America are the chief source of mahogany, rosewood, greenheart, and ironwood. Quebracho — 'the axe-breaker' — comes from Paraguay. The small country of British Honduras is an important exporter of mahogany, which is also found in equatorial Africa and in South-East Asia.

The time element is an important factor in forest conservation and land use. This factor must influence, in different and often opposing ways, governmental policy towards forests, and the commercial organizations and interests concerned. It has been estimated that a commercially useful growth rarely matures in 'under 60 to 80 years in the tropics, and in the montane and sub-tropical variants

frequently not under 100 to 180 years'.[8] In Nigeria's Western
Region the forestry cycle of operations is a hundred years, and in
her Eastern Region eighty years. Tropical timbers are noted for the
beauty of some of their members and for the durability of others.
Greenheart, for instance, is exceptionally resistant to water action.
The gates of many of the canal locks and ocean docks of the world
are made exclusively of this timber.[9] The name Demerara greenheart indicates its country of origin: Guyana has almost a monopoly
of the commercial production of this timber. Countries such as
Nigeria, with an extensive latitudinal range, include large areas of
tropical and subtropical forest within their borders.

Teak is the leading hardwood of southern Asia, and its chief source
is Burma. Its durability and resistance to weather give it a sure
future, while the dyewoods and cabinet woods of the tropics can
also presumably expect a satisfactory demand from more affluent
communities.

Much of the natural cover of deciduous Europe has been cleared,
often owing to wasteful and thoughtless exploitation, but also, on
occasion, because of the exigencies of war. Britain's oaks, once the
raw material for building warships, are now sadly depleted. The
proportion of forest land in Britain today is very small — less than
in any other country of Europe. Even small States, such as the
Netherlands and Denmark, which are renowned for the intensity of
their farming efforts, have proportionately much more woodland.

Comparisons with Scandinavia

The timber resources of foreign lands have a longer tradition of
efficient organization than our own. The immensity of the forest
wealth, particularly of the coniferous lands, has stimulated organization. Steam power was applied to the Swedish sawmills in the
1850s, providing an enormous impetus to production and export.
It has been found with most of the great timber producers that
governmental intervention has been necessary to safeguard supplies.
This has been chiefly because of the time factor. Within the lifetime
of one operator it is often not possible to see through the complete
cycle of a single important tree: this in an industry where controlled
cutting and replanting are essential to conservation and planning.
On the other hand, there are few enterprises where quick, uncon-
trolled returns are so large and so tempting. As a result, for instance

in the Scandinavian countries, there has been massive intervention by public bodies. In Finland 35 per cent of forests are owned by the State or by municipalities; in Sweden the figure is 25 per cent; in Norway over 17 per cent.[10]

The Forestry Commission

Britain's Forestry Commission dates only from 1919. Its creation had been hastened by the accelerated depletion of domestic reserves during the First World War. The work of the Commission, although belated, was on a considerable scale. Stamp and Beaver relate that at the time of the thorough census taken over the years 1921–26 by the Commission, it was discovered that there were in England and Wales about 1·9 million acres of woodland; but this included poor scrub. The size of the national problem was such that the planners of 1919 embarked upon a project lasting eighty years, to afforest 1,777,500 acres.[11] In Scotland about 1 million acres of woodland already existed. The position in 1962 was that the first cuttings, in the shape of 'thinnings', were only just coming on to the market in any quantity. Particularly in Scotland, in the Lake District, and in Wales, Forestry Commission holdings have been planted with conifers, and even with these a quarter of a century needs to elapse before thinnings become practicable. The U.K. still depends on imports for 90 per cent of her timber needs, but by 1980 production from softwood holdings of the Commission will increase from the 18 million of 1961 to 72 million cubic feet per annum. Privately owned woodland will increase production during the same period from 26 million to an estimated 44 million cubic feet. Hardwood production is unlikely to increase much over the present 40 million cubic feet.[12] In February 1964 a Member of Parliament stated that 'many of the great forests of Wales were approaching maturity. Next year, 4,600,000 cubic feet of new timber would be available. In 1970, it would be 5,800,000; 1975, 8,700,000; and in 1980, 12,500,000'.[13]

The scale of the Forestry Commission's holdings also can be judged by the fact that in the year ending September 1964, land owned by the Commission had reached a total of over 2·6 million acres, of which 1·5 million were already under plantations. The original objective of the planners of 1919 was approaching completion. In north Scotland there had been tremendous progress, with the densest plantings to be found in Argyll and large forests located in the districts to the west of Aberdeen, north of Glen

More, and on the coast around the Moray Firth. On the west coast, near Fort William, is Britain's first integrated pulp and paper mill.

FOOD FROM THE SEA

Fishing is an activity with one of the greatest seasonal fluctuations. It is an industry where there is room for the big operator in deep-sea fishing, just as there is also a place for the one-family inshore unit. In some lands the catching, landing, processing, and marketing of fish are mechanized to a high degree. Elsewhere, fishing is a part of a subsistence economy, often providing the richest element in an inadequate diet. In marginal regions, as in China and India, fish ponds are unfortunately subject to the effects of drought, just as are the peasants' tiny fields. Fish die, and so may the fishermen. Elsewhere in these lands, for instance in Cambodia's Tonlé Sap, lakes may provide an enormous seasonal accumulation of exploitable wealth. Fish farming — feasible in most countries — has a growth potential that could transform some national diets. It has been said that fish production from farms and inland waterways in the Soviet Union yields 'about a million tons of fish a year'.[14]

Landings of Fish — The Two Leading Nations[15]
('000 metric tons)

		1962	1963	1964
Peru	. .	6,957	6,900	9,131
Japan	. .	6,867	6,695	6,335

The United Kingdom

Britain's fisheries are an important part of the economy. The investment in boats alone amounts to some £50 million. There has been an unwelcome decline in the catch since 1957. Britain's most important pelagic fish (found near the surface of the sea) are the herring, pilchard, and mackerel. By far the most important of the demersal fish (living on or near the sea bed) of the North Atlantic is the cod. This accounts for more than half of the demersal fish caught by European countries. In the area fished by the British deep-sea fleet the most prolific area for cod is in the waters around Iceland; but the next-highest yield comes from the waters around Bear Island, north of Norway. This latter sailing involves a round journey from Grimsby of about 3,000 miles; but vessels go even

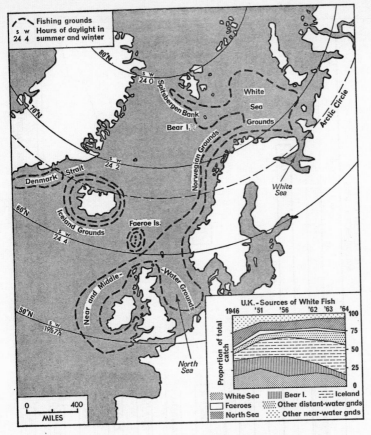

FIG. 3.2   U.K. — major grounds for white fish

Great distances are involved in journeys to the distant fishing-grounds, but a breakdown of the total catch shows the increased importance of the Iceland grounds.

further — to the west of Greenland, for instance — entailing a round journey of as much as 4,900 miles (Fig. 3.2).

Other Nations

Fishing is important to Britain, but it is more vital to Peru (Fig. 3.3), and very much more to Iceland, where it is by far the largest industry. Fish — frozen, salted, or cured — represents nearly 80 per cent of the total value of Icelandic exports. It is not surprising, therefore, that Iceland is particularly sensitive about fishing rights

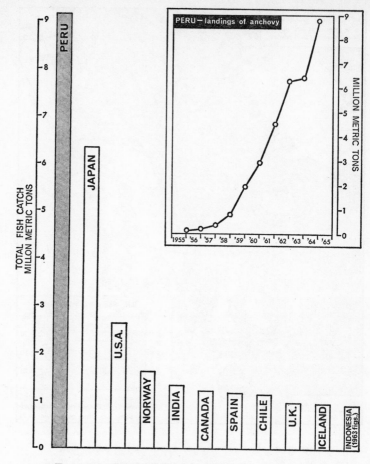

FIG. 3.3   Leading fishing nations — total catch

Peru and Japan are far ahead of other fishing nations. Peruvian
production has increased spectacularly since the late 1950's.

around her shores, where she has promulgated a twelve-mile
territorial limit.

Japan's well-diversified industry has had huge catches of whales,
from both the North Pacific and the Antarctic, as many as 20,000
having been taken in a year from the North Pacific and around
Japan. The annual whale-oil procurement of the Japanese Antarctic
fleets has been as much as 100,000 tons. The Japanese obtain rich
hauls of salmon and crab, not from their old grounds in the Sea of

FIG. 3.4   Fishing industry of Peru

Peru's fish catch is almost entirely (98 per cent in 1964) anchovy.
Nearly all is landed at ports north of Lima.

Okhotsk, but from the North Pacific.[16] There are also important
crab-fishing areas in Bristol Bay, off Alaska. Tuna fishing also
expanded greatly between 1952 and 1960.

It is not surprising that the greatest ocean in the world — the
Pacific — should contain fishing grounds even more prolific than

45

those of the Atlantic and its tributary seas. The United States and
the Soviet Union also share in the wealth of the sea off Alaska, and
the U.S.S.R. has naturally taken over the operation of the fisheries
pertaining to those territories acquired from Japan after her defeat
in the Second World War — namely southern Sakhalin and the
Kuriles. These waters are particularly rich in salmon and crab.
Japanese boats fish the length of the Kuro Siwo current, and operate
around Hawaii and in the Indian Ocean. Fish forms the main
element in the Japanese people's diet.

The story of Peru is one of remarkable progress, which has now
made that country supreme in the world fishing industry (Fig. 3.4).
She is notable for specialization in her catch, as well as for its
magnitude: 95 per cent of the haul in 1960 was in anchovies;[17] in
1964 the figure was 97 per cent. Another outstanding feature of the
west-coast industry of South America is that the anchovy fishermen
are in competition with sea fowl, especially the guanay, the sea birds
being estimated to have taken 1·8 to 2·8 million tons of anchovy
per year in the period 1961–63. The main catch of anchovy, by both
birds and fishermen, is between latitudes 8° and 14° S. The anchovy
is processed into fishmeal (six tons of fish yield one of meal), and in
1964, 9 million tons of anchovy were landed in Peru.

Fishing is highly important in both China and the U.S.S.R.,
despite the fact that many of their people have never seen the sea.
The U.S.A. possesses a two-ocean fleet, as she has a two-ocean
Navy: notable fishing areas are off Alaska and the Aleutians, off
southern California, and off the coast of northern New England.
Russia has a rapidly growing fleet — to be found in the various seas
to which she has access — the Baltic, the Black and White Seas, the
Arctic, and the Pacific. Soviet salmon fishing now rivals in scale
that of the other Pacific Powers: Japan, the U.S.A., and Canada.
It is worthy of mention that trawlers may have a multi-purpose
design: the creation of vast trawler fleets has more than once been
mentioned in *Jane's Fighting Ships*. The Russians have been taking
more fish from New England waters (using the latest types of deep-
freeze vessels) than have the Americans.[18] Some of the Russian
vessels are as much as 2,500 tons.

New Vessels
and Old
Fishing
Grounds

The increased size and range of vessels are impressive. The new
British fleets include stern-fishing trawlers, like the *Junella*, costing
up to £500,000 each, equipped to deep-freeze the catch on board.

Heavy and sometimes over-fishing of traditional grounds has not diminished the importance of the U.K.'s main source of supply — the waters around Iceland. But there has been a considerable fall, both absolutely and relatively, in the share of production from British coastal areas. The industry here has been seriously affected by the restrictions imposed by the Icelandic Government, which puts serious pressure on the fishing grounds of the West and of the North Atlantic. It has been suggested that as a result of the general adoption of twelve-mile fishing limits, the British distant-water trawlermen will by 1972 have lost 9,000 square miles of profitable grounds.[19] There has been a move to explore the possibility of British vessels being able to use the South Atlantic, and the latest Russian vessels — the 'Tropic'-class trawlers — are equipped to take any size or type of fish.

The industry in general is controlled by the century-old appearance of the herring shoals in the same localities year after year. The result is that the traditional grounds are not subject to human choice. The other fishing nations of the Continental Shelf are also entitled to sail the grounds outside U.K. territorial waters — extended, since 1964, to six miles from the shore — and there are, in fact, important landings of herring into this country from Norway and Sweden, but much larger landings from the Republic of Ireland.

There was a time when the herring was one of the principal British exports. Before the First World War as much as 75 per cent of the catch was exported.[20] Now the position is very different: 22 per cent only was exported in 1961, and 26 per cent in 1962. Fluctuations in such sales are caused chiefly by the scale of foreign landings by other fleets from other grounds.

The seasonal pattern of this still important British industry emphasizes the continued supremacy of the Scottish ports. The autumn and winter catches are notable for the achievement of the smaller centres of the Hebrides in the areas of the North Minch (Stornoway, Ullapool, and Gairloch) and the South Minch (Mallaig, Oban, and the Outer Isles).

1. Dept. of Scientific and Industrial Research, *A Handbook of Softwoods* **NOTES** (H.M.S.O., 1957), pp. 49–55.

2. *Financial Times*, 8 Jan. 1963.

3. *Geographical Notes on the Soviet Union*, Soviet Booklets (London, 1960), p. 23.

4. Peter B. Meyer, 'The Timber Industry', *Financial Times*, 19 Nov. 1962.

5. Thoman, *The Geography of Economic Activity*, p. 381.

6. Ibid., p. 383.

7. J. Phillips, *Development of Agriculture and Forestry in the Tropics* (Faber, 1961), p. 128.

8. Ibid.

9. F. H. Titmuss, *A Concise Encyclopedia of World Timbers*, 2nd (rev.) ed. (Technical Press, 1959), p. 95.

10. Federation of Norwegian Industries and Norwegian Ministry of Foreign Affairs, *Norway's Industry* (Oslo, 1958), p. 18.

11. L. D. Stamp and S. H. Beaver, *The British Isles*, 5th ed. (Longmans, 1963), p. 157.

12. E. G. Richards, 'Timber: Britain's Home Resources', *Financial Times*, 19 Nov. 1962.

13. *Hansard*, 8 Feb. 1964.

14. *The Times*, 23 Sept. 1965.

15. F.A.O., *Yearbook of Fishing Statistics, 1964*, vol. 18., p. a-35.

16. Japanese fishing in areas adjoining the Okhotsk Sea is agreed annually with the U.S.S.R.

17. J. P. Cole, 'The Growth of the Peruvian Fishing Industry', *Geography*, vol. xlvii, pt. 2, no. 215 (April 1962), pp. 186-8.

18. 'Russia Shows the Way to Catch Fish', *The Times*, 22 Sept. 1964.

19. *Financial Times*, 12 July 1962.

20. Stamp and Beaver, *The British Isles*, p. 271.

Food for the millions. Ploughing for rice in Kyushu, Japan.

Cereal farming contrasts

above : Combine harvesters at work in Denmark
below : A donkey brings in maize in Egypt

Food and drink production. A large labour supply is often needed.

above : Cacao in Ghana
below : Yams on a commune in southern China

Hand labour in plantation production

left : Cutting budwood in a
    Malayan rubber nursery
below : Cutting sugar cane in
    the West Indies

Coffee plantation layout. Plantation production requires a high degree of order and organisation.

above: Brazil   *below:* Kenya

Water supply

above: The Thames — water pumps at Ashford Common
below: An Indian water cart, pulled by bullocks

Timber

above: Pulpwood for paper being cut and loaded on site in Newfoundland
below: Timber for building in Peking, where one-storey houses are being replaced by
much taller buildings

Copper mining. A highly mechanised operation, often from deep mines.

above: Chibuluma, Zambia
below: Mount Isa, Queensland, Australia

Mining — contrasting surface scenes

above: The Slochteren gas field, Netherlands
below: Mufulira copper mine, Zambia

Steel production in 'advanced' countries, and usually in underdeveloped ones also, is a big-scale operation, requiring large amounts of capital

Bloom passing through the Intermediate Mill en route for the Continuous Billet Mill (East Moors, Cardiff)

Adding cold steel scrap from a charging pan into a Kaldo furnace (Rotherham)

Contrasts in building methods

above: Making bricks in Chainsa village, near Delhi, India
right: Building a hydro-electric power station. Bratsk, on the Angara River, Siberia.

Textile production

above: Old-style. Warping of cotton yarn, Birla Mills, Delhi.
below: New-style. Testing nylon yarn, Brockworth, Gloucestershire.

Labour and production

above : Assembling radio telephones in a Cambridge factory
below : Picking tea in Assam

Aerospace industries

left : Lowering the protective
shroud of a Mariner spacecraft
(Sunnyvale, California)
below : Building Spey aircraft
engines (Derby)

Aircraft manufacture and operation

above : Fitting panels to the Concord fuselage (Filton, Bristol)
below : Mechanical handling of air cargo (Haneda International Airport, Tokyo)

The gas industry

left : Neptune I drilling rig flares off
gas in block 49/26 of the
North Sea gas field
below : Gas reforming plant at
Southall, Middlesex

Chemicals

above: A chemical derivative — nylon. Sampling nylon polymer (Pontypool, Monmouthshire).

below: A basic chemical material — sulphur. The world's largest sulphur-producing unit (Lacq, France).

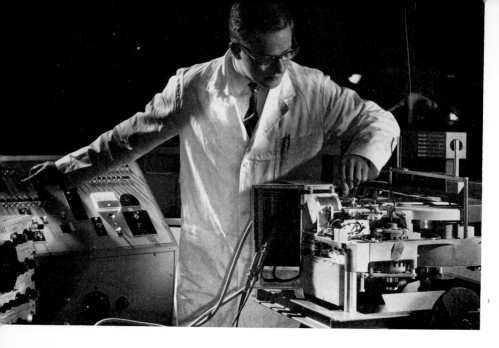

Electronics — manufacture and use

above : Checking a computer in a Greenock factory
below : Operating the automatic control system of a modern power station at Tilbury

Industrial location

above: A chemicals-fibres factory on a spacious site near river and sea (Wilton, near Middlesbrough)

below: A steel-tinplate complex, on a head-of-valley site, alongside a high-density residential area

Energy production

left: Materials assembled for building the Sanmenshia hydro-electric dam, north
    China, which involves the temporary diversion of the Yellow River
above: Kingston thermal power station on Watts Bar Lake, Tennessee. (Coal con-
    sumption — over 4 million tons per year.)

Transport — man and machine

above: A standard container is unloaded from ship to lorry in the southern U.S.A.
below: An Indian method of carrying milk or other liquids

Transport — animal and mechanical traction

above: Egypt. A wooden sleigh in use in the Nile Delta region.
below: New York. Goods and passenger traffic at the exit from the Holland Tunnel.

Railway development in Britain

above: Overhead electrification on the Euston–Liverpool line

left: Colour signalling
at Faversham,
Kent

Traffic problems in great American cities

above: The busiest intersection in the United States, at the meeting of 6th Avenue, Broadway, and 34th Street, New York

below: Chicago's Congress Expressway, divided by Rapid Transit electrified lines

Bridges

above : Road-rail bridge over the River Indus Rohri Channel, West Pakistan
right : The viaduct section of the M4 Motorway, west London

Inland water transport

above: Sailing barges on the Sweetwater Canal, Egypt
below: Diesel-driven barges on the Mittelland Canal, West Germany

From ship to shore

By mobile crane, Port of London

By surf-boat, Ghana

Automation

A hot-steel strip
process is operated
automatically.
Aliquippa,
Pennsylvania

Plantation Farming   Chapter 4

Much of the commercial production in tropical agriculture is in the form of plantation farming. This type of production was born out of a realization of the geographical potential of the tropical zones as well as out of demand in the metropolitan countries. Commercial exploitation of favourable sites began as an activity of private enterprise. Like other linked activities, it ultimately became the concern of the Imperial Powers. Plantations depended upon the availability of very large amounts of capital, derived originally from the savings made possible by technological advances at home.

The Organization of Production

Commercial plantation agriculture today is typically large-scale and geared to industry. The total cost of preparation, of equipping the site, of tillage and maintenance — not to mention materials and labour — is high. The owner must be prepared to wait for results, but the ultimate profit may be very large. Plantation agriculture in the tropics has not been a monopoly of foreign interests, but the time-lag between original investment and eventual return is common to all plantation organization. With the necessity of progressive planting and picking, the commercial risks involved belong chiefly to the early period of operations. Afterwards, the hazards of cultivation are covered by the proceeds from previous crops. Tropical countries have seen large-scale units controlled by native landlords: 'usually not centrally operated estates, but divided into family-type tenant farms'.[1] Plantations, whether in the United States or in the West Indies, in India or Malaya, have been great employers of labour: where this has been inadequate or unsuitable, the human reservoirs of neighbouring areas have been tapped. A consequence of this in Malaya is the very large local preponderance of Chinese.

The utilization of the best land for industrial crops may produce a real shortage of food, leading to imports from distant rice- or other cereal-growing areas. Not every tropical region has the versatility of Java and is able to grow rice and a wide variety of plantation products. Many zones have been leached over the years — the chemical value of their soils diminished, as plant nutrients have been

C H.G.P.

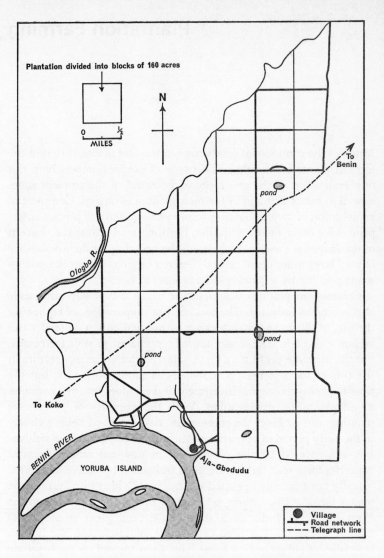

Plantation divided into blocks of 160 acres

N

0   ½
MILES

To
Benin

pond

Ologbo R.

pond

pond

To Koko

BENIN RIVER

YORUBA ISLAND

Aja-Gbodudu

Village
Road network
Telegraph line

FIG. 4.1   West African palm-oil estate

The Cowan Estate, in Nigeria, belonging to Unilever Ltd., is laid
out in blocks of a quarter of a square mile. For harvesting control
purposes, these blocks are divided into strips of 40 acres each.

drained away. This has happened in the Congo Basin and in
Amazonian Brazil.

There is a wide range of efficiency between the small plantation, organized by the native producer, and the very large commercial concern, often owned and managed by a foreign company. A United Africa Company publication has expressed a typical result thus: 'The quantity of palm oil obtainable from a given amount of fruit in a power mill in West Africa is over 90 per cent of the oil content, compared with only 45·5 per cent by primitive African methods'.[2] Heseltine has provided even more striking figures for coffee on European plantations in Kenya and on African holdings in Tanzania and eastern Malagasy, the yields from the European units being three to four times greater than those from the African.[3]

The Organization of Production

The order and uniformity introduced by the intervention in the tropics of large-scale commercial interests is illustrated in the 160-acre blocks of the Cowan Oil Palm Estate, laid out by the Benin River in Nigeria (Fig. 4.1); but many 'plantation crops' are in fact mainly grown by peasant farmers. Almost all tea production is from plantations, but cacao in Ghana and Nigeria is very largely a small producer's crop. Groundnuts are mainly peasant-produced; but most Pacific Ocean coconuts come from plantations.

Control of plantation development by climate is a reality, whether exercised directly, as in the determination of the location of a crop that is inhibited by susceptibility to frost, or indirectly, through the reaction to climate of soil composition and behaviour. Generalizations are dangerous, perhaps most seriously in the case of 'average rainfall' — 'a commonly used expression of little practical value', as Wrigley says. 'Distribution and reliability are more crucial factors'.[4] The temperature requirements of plantation crops can be so specific that only in the belt on either side of the Equator — 'six or seven degrees north and south' say Tempany and Grist — does one find the temperature conditions in which the efficient propagation of hevea rubber may proceed, and 'cocoa is almost equally sensitive'.[5] But such areas may have a marked seasonal variation in rainfall. On the other hand, coffee, bananas, and tea are comparatively tolerant of temperature variations: tea, especially, has a wide distribution, in terms of both latitude and altitude. It is found in the equatorial zone at over 6,000 feet and in latitudes of 30° or even more to north and south of the Equator. The tropical tree crops are particularly vulnerable to severe drought.

Climatic Control

Much of the work required in the investigation of soil conditions in the equatorial and subtropical zones has been organized by plantation interests; other valuable material has been collected by investigators for the World Bank. Certain of the chemical factors involved are derived from the composition and behaviour of the underlying parent rock. Soil make-up is likely to differ as widely as do the rock types of the temperate zones. Tempany and Grist show a Rendzina soil, in profile, resting upon the parent limestone in Jamaica, and in contrast a striking profile of Kikuyu red loam from the Kenya highlands. The loam is far deeper than the Rendzina and is formed from volcanic ash deposited in water.[6] The leaching effects of heavy rainfall are serious: the older the rock base, the more drastic the results.

Twyford and Freitas have shown what can be done as regards soil improvement in banana–cacao country on the Windward Island of St. Vincent. Here erosion has bared the parent rock — a consolidated volcanic ash — and the region is exposed to an annual rainfall of between 60 and 150 inches. Reclamation takes the form of an attack on the bedrock, this process resulting in the accumulation of a new wealth of soil.[7] Nature, in different circumstances, performs a similar service, but over a longer period, by adding the nutrients from decomposed vegetation to the reservoir of food in the subsoil.

Fertilizers The commercial concern is at an enormous advantage as regards the purchase of expensive fertilizer. The most chronic fertilizer hunger is in the equatorial lands, though, as Wrigley says, more phosphate and potash are used in Britain than in the whole of the tropical zone. At the same time, he supplies evidence of the beneficial effects of nitrogen fertilizer on tea plantations.

Nitrogen Application in Tea Cultivation[8]

Nitrogen applied annually (lb. per acre)	Average annual gain in tea crop (lb. per acre)
40	256
80	535
120	721

It is notable that the gain is steady through the whole range of input from 40 to 120 lb. per acre. He gives further evidence of a significant increase in the yield of shelled groundnuts in West Africa — from 700 to 900 lb. per acre — as the result of a single application of superphosphate.[9] There has been a 100 per cent increase in the yield of thirty-year-old oil palms in Nigeria's Eastern Region after one application of 5 cwt. per acre of potassium chloride.[10] There is a possible new source of phosphatic fertilizer in the shape of the phosphate rock found in West Africa. Tests have shown that it may be possible to utilize these deposits on a large scale by mixing them with sulphur, so providing a fertilizer that will give plants the phosphorus intake they need.

The Organization of Production

It is remarkable how commercial organization has shifted production in major commodities from one hemisphere to the other. There have been a number of factors bearing upon this transference — market situation and demand, labour supply, and the incidence of disease — but there was a common geographical factor to the changes. Sugar moved from the Old World to the New; rubber was taken, with conspicuous success, from Brazil to Malaya; tea, originating in South-East Asia, was transplanted in Africa; coffee-growing was imported into South-East Asia: all moved to congenial, and familiar, physical and climatic environments.

Not only crops, but also systems, may be mobile, and Gregor[11] has stressed the spread of plantation organization from the tropics into North America, Central Asia, and even into Europe. The nature of the crop, he holds, is less important in deciding on definitions than is the degree of specialization, rationalization, and capitalization associated with plantation farming.

Changes in Location

1. Rainer Shickele, 'Land Economics Research for World Agricultural Development', *Symposium on Land Economics Research* (Johns Hopkins Press, Baltimore, 1962), p. 104.

2. United Africa Company, *Statistical and Economic Review*, no. 9 (March 1952), p. 10.

3. Nigel Heseltine, 'Investment in Agriculture (2)', *World Crops*, vol. 18, no. 1 (March 1966), p. 72.

4. G. Wrigley, *Tropical Agriculture: The Development of Production* (Batsford, 1961), p. 53.

5. Sir H. Tempany and D. H. Grist, *An Introduction to Tropical Agriculture* (Longmans, 1958), p. 5.

6. Ibid., pp. 23–24.

NOTES

**Plantation
Farming**

7. I. T. Twyford and C. L. Freitas, 'Extension Methods, Soil Conservation and Land Productivity in St. Vincent, West Indies', *World Crops*, vol. 15, no. 3 (March 1963), pp. 89–90.

8. Wrigley, *Tropical Agriculture*, p. 105.

9. Ibid., p. 108.

10. E. W. Bolle-Jones, 'P²O⁵ — A New Phosphate Fertilizer for Use in Less Developed Countries', *World Crops*, vol. 15 (Sept. 1963), pp. 326–7.

11. Howard F. Gregor, 'Plantation Farming and Agricultural Classification', *Abstracts of Papers, 20th International Geographical Congress*, ed. F. E. Hamilton (Nelson, 1964), p. 217.

Commercial Cereal Farming   Chapter 5

The main world areas of white settlement are strikingly differentiated, in their typical production patterns, from the zones of tropical farming. Commercial cereal production is the normal form of agricultural organization in large areas of North America, the Soviet Union, Argentina, and Australia, where most output is for the market. In Britain the proportion of arable land is particularly high in the Holland division of Lincolnshire.

The climatic requirements of cereals are markedly different, so that rice is normally confined to the tropics and subtropics, whereas wheat is associated with semi-arid conditions. Maize, on the other hand, is unsuited to the relatively low temperatures of Britain's summers, but thrives in the humid warmth of France's south-west, the Po Valley, and the Danube Basin, while the United States produces almost one-half of total world output. Maize, much more than wheat, has a regional crop emphasis. It is climatically much more fastidious than the temperate cereals — wheat, oats, and barley — which thrive over a wide area of the mid-latitude lowlands.

Crop Emphasis

It has been said that crop specialization is one of the distinguishing features of commercial grain farming: 'the comparatively few sizeable regions engaging in this type of agriculture tend to specialize in the production of one particular grain crop, growing it almost entirely for commercial markets'.[1] On the other hand, there are important districts, such as the 'wheat belt' of Western Australia, where 'wheat . . . is still the most important crop and is likely to remain so, but its dominance is less marked now than it was 25 years ago'.[2] Another source has spoken of the specialization in grain production of the American Middle West, particularly in the Corn Belt, where farmers 'have virtually no rotations, alternative husbandry or ley farming being unheard of, and livestock are an incidental'.[3] This is indicative of crop emphasis rather than a complete devotion to a single crop. In Iowa, which specializes in

Commercial Cereal Farming

maize, there is a very large production of oats; but in Illinois maize production is about five times that of oats. In much of the Corn Belt the two crops are used largely for animal feed; in fact, says Thoman, four-fifths of American maize is used on the farm, and half of the grain so used goes to pigs.[4] But in the market area of Chicago, as around the major centres of Springfield and Peoria, much of the maize moves from farm to town and city.[5]

Crop emphasis can change drastically. In Kansas, before the First World War, maize was the leading crop, whereas that state now leads the nation in wheat production. In the Soviet Union governmental intervention in the 1950s led to the controversial decision to plant vast new areas with maize.

Mechanization

Farming geared to market demand has become increasingly mechanized. The improvement of ploughs has gone hand in hand with increased knowledge of soil structure and behaviour. Soviet scientists have been to the fore in the examination of the nature of soil; their geographers have led in the mapping of soil types, on a world scale.[6]

Progress in farming is not merely a question of applying capital to land: this must be done scientifically and knowledgeably. The largest producer is not necessarily the best; not the biggest-scale but the correct treatment is required. It is no surprise that machines play a vital role on the extensive farms of cool temperate lands, but it is interesting to note the growth of mechanization in the United States Wheat Belt northwards from Kansas, through Nebraska to the Dakotas.

British farming is already the most mechanized in Europe, and the degree of mechanization is still increasing: in the period 1950–62 the number of tractors on British farms increased by around 30 per cent; the number of combine harvesters was trebled; the number of ground-crop sprayers increased five times, and of pick-up balers seven times.[7] The result is that 4 per cent of the working population is able to satisfy two-thirds of the British market for temperate foodstuffs.[8]

The contrasts in the degree of mechanization between the different food-producing zones are very marked. In 1964, the United States had three and a half times as many agricultural tractors as the Soviet Union, although in 1955 she had had six times as many as the Russians. But, in 1964, the Soviet Union still had more tractors

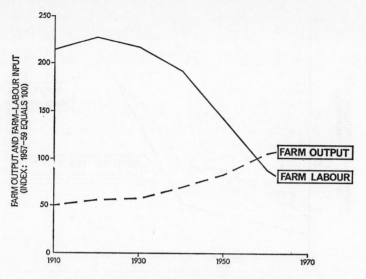

FIG. 5.1   Labour productivity on American farms

Farm productivity has increased dramatically, with an increase in output accompanied by a drastic decrease in farm workers employed.

Fertilizers and Production

than all the rest of the world outside Europe (excluding Russia) and North America. The intensity of mechanization shown in the acreage of arable land per tractor is even greater in Europe than in North America. Comparative progress over a third of a century is shown in the fact that Russia's tractor fleet increased twenty times between 1930 and 1964; North America's, only a little over five times.[9] But the result of American effort is seen in the advance of farm output achieved by a still rapidly shrinking labour force (Fig. 5.1).

A wide range of fertilizers is now available to the farmer, and there has been a spectacular increase in their use. For instance, Britain's consumption of nitrogen quadrupled between the years 1939 and 1954.

There are contrasts in fertilizer use, even among the advanced nations. Russia is notable for her low consumption, contrasting with her huge crop acreages, while American use of potash is considerably greater than that of any two other consumers combined. The United States is singularly fortunate in being self-sufficient in the major base

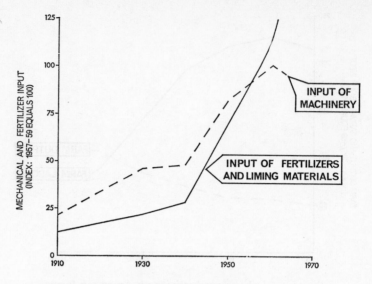

FIG. 5.2   Development of mechanization and fertilizer
use on American farms

The impressive growth in productivity has come from increases
in mechanization and in the utilization of chemical aids.

materials. A more intensive use of fertilizer has, in the past, accompanied increased mechanization, but recently fertilizer sales have continued to rise in America, whereas, in some items, machine sales have actually reached saturation (Fig. 5.2). In Canada extraordinary results have been reported from the use of herbicides, particularly after the application of triazine to maize production, in a cereal–stock-rearing area. In Ontario, farms of 500 to 700 acres, 'growing only maize year after year, where a single man did all the planting, chemical treatment and harvesting', were able to support '400 to 500 beef cattle or 600 to 700 pigs a year.'[10]

By no means all the land from which greater food supplies are required can withstand increased applications of fertilizer. Water supply must be adequate to deal with the sudden increase in mineral food. West European farms can meet these requirements, but even in the United States there are important limits upon fertilizer use. Rainfall is a limiting factor in the Dakota–Kansas region, where application of fertilizer in the mid-1950s was far less intensive than in the better-watered New England states;[11] but since that time there has been a huge development in the use of fertilizer in the drier Middle West. Use of nitrogen in North Dakota, for instance, increased ten times between 1950–54 and 1961, and phosphates four times. Over the same period, in Connecticut and Maine, fertilizer consumption fell.[12] World nitrogen output increased by half between 1957 and 1963, while total world fertilizer consumption increased by fourteen times over the period 1905–61. The United States, despite its climatic range, has by far the largest consumption in the world, nitrogen compounds in the 1962–63 season being more important than any other.[13] The statistics for the following season illustrated the contrast between the inputs of the United States and the Soviet Union.

Fertilizer Consumption, 1963–64[14]
('ooo metric tons)

	Nitrogenous	Phosphatic	Potash
U.S.A. .	4,028	2,984	2,542
U.S.S.R. .	1,360	969	901

In the temperate zone, yields vary from country to country, from farm to farm, and even from field to field. The conditions for growth differ greatly between favourable and unfavourable areas. The warp soils of Lincolnshire yield well; so does the loess of the 'Bays' along the southern edge of the German Plain. Yields can be increased by husbanding the soil and by the input of capital. In the Netherlands and in Denmark, with very limited areas of arable land, the application of quantities of fertilizer, backed by efficient organization and unlimited effort, has produced yields higher even than those in Britain, where arable farming is very competent by most standards. What are notable on the world scale, especially with wheat and barley, are the relatively low yields of the United States and the still lower yields of the Soviet Union (Fig. 5.3).

In the arid and semi-arid areas of commercial grain growing, farms tend to be large and yields low. In optimum soil conditions farms are smaller and yields higher. In West Germany there are nearly 3 million acres occupied by farms of 25 acres and less, and this is an improvement on conditions in the immediate post-war period. In France farms have become excessively small, owing to the working of the inheritance laws. In Sweden three-quarters of arable production is from farms of less than 25 acres. Farm size in Britain is a

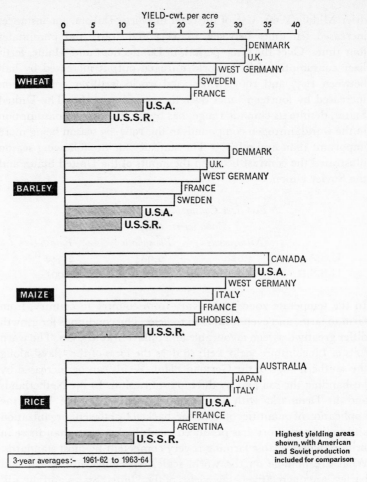

FIG. 5.3 World cereal crop yields

The performance of Denmark is outstanding. Canada and
Australia lead the productivity table for maize and rice respectively, but their production of these commodities is small. There
is evidence here of the poor general performance of Soviet, as
compared with American, farming.

picture of contrasts: more than half of our farms are under 60 acres,
but these comprise less than 15 per cent of the total acreage under
crops and grass. Grigg has portrayed the geographical distribution
of the large (over 500-acre) farms of England and Wales, showing
a very notable concentration in the Hampshire Basin, in Wiltshire

and Berkshire, and in the cereal lands of eastern England. In the United States Winter Wheat Belt the pressure of competition has increased the size of farms: the average went up from 244 acres in 1910 to over 500 acres in 1960. There is a very marked progressive increase in farm size as one proceeds northwards from Kansas into the Dakotas. Consolidation of production in Canada has entailed the reduction in the number of farms and an increase in their size. In Saskatchewan, which is responsible for 70 per cent of Canadian wheat production, the average farm size is now 690 acres, and the 90,000 farms are diminishing in number at the rate of 2,000 a year.[15]

In a given cereal region, especially in the densely populated parts of Western Europe, there may be a vivid contrast in the size of holdings. The position in the context of a modern society is rendered socially explosive where a number of huge holdings exist side by side with a multitude of tiny, intensively worked properties. The situation in post-war Italy was such as to call forth a measure of land reform; but by 1955 this had achieved only a partial success in the division of the largest properties.[16]

In Britain there is some correspondence between the distribution of large farms and of company holdings (farms operated by joint-stock companies, with the help of farm managers). Coppock has shown a marked concentration of company farms among the orchards and hop gardens of the South-East, where farm size is not large.

Very large amounts of money are involved in the big high-yield farms of Britain, as also in the much larger prairie units of North America and the Southern Hemisphere. In Kansas, it has been said, there are 'many companies owning from 40,000 to 70,000 acres'.[17]

In Britain nearly all cereal output is transported a considerable **Production** distance from the farm. In countries where subsistence farming is **for the** normal, for example in India, by far the largest part of production **Market** is for the family or village. Production for the market depends upon the presence of objective conditions — chiefly of climate and soil — to permit cultivation, and upon the pull of demand from the great body of consumers. For output to grow, and for the crop to reach its destination, efficient and adequate transport is needed. The railway has been especially important in the opening-up of the grain lands: this has applied in both South and North America. Production expanded as railway building extended.

Commercial Cereal Farming

Trade in Grain

There are contrasts in the extent to which the different cereals enter into international trade. Trade in rice is very small in relation to production. Some significant areas, it is true, such as Louisiana and the French Camargue, may rely upon steady exports. In America the area devoted to the rice crop increased, in 1962–63, by nearly 1·8 million acres, 'in anticipation of heavier foreign demand, especially under foreign-aid programmes',[18] and the United States is now the third world exporter, more than half of her production finding its way eventually to the market. But the great rice-producers — India and China — are also major grain importers. India imports about 2 per cent of her rice needs but — in bad years — as much as one-third of wheat consumption. China exports some good quality rice — she has recently been the fourth world exporter — and buys even more wheat than India. Burma, the chief world rice-exporter, consumes two-thirds of her product.

Wheat production, on the other hand, often from food-surplus and from relatively thinly populated areas, is commonly geared to exports. Prosperity of communities in the semi-arid lands of both Northern and Southern Hemispheres may depend upon sales abroad.

The volume of trade varies considerably from season to season. In recent years, shortages in the Soviet Union, in China, and in India have led to very large shipments from the New World and from Australia. In 1965 arrangements were made for the Canadians to ship 195 million bushels of wheat to China and 222 million bushels to the Soviet Union.[19] One of the important factors in grain movement and trade is the ability to store vast quantities of the season's product in anticipation of later demand. The size of elevators is great, as is the total scale of their holdings. The recent massive Canadian wheat shipments have led to the construction of considerably more storage space 'at Montreal and at other places down river'.[20]

NOTES

1. Thoman, *The Geography of Economic Activity*, p. 132.
2. Western Australian Dept. of Agriculture, *Agriculture in the Cereal and Sheep Areas of Western Australia* (Perth, 1963), p. 2.
3. 'Agricultural Topics', *The Times*, 28 June 1965.
4. Thoman, op. cit., p. 303.
5. Ibid.
6. See I. P. Gerissamov and N. N. Rozov, 'A System of World Soil Maps', *Abstracts of Papers, 20th International Geographical Congress*, ed. Hamilton.

7. F. Appleyard, 'Anglo-Soviet Teamwork in Agriculture', *Board of*
Trade Journal, vol. 186, no. 3489 (H.M.S.O., 31 Jan. 1964), p. 191.

8. Ibid.

9. F.A.O., 'Progress in Farm Mechanization', *Monthly Bulletin of Agricultural Economics and Statistics*, vol. 15, no. 5 (May 1966), p. 1.

10. 'Agricultural Topics', *The Times*, 8 Nov. 1965.

11. *The Shorter Oxford Economic Atlas of the World*, p. 85.

12. U.S. Dept. of Agriculture, *Agricultural Statistics, 1965*, pp. 489–90.

13. *U.N. Statistical Yearbook*, 1965, p. 511.

14. F.A.O., *Production Yearbook, 1964*, vol. 18, pp. 293, 296, 299.

15. *The Times*, 4 Nov. 1965.

16. V. Lutz, *Italy: A Study in Economic Development* (Oxford U.P., 1962), p. 136.

17. *Statesman's Year-Book*, 1959, p. 683.

18. Commonwealth Economic Committee, *Grain Crops*, p. 130.

19. *The Times*, 29 Oct. 1965.

20. *Financial Times* supplement on 'Canada', 4 Oct. 1965.

Chapter 6 Farm and Nation

Farming and Government

Farming is a strategic activity and farmers have been able to claim, with some justification, that they are entitled to special protection against foreign competition. But Britain is still heavily dependent upon imports of food (Fig. 6.1). In the temperate regions many farming industries are supported by subsidies. This may work through a guaranteed price, which the government will sustain. A government may buy and store grain; it may also impose duties on cheap grain from abroad. The policy of the great shippers such as the Americans and Canadians is particularly important. They in turn are dependent upon prosperity and government policy in Western Europe. In recent years a vital question has been the price regulations affecting farm production in the E.E.C. countries. The French and Germans found it hard enough to agree between themselves on price policy, and even more difficult to produce a common attitude towards the question of Britain's agriculture.

Two points have been especially important as regards farming in this country: Commonwealth preference and farm subsidies. The effect of preferences has been threefold: to commit Britain and British industrial consumers — the chief of these being the millers — to a certain pattern of trade; to support the economies of major exporters like Canada and Australia; and to deter competition from European and other producers. Subsidies have often been criticized as protecting the inefficient by smothering the natural effects of free competition. They have been defended on national and strategic grounds. British yields have been high, but higher expenditure has to be set against increased output.

The contemporary trend is towards the establishment of very big trading units: the United States and her Latin American partners, the Soviet Union and the Comecon countries, the British Commonwealth, E.E.C., and E.F.T.A. The effect of policies of protection is to assist farming within these large groupings. British farmers have received very large sums in subsidies and have been a powerful influence on government policy. The same applies to the farm

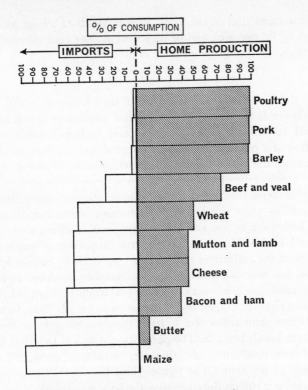

% OF CONSUMPTION

← IMPORTS ─ HOME PRODUCTION

Poultry

Pork

Barley

Beef and veal

Wheat

Mutton and lamb

Cheese

Bacon and ham

Butter

Maize

FIG. 6.1   Britain's food — dependence
on imports, 1965–6

Home production supplies nearly all Britain's
barley consumption, but all her maize requirements and nearly all her butter have to be bought
abroad.

lobbies of France and the United States. There may be conflict
between the policies even of associated States: inside the E.E.C.,
before agreement on common prices was reached in 1966, the
farmers of France and West Germany and of Italy and the Netherlands had great difficulty in reconciling what they consider to be
their respective just demands. The French are in a special position
as regards exports of cereals, as they possess a very large surplus of
production. They plan to export even to West Germany. France's
farm population is now less than half what it was at the end of the
First World War; but the farming community represents 21 per cent
of the active population — twice the percentage of West Germany

65

and four times that of the U.K. French yields of wheat have improved by 62 per cent and of barley by 85 per cent, as compared with 1938, and maize yields have doubled.

The Soviet Union

Under the Soviet system, ownership of land is vested in the State, which controls all sources of finance and investment and is able to demand subordination of all local and sectional needs to the operation of a plan conceived and directed perhaps from far away.

Although the general picture in Soviet society is one of overall central political direction, the agricultural scene shows some variety. Collective farms produce the bulk of agricultural output. They are very large — 5,000 acres is quite common; some, specializing in grain, have over 25,000 acres. Even smaller collectives, such as the kolkhoz Ukraina (Fig. 6.2), have a large proportion of arable land. Farmers on the collectives retain their own plots, of half an acre to an acre, but tractors, combines, and the other machines required are procured from the State's machine and tractor station (M.T.S.). Collective farms elect their own Management Boards. State farms — often bigger than collectives — have been responsible for most of the Virgin Lands projects. The percentage shares of the State farms in total farm production in 1961 were: cereals, 43; meat, 28; milk, 32; wool, 31 per cent.[1] The figures show that overall emphasis in organization is still on the collective, the kolkhoz. Relations between the kolkhoz and the centre, as represented by the regional government, are in the form of an annual contract for the delivery by the collective of stated quantities of specified commodities. 'This contract has the force of law: there appears to be no particular penalties for failing to reach the target (other than the normal economic ones) and reliance appears to be placed entirely on generous bonuses for over-fulfilment'.[2] The contract provides for a planned delivery from the farm, and there is a separate delivery to the M.T.S. on account of work done. To finance operations, first advances are made by the State Bank on conclusion of the contract.[3] The less efficient or less successful farm may not be able to afford to call in the services of the M.T.S.

China

The Communists' victory in 1947–49 was the result of successful rural work over the long period when they ruled large areas of northern China. The revolutionary reorganization of agriculture

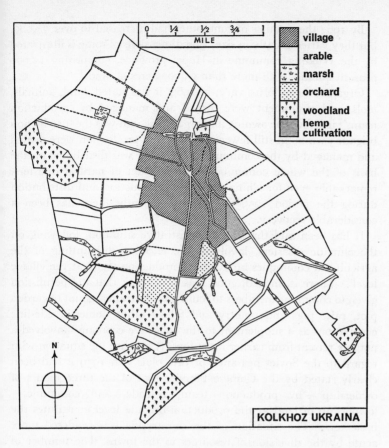

FIG. 6.2   A Soviet collective farm
This Ukrainian collective is nearly all given over to arable farming.

was to involve the creation of communes. These, instituted in 1958, were said to have evolved from successful experience, particularly in the province of Honan. The decision to introduce them nationally followed a number of preparatory steps: (i) the development of 'mutual-aid teams'; (ii) the construction of elementary agricultural producers' co-operatives, pooling land, and practising 'unified management and distribution of income'; and (iii) the introduction of 'advance co-operatives', where the 'major means of production were pooled at their money value and turned into the collective property of the co-operatives'.[4]

By 1963 the number of communes had increased to over 74,000, but they varied greatly in size. The dimensions of some is illustrated by the Wukung commune in Hopei province, comprising 13,000 peasant families with more than 25,000 acres of land.[5]

Organizational forms vary; in 1963, it was stated, land, animals, tools, and equipment were owned and managed by 'production teams'; in a few, the owning and organizing unit was the 'production brigade', while 'in still fewer, the means of production were owned and managed by the communes and income was distributed on the basis of the whole commune'.[6] A succession of natural disasters, remarkable even for China, dislocated production and distribution during the period 1959–61, but subsequently there has been a considerable recovery.

It has been said that the administrative situation, following on the climatic disasters, involved 'the effective dismantling of the agricultural communes in favour of production teams at the village level'.[7] There is, indeed, good reason to think that the permission given to commune members to 'cultivate a certain amount of garden plot, raise pigs and poultry and follow other domestic side-line occupations as a supplement to the collective economy' involved a notable retreat from earlier intentions. (Compare the situation with regard to the Soviet peasants' private plots.) In 1959 it had been clearly stated by the Chinese Premier that of the three modes of ownership — by production team, brigade, and commune — 'ownership of land at the production-brigade level constitutes the basic use'.[8] The situation in the countryside was rendered more acute by the diversion of resources to the towns. The number of industrial 'workers and staff increased by nearly 20 per cent' during the period 1957–59. Most of these vast numbers came from the villages. The result of the crisis in the fields was a decision taken at national level in September 1962 to re-allot priority to agriculture.

In agriculture emphasis has been placed on mechanization and, still more in many areas, on irrigation: 'the linking up of large numbers of existing reservoirs, ponds and canals into integrated irrigation systems, repair of existing irrigation facilities and building key water-control projects in important grain and cotton producing regions'.[9] In north China's winter-wheat belt, 5 million more acres were sown in 1963 than in 1962.

One of the more interesting administrative decisions taken during the agricultural crisis in China was to concentrate investment 'on the most fertile farming areas and those naturally least susceptible to damage by flood and drought'. This is to put realistically into perspective the large-scale schemes that attract publicity. In rural mechanization, likewise, the emphasis is on 'small versatile machines and on irrigation pumps using power made surplus by the decline of industry in the towns'.[10]

China

The first of modern Israel's more than 250 *kibbutzim*[11] (singular: *kibbutz*) was founded in 1909, in the malarial swampland south of the Sea of Galilee, with 'six ploughmen, two watchmen, a secretary-accountant, a reserve worker and two women for housekeeping'.[12] These associations are the product of voluntary dedication to the idea of collective production and community living. The *kibbutzim* are self-governing groups, the members of which may come from an extreme variety of physical and historical circumstances. The early pioneers were Socialist refugees from Tsarist Russia.

Israel

In the first days of Israeli independence after 1949, communal settlements served as defence points near to the new frontiers (including the Gaza Strip; see Fig. 6.3). The *kibbutz* organization presents a picture of a tightly-knit community easily adaptable to the requirements of national defence.

Nearly all — 92 per cent — of land in Israel belongs to the State and is leased to the *kibbutzim*, 'as to others for renewable 49-year periods at a minimal rent'.[13] The strictest collective practices have declined in the circumstances of increased national stability, but the *kibbutzim* are important enough to account for some 30 per cent of total agricultural and 6 per cent of industrial production.[14]

New settlements are being pushed further and further south, with the extension beyond Beersheba of the Yarkon–Negev pipeline. Further momentous developments will follow the flow south from the pipeline being built to carry Jordan water via Galilee and the Plain of Sharon. In a number of districts cereals will not be the main crops. Industrial crops — including sugar beet and cotton — are already being grown under irrigation, as in the Imperial Valley of California, along with deciduous fruits, oranges, almonds, and figs. This is illustrated in the development of the Lachish region, south-west of Jerusalem.[15]

The *kibbutz* has always been linked with the Zionist movement, so acquiring its peculiar socio-political flavour; but in Lachish one farming enterprise, from being a *kibbutz*, has been transformed into a *moshav*, a 'community of individual family-type farmers supported

69

FIG. 6.3 Communal settlements
(*kibbutzim*) in Israel

There are marked concentrations on the north-
eastern and south-western borders and around
Jaffa–Tel Aviv.

by a strong multi-purpose co-operative organization'.[16] The
moshavim are seen by the enthusiast as lower forms of organization;
but the small-holders' villages hold twice as many people as do the
collectives. There exists a third type of village — the *moshav-shitufi* —
combining the collective and private elements of the two main
forms.

Israel

1. A. Filipchuk, *Agricultural Development in the U.S.S.R.*, Soviet Booklet
no. 98 (London, 1962), p. 15.

2. Hemy, *Cotton Growing in the Soviet Union*, p. 54.

3. Ibid.

4. Liao Lu-Yen, 'Collectivization of Agriculture in China', *Peking
Review*, no. 44, 1 Nov. 1963.

5. Hsinhua News Agency, 8 Dec. 1963.

6. Liao Lu-Yen, op. cit.

7. *The Times*, 5 Dec. 1963.

8. Chou En Lai, 'Report on China's 1959 Economic Plan', *China
Reconstructs*, supplement (Peking, Oct. 1959).

9. Hsinhua News Agency, 17 Dec. 1963.

10. The Hong Kong and Shanghai Banking Corporation, *Annual Report*
(1964).

11. Hebrew *kibbutz* = a group.

12. *The Times*, 15 Oct. 1959.

13. Moshe Kerem, 'The Kibbutz', *Israel To-day*, no. 27 (Jerusalem,
1964, p. 10.

14. *The Times*, 15 Oct. 1959.

15. *Operation Lachish* (Tour Ltd., Jerusalem, 1960).

16. Schickele, 'Land Economics Research for World Agricultural
Development', *Symposium on Land Economics Research*, p. 109.

NOTES

Chapter 7 Iron, Steel, and Alloying Metals

The world's mineral wealth is not inexhaustible and there has been a great increase in consumption in recent years. Industrialization requires more metals; the enormous increase in canning calls for steel, as well as tin; technological developments have led to important changes in the demand even for such 'old' metals as copper and lead. Over the past thirty years there has been a sensational expansion in the production and demand for aluminium, which has ousted copper from sections of the electrical industry, including power transmission. But at the same time total demand for copper has continued to rise fast, though not quite so quickly as in the early years of expanding electrification.

IRON AND STEEL Steel is an index of industrial strength, as it is of political power. Between 1946 and 1965 world steel production increased four times; in recent years total output has been rising by an average of over 8 per cent per annum.

Iron Ore Iron is one of the few important minerals in which most of the leading industrial nations could, if necessary, be largely self-sufficient, Japan being the obvious exception. The leader in iron-ore output is the U.S.S.R. (Fig. 7.1). The iron industry contains something of a balance in bulk between raw material and fuel supplies so that smelting may occur on either the coal or iron-ore field. An equilibrium of locational factors is seen as between Lorraine and the Ruhr and, over much greater distances, between the Urals and the Kuznetsk field in Soviet Siberia.

In Britain, the main trend of pig-iron production has been: (i) towards the ore fields, as at Scunthorpe and Frodingham; (ii) continued development on the North-East Coast, especially on Teesside; (iii) the construction of large units in South Wales.

72

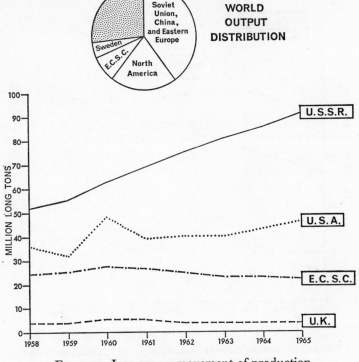

WORLD
DISTRIBUTION

FIG. 7.1   Iron ore — movement of production
(iron content)
The Soviet Union continues to increase her share of world
production.

Some of the most spectacular recent finds of ore have been in
South America, notably in Bolivia and Brazil; but Canada may
eventually rank as second in world ore reserves: the proved total
there, it has been said, could amount to as much as 30,000 million
tons.[1] Bare statistics of production do not indicate the richness of
the ore — whether it is 'lean', like the Jurassic supplies of eastern
England, or rich, like the Swedish or the Soviet ore, which have on
the average twice the iron content of British ores. Ore which is far
from conceivable transport facilities has to be disregarded in evalu-
ating mineral wealth; but new resources are still being confirmed
and, in Western Australia's Pilbara region alone, there has been
found 1,000 million tons of ore, 'which can be profitably mined and
shipped without processing'.[2]

Iron, Steel, and Alloying Metals

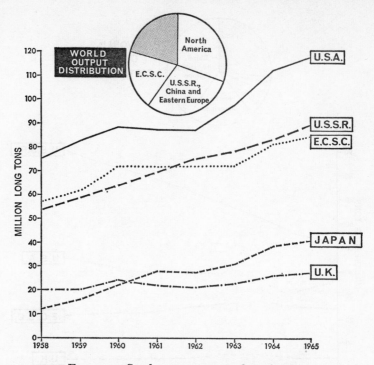

FIG. 7.2   Steel — movement of production

Britain's performance shows up unfavourably in comparison with that of her more powerful competitors.

Steel Production

The United States still leads the world in steel production, but Soviet steel output has risen impressively, and Communist China is also now a significant producer. In Eastern Europe there has been a notable growth: in Czechoslovakia, for instance, in Poland, and in East Germany. The Comecon countries have produced an ambitious plan for 500 million tons of steel by 1980, half to come from the U.S.S.R. In the European Coal and Steel Community (Fig. 7.2), West Germany is still supreme. German domestic ore supplies are not negligible; since the Second World War mining has been greatly stepped up. Ore imports decreased by over a quarter during the period 1960–63, France and Sweden together supplying over half of them. Today West Germany has been overtaken in the table of world producers by Japan — this despite the fact that Japan is deficient in iron and has to buy more than half of her consumption of coking-coal. Nearly a third of Japanese scrap also comes from abroad. The French achievement has also been considerable, output having increased from 11 million tons in 1952 to almost 20 million tons in 1964 and 1965.

Along with other major industries, steel has made most important technological advances in the past decade, particularly in the L.D. process (named after the Austrian towns of Linz and Donawitz, where it was first developed) and the Kaldo converter (named after its inventor, Professor Kalling, and the Swedish steelworks, the Domnarfvets Jernwerk, where it was first used). The substitution of large quantities of oxygen for the hot-air blast that was formerly used in making steel has cheapened its manufacture. A striking increase in the fuel efficiency of blast furnaces has reduced the amount of coke needed to make each ton of pig-iron. In Britain this figure stood at 22·1 cwt. of coke, per ton of pig-iron, in 1946. By 1961 it had been reduced to 16·4 cwt. Britain has also been to the fore in the development of continuous casting processes, in which molten steel is converted into a semi-finished product in a single operation.[3]

There are two giants in steel production, the United States and the Soviet Union, but the productive capacity of the Americans is still far superior. The largest unrealized potential lies in South America, Asia, and Africa. Perhaps the greatest increases in the immediate future are to be anticipated in China, India, and Brazil. China's industrial leap forward was based upon steel, the new Communist rulers having appreciated its strategic role. In their ambition to make China one of the leading World Powers, they adopted industrial and military policies that called for considerable increases in steel supplies.

1. The United Kingdom
    There have been considerable changes in the location of the United Kingdom industry. The iron-making that preceded steel was concentrated where iron and charcoal were available, as in the Forest of Dean. Later, the industry moved to the more considerable raw-material supplies of the coalfield clayband and blackband ores. The availability of large supplies on the continent of Europe encouraged the setting-up of steel installations on the coast of the

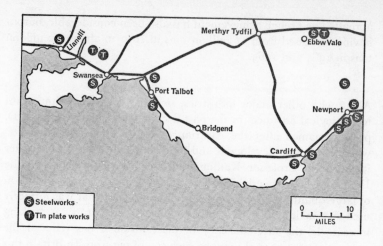

FIG. 7.3   South Wales iron and steel industry
Some of Britain's biggest and newest steelworks are located in
South Wales. Most of them near the sea.

U.K. The growing significance of imports of ore and scrap, as well
as the presence of iron in the Cleveland Hills, supported the steel
industry of the North-East, although for many years the phosphoric
nature of the local ore prevented its use in steel. However, the work
of Thomas and Gilchrist disposed of that difficulty; and the excellent
Durham coking-coal has helped to keep the industry here, even
with the decline and disappearance of the Cleveland ore supplies.
   During the inter-war years, one of the chief developments in the
industry was the growth of production using Jurassic ores, as at
Appleby–Frodingham, in Lincolnshire, and at Normanby Park and
Corby. The production position in 1938 showed the Lincolnshire
steel mills as having gone ahead of those in Lancashire or in Stafford-
shire. Since the Second World War there have been spectacular
developments, first in the North-East and, most recently, in South
Wales. Production in No. 8 (the Welsh) District of the British Iron
and Steel Federation is now much greater than that of any other
region. In South Wales are the tide-water locations of Port Talbot
and Margam, of Cardiff and Llanwern (Fig. 7.3). During the past
quarter of a century, production has increased faster in South
Wales than anywhere else in the United Kingdom; and inside South
Wales there has been a very marked shift to the east, away from
Llanelli and Swansea.[4] Steel output in South Wales has almost

trebled since 1938. Imports of iron and other ores from abroad into this region more than quadrupled in the period 1938–61.[5]

Much of South Wales steel is consumed locally, notably by the tinplate works at Ebbw Vale, at Trostre, and at Velindre. The most important movement of strip steel from South Wales is to the car-manufacturing centres of the English Midlands.

Defence, and the newer space industries, are important consumers of steel, often in alloy form. Tradition and know-how still count for much. Some of the older producing districts can profit from the utilization of fresh techniques to maintain themselves, and one of the largest single developments in recent years has been at Rotherham, where the Park Gate Works uses the latest Kaldo converters.

2. The United States

The growth of the steel industry of the United States was closely connected with the city of Pittsburgh and with the person of Andrew Carnegie, one of the great steelmasters of the world. Around his creation, the Carnegie Steel Company, was eventually constructed the United States Steel Corporation, which is still one of the key producing units of the non-Communist world.[6] Iron had been found in the Monongahela Valley in the last decade of the eighteenth century, but the steel of Pittsburgh was founded, above all, on the availability of Pennsylvanian coking-coal. With the exhaustion of local supplies, it was soon seen to be feasible to bring in the plentiful coking supplies that had long been known to exist both to the west and to the south of Lake Superior. Upon these reserves were built the later steel industries, not only of Pittsburgh and Wheeling, but also of Youngstown, of Cleveland on Lake Erie, of Buffalo near the Niagara Falls, of Chicago–Gary, and of Detroit (Fig. 7.4).

When one speaks of the movement of supplies across a country the size of the United States, it is necessary to remember the conti-nental scale of the procedures involved. In many instances the distances are comparable to those taken by Britain's imported ores. Of recent years the Americans have become more and more conscious of the finite nature of their own plentiful natural wealth. Imports of ore into the U.S.A. have assumed greater and greater significance for her production–consumption pattern. Among imports, of course, have to be considered the purchase and move-ment of iron that may have come only a comparatively short distance from Ontario, or, still along Canadian railways and the St. Lawrence, from the plentiful supplies of Labrador.

Iron, Steel, and Alloying Metals

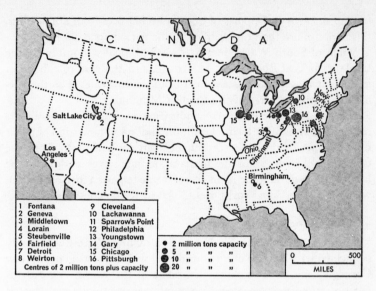

FIG. 7.4   U.S. — location of steel production

American steel output is still overwhelmingly concentrated in the region between Chicago and Philadelphia.

In the southern Appalachians are to be found the blast furnaces of the town of Bessemer and the steel mills of Birmingham, Alabama. The East Coast industry includes the steel of Bethlehem, Pennsylvania, and Sparrow's Point in Maryland: both of these centres belong to the Bethlehem Steel Corporation. Since 1912 the coastal works have utilized ore brought in cheaply from South America.[7] Originally supplies came from Chile, but now, the United States is a customer for the very important supplies of Venezuela. In fact, in 1961 virtually all of the Venezuelean production — the largest in South America — went to the United States, but in 1962–63, the South Americans lost ground in the United States market to Canadian exporters. The American industry also has significant centres in the West, in Utah and in Colorado, and at Fontana in California.

American achievements are subject, inevitably, to comparison with those of the Soviet Union. After falling back in the early 1960s, American production went ahead again in 1964, increasing by 16 per cent over the previous year, to an output of 113 million tons and it increased again, in 1965, to 117 million tons. American industry could, if necessary, produce much more even than this.

Some American steel consumers have been buying heavily from abroad: total steel imports in 1965 were over 10 million tons — four million from Japan alone.

3. The Soviet Union

There are three main areas of European Russia where natural advantages of raw material or fuel wealth have produced a very large metallurgical industry: (i) in the Donetz Basin; (ii) at Krivoi Rog, the largest iron-ore field east of Lorraine–Luxembourg; (iii) in the Urals. There are also big ferrous metallurgical centres in or near the Kuznetsk Basin, and at various points on the Volga and its tributaries — notably at Volgograd, Gorki, Noginsk, and Cherepovets. As in the case of the United States, ore or fuel may have to travel great distances. The distance from the iron of Krivoi Rog to the coal of the Donetz is a mere 500 km.; but from the ore-field that Chelyabinsk (in the Urals) utilizes, the distances to major coal reserves are vast: 1,150 km. to Karaganda; 1,500 km. to Kuznetsk.[8] Similar problems are involved in the movement of ore from the southern Urals to Kuznetsk. Cherepovets is near neither iron nor coal; but it is convenient for the express rail routes to Leningrad and Moscow. Coal has to come from the Arctic Pechora field, and iron from the equally distant Kola Peninsula.

The Soviet planners are fortunate in having a diversity of choice in determining the location of industry, and their choice is greater than it was half a century ago. For instance, there are good prospects of the economic transformation of much of Siberia, in which the power and metallurgical industries will play a very large part. Coke is relatively dear in eastern Siberia, where cheap hydro-electric power favours the use of electric furnaces.[9] An iron and steel plant is being built at Tayshet, east of Krasnoyarsk, using the iron and steel deposits that lie near the junction of the Angara–Ilim rivers. (These deposits hold a reserve of 1,000 million tons of haematite, and have a ferrous content of 40 per cent.)[10] Soviet steel production has continued to advance at a rate of rather more than 5 per cent per annum, to reach nearly 90 million tons in 1965.

4. Japan

Japan is now the third world producer of steel, with over 40 million tons in 1965. The Japanese industry is inescapably dependent upon imports of ore, principally from Malaysia, India, and the Pacific coast of South America. The limited supplies of native coal

Iron, Steel, and Alloying Metals

1 Muroran	9 Amagasaki
2 Kamaishi	10 Kobe
3 Chiba	11 Hirohata
4 Kawasaki (3)	12 Kure
5 Ueno	13 Kokura
6 Wakayama	14 Tobata
7 Sakai	15 Yawata
8 Osaka	

Centres of ¾ million tons plus capacity

● Up to 1 million tons capacity
● 1 to 2 ,, ,, ,,
● 2 to 3 ,, ,, ,,
● 3 to 4 ,, ,, ,,
● 5 ,, ,, ,,

HOKKAIDO

SEA OF JAPAN

Hakodate

Sendai

Toyama

TOKYO

Nagoya

Osaka

Hiroshima

Yawata

SHIKOKU

KYUSHU

Nagasaki

PACIFIC OCEAN

0   100   200
MILES

Fig. 7.5   Japan — location of iron- and steel-works
Nearly all Japan's steel production is located along an axis
Tokyo–Yawata.

have led to great stress being placed on the economic use of fuel.
In 1963 the amount of coke needed, on the average, to produce one
ton of pig-iron in Japan was 22 per cent less than that required in
the United States.[11] There are heavy concentrations of production:
(i) around Osaka and Kobe (Fig. 7.5); (ii) in the Tokyo–Yokohama
region; (iii) in the north of Kyushu, including the largest and oldest
Japanese steel-making unit, at Yawata, which had an annual
capacity of nearly 5 million tons in 1964. But almost as large is the
Kawasaki Corporation's installation at Chiba on Tokyo Bay.

80

5. *West Germany*

The West German steel industry is concentrated in the Ruhr to
the extent of about 70 per cent of production. Pig-iron production
is centred there to a slightly less degree. Easily the next most
important region is in the Saar which, twice during this century, has
been under largely French control. About five times as much pig-
iron is produced in the Ruhr as in the Saar basin — and about six
times as much steel.

Most Ruhr steel, as Pounds[12] has said, is produced at either end,
east and west, of the coalfield. The biggest concentration is near to
Duisburg–Ruhrort, the next most important centre being Dortmund. The main producing areas are dependent upon good communications by rail and, still more, by canal. There are two vital
east–west canals crossing the Ruhr, and Dortmund is also connected
direct with the sea by the Dortmund–Ems Canal. Essen, although
no longer having the status in the industry that it once possessed, is
still important as a producer of special steels. On the northern plain,
north-west of Hanover, there is a steel complex using the minette
ores of Ilsede. Its situation may be compared with that of the Corby
Works in Britain. Steel-making as well as shipbuilding is carried on
in the Lower Weser region; the two industries are of course interdependent.

6. *France*

Lorraine is almost as important to French steel production as the
Ruhr is to Germany. About two-thirds of France's steel is made
there. Lorraine is proportionately even more important in pig-iron.
This is logical, since the smelting works are near the great supplies
of minette ore. The next most important district in France is on her
northern coalfield, where the main producing centre is Valenciennes.
Here steel is more important than pig-iron. In the Lorraine area,
which was first developed on a large scale by the Germans after
1871, the mines, the blast furnaces, and the steelworks are found on
either side of the heavily wooded valley of the Moselle. The trend
since the 1930s has been towards increased concentration on the
western side of the river. The ore-field has for long been inter-
nationalized between the Powers and interests that in 1926 formed
the International Steel Cartel, and after the Second World War the
European Coal and Steel Community.

The Moselle Valley producers are now beginning to benefit from
the construction, with French and German capital, of the Moselle

D   H.G.P.

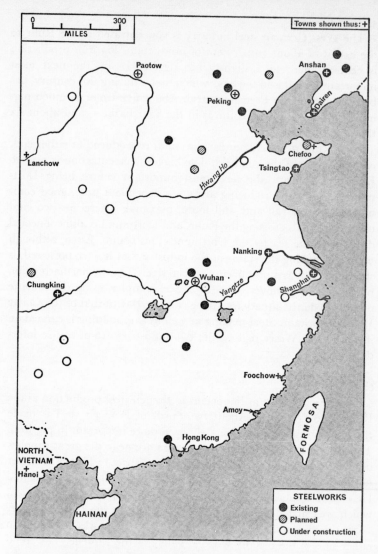

FIG. 7.6   China — location of steel industry

Chinese steel production is widely dispersed and new units are being added in the west and north-west.

Canal. This allows barges of 1,500 tons to reach Thionville from Rotterdam via Duisburg and Koblenz. The Lorraine ores are lean. To enrich them it is usually necessary to import ore that has come from afar. The expected saving to Thionville producers, who can now use the new canal for the transporting of Venezuelan ore, was in 1963 estimated at nearly 10 per cent.[13] But the wholly seaborne ore supplied to coastal installations is still cheaper.

7. *Belgium–Luxembourg*

There are close commercial and financial links — antedating the creation of the Common Market — between the Belgian and Luxembourg steel industries. An example of the co-ordination is Didmar, the steel complex being built outside Ghent. Its main partners are the Belgian Cockerill-Ougrée and the Luxembourg Arbed companies. The mills of the two countries have been manufacturing over 11 million tons of steel a year since 1962. In 1963 they formed the leading exporting unit in the world — bigger even than the Japanese.

8. *China*

The Chinese Communists inherited a steel industry largely grouped in Manchuria around the Anshan works, which the Japanese had organized during their occupation. The Chinese have since developed complexes at Paotow on the Mongolian side of the Yellow River, and at Wuhan on the Middle Yangtze (Fig. 7.6). National production went ahead, impelled, as in the early days of the Soviet Union, by a ruthless drive to establish the industrial bases for further growth; but since 1960 steel has been recovering from the reaction against the 'backyard furnaces' plan. For a time, this had boosted output by a policy of steel at any price and, apparently, of any quality. The Chinese subsequently admitted that the resulting product was 'not really steel at all'.[14] Output in 1964 is estimated to have been less than 10 million tons. The major producing centres as listed by K. P. Wang are, in order of size: Anshan, with total output in 1963 of 4·5 million tons; Wuhan (3·5 millions tons); Paotow; Shanghai; Shihchingshan; and Chungking. The Wuhan works were two-thirds completed in 1963, and only working at half capacity.[15]

The steel industry depends very largely for its operation upon the availability of alloy metals. *Manganese* is important as a cleansing agent in the smelting of steel, ridding the metal of the oxygen and sulphur that would otherwise remain in the form of ferrous sulphide and ferrous oxide; manganese also increases its tensile strength and resistance to abrasion. This mineral's strategic significance arises first from its position as the leading ferro-alloy; secondly, from the lack of manganese supplies in the United States; thirdly, from the surplus in the Soviet Union.

Chromium is needed to make steel stainless and also to render it stronger and more resistant to wear. The Soviet Union produces far more *chrome ore* than any other country, but the great bulk of world reserves lies in Africa, south of the Sahara — some in Rhodesia, but most in the Republic of South Africa. The principal South African site is at Rustenburg, in the Transvaal. The major Soviet source is Khrom-Tau, in Kazakhstan. The United States is vulnerable in respect of this mineral also, being almost entirely dependent upon imports from the Eastern Hemisphere: normally, Rhodesia supplies half of her requirements.

The largest *nickel* reserves in the world are located in Cuba, but processing of the Cuban ore — containing up to 50 per cent of iron — is difficult and costly. During the period 1960–66, Canada's Sudbury mines supplied 80 per cent of the non-Communist world's consumption. However, the Soviet Union and Cuba between them mine about a third as much as Canada. Nickel is a vital requirement for the manufacture of ordnance and ammunition, and it is one of the raw materials of the satellite and missile programmes of the Great Powers. The discrepancy between the production and consumption of minerals — even in developed countries — is well illustrated by the contrasting positions of nickel in the United States and Canada: the United States is without nickel ore, but accounts for 50 per cent of its consumption in the non-Communist world; Canada makes massive exports to the United States, but consumes little herself.

U.S.A. and Canadian Consumption of Nickel
(million lb.)

			1961	1962
U.S.A.	.	.	227	240
Canada	.	.	12	13

Tungsten, obtained chiefly from wolframite, is used in the manufacture of armour-piercing projectiles, its most important property being resistance to heat: tungsten has the highest melting-point of any metal. It is used in ferro-alloys, and also together with cobalt, chromium, copper, and silver.[16] Tungsten carbide, made by adding a small amount of carbon to tungsten powder, is the hardest metal, which explains its role in tank manufacture. Since 1914 China has been the leading producer in the industry, and the Communist Powers today are responsible for over half the total world output. By the dumping of subsidized cheap concentrates in the West, the Communists have been able to put marginal producers out of business,[17] but the position for the West has improved relatively since the discovery of large reserves of high-grade ore in the Flat River Valley of Canada's North-West Territories.[18]

The distribution of *molybdenum*, another essential ingredient in steel manufacture, is highly uneven. The Southern Hemisphere apart from Chile has almost none. Ninety per cent of non-Communist supply comes from the United States, and three-quarters of this from the single Climax mine, in Colorado. Molybdenum can be used as a substitute for tungsten.

Cobalt is required for alloying with chromium, tungsten, or molybdenum, and for making cobalt steel. It is usually found alongside copper and silver, the oldest-established location being at the town of Cobalt in Ontario; but Katanga is estimated to contain more than twice the reserves of all Canada; moreover, the Katangan ores are much higher-grade than the Canadian.[19] The second most important Commonwealth source is the Zambian Copperbelt.

As with molybdenum, most of the alloy mineral *vanadium* comes from the U.S.A. — more than half, in fact, in 1960. The only other significant producers are South-West Africa, the Republic of South Africa, and Finland.

We have been told that 'there is . . . no foreseeable shortage of *titanium* minerals in the world',[20] though their distribution is uneven. In 1950 the U.S.A. was producing twice as much ilmenite — the main source of titanium — as India, the next most important source in the non-Communist world. But there is a great discrepancy between published figures of production. Ogden and Gonser have pointed to the very large potential of eastern Quebec.[21] More information about these deposits, at Lac Tio, and their recovery, is to be seen in an article by Barksdale.[22] Ninety per cent of the world's rutile — a source of titanium dioxide, and the raw material for the manufacture of titanium tetrachloride — comes from Australia.[23] The development of titanium processes in Utah and Nevada, during the course of the Second World War, is discussed by

Jewkes, Sawers, and Stillerman.[24] The importance attached to the metal by a United States Senate Committee was expressed as follows: 'We recommend increasing the production goal for titanium to 150,000 tons annual minimum without delay. Titanium is a new wonder metal. This is a military must. . . . This metal can become the basis for a 5 to 10 billion dollar new civilian industry. Production of the long-range supersonic speed bombers and the necessary fighter planes will make obsolete any nation's air equipment built without it'.[25] 'One of the greatest technological achievements of the A.11', says *Flight International*, speaking of the Mach-3 Lockheed aircraft that first flew in 1963, 'is the fact that practically the whole primary structure is of titanium. A far greater proportion of the airframe is of titanium and its alloys than anything achieved previously. . . . Structural temperatures at Mach 3 at 70,000 ft. are likely to reach 275° C. (520° F.), which is beyond the limit for any aluminium alloys currently available'.[26] And even these achievements may be surpassed by imminent developments in space technology. In the course of re-entry after space flight, nose cones, we are told, 'may be expected to encounter for short periods, temperatures of 3,500° F. (1,930° C.) and higher'. New elements, new alloys, are needed: 'uses of titanium-base alloys to 1,600° F. (870° C.), cobalt-base alloys to 2,500° F. (1,370° C.), molybdenum-base alloys to 3,400° F. (1,870° C.) are possibilities under study and development'.[27]

NOTES

1. *Structural Change in World Ore* (B.I.S.F., 1963), pp. 4, 11.
2. *The Times*, 7 Dec. 1965.
3. *The Times*, 5 Aug. 1965.
4. Leslie Jones, 'Llanwern and the South Wales Economy', *Financial Times* supplement on 'The Spencer Works', 26 Oct. 1962.
5. Ibid.
6. Norman J. G. Pounds, *The Geography of Iron and Steel*, rev. ed. (Hutchinson, 1966), p. 122.
7. Ibid., p. 130.
8. A. E. Probst, in *The Location of Communist Industry*, ed. G. W. Hemy (Joseph Crosfield, Warrington, 1963), p. 6.
9. Ibid., pp. 105–6.
10. Paul E. Lydolph, *Geography of the U.S.S.R.* (Wiley, 1964), pp. 358–9.
11. Shigeo Nagano, 'Steel Industry Forging Ahead of Europe', *The Times* supplement on 'Japan', 21 Sept. 1964.
12. Pounds, *The Geography of Iron and Steel*, p. 130.

13. Ernest Broes, 'European Steel: The Impact of U.S. Coal', *The Times Review of Industry* (Feb. 1963).

14. B. Crozier, *China and her Race for Steel Production* (B.I.S.F., July 1959), p. 11.

15. K. P. Wang, 'The Mineral Industry of Mainland China', *U.S. Mineral Yearbook*, vol. iv (U.S. Bureau of Mines, Washington, D.C., 1963), p. 1287.

16. K. C. Li and C. Yu-Wang, *Tungsten* (Chapman & Hall, 1955), p. 3.

17. 'The Wolfram Market and Supplies from behind the Iron Curtain', Beralt Tin and Wolfram Ltd., *Annual Report*, 6 Nov. 1962.

18. Commonwealth Economic Committee, *Iron and Steel and Alloying Metals* (H.M.S.O., 1965), p. 162.

19. Ibid., pp. 198–9.

20. A. D. and M. K. McQuillan, *Titanium* (Butterworth, 1956), p. 3.

21. H. R. Ogden and Bruce W. Gonser, 'Titanium', in *Rare Metals Handbook* (Reinhold, New York, 1954), pp. 456–7.

22. Jelks Barksdale, 'Titanium', in *The Economic Geography of Industrial Materials*, ed. A. S. Carlson (Reinhold, New York, 1956), p. 214.

23. *Financial Times*, 27 Sept. 1965.

24. J. Jewkes, D. Sawers, and R. Stillerman, *The Sources of Invention* (Macmillan, 1958), p. 398.

25. 'Critical Materials: Factors Affecting Self-Sufficiency within Nations of the Western Hemisphere', Supplement to *Senate Report 1927* (U.S. Govt. Printing Office, Washington, D.C., 1956), p. 4.

26. 'A.11, Some Thoughts on a 2,000 m.p.h. Aircraft', *Flight International*, 12 March 1964.

27. J. H. Scarff, 'Coming Developments in Metals Technology', in *American Enterprise*, ed. M. R. Gainsbrugh (Macmillan, New York, 1961), pp. 284–5.

Chapter 8 Non-ferrous Minerals and Metals

Some minerals are important because they are required as alloy materials, to impart special and individual qualities to steel. Other strategic items are just as important, either in their own right, or alloyed among themselves. Thus copper is often found alloyed with tin, to produce bronze, one of the world's oldest mineral admixtures. More common today is brass, a mixture of copper and zinc. Bronze itself can be combined with numerous minerals or metals — among them manganese, aluminium, and nickel — to produce special alloys.

Copper   Increasing mechanization and improvements in copper mining techniques have made practicable the working of copper deposits that were previously uneconomic. The biggest producers are the United States and the Soviet Union, the leading exporters Chile and Zambia. Distance from the markets in the highly industrialized countries has promoted the development of post-primary processes, like those near the Chilean mines. The main centres of production there are not owned by the Chileans; in 1960, 89 per cent of production came from American-owned mines. The United States is therefore in a position to dictate production policy.

Copper passes first through a concentrating mill, then through a smelter. The amount of waste matter in the copper ore makes it economical to carry on both concentration and smelting near the producing centre. Materials for the electrical industry need to be especially pure, so the blister copper from the smelter passes to an electrolytic refinery utilizing plentiful electric power. Conditions now exist in Central Africa, in the Great Lakes region of North America, in the Urals, and in Soviet Central Asia for the provision of adequate electrical power, often from hydro-electric stations.

One commercial risk is that substitute materials will be found, to undercut the price at which the miner can produce. The chief such competitor to copper is aluminium. There are many items of domestic use in which aluminium has supplanted its rival. Another Copper and growing alternative is afforded by plastics.

Fortunately for prices, a number of the important industrial countries have little or no copper-mining, and one of the main producers — the Soviet Union — must seek considerably to supplement production by imports. In 1962 the Russians made tentative approaches to Chile to import 300,000 tons of ore over the succeeding five years, but discussions failed over a disagreement on price.[1] Britain has to import all of her copper ore. The Americans and Russians too, despite large outputs, have to import sizeable quantities of ore. The Japanese are significant producers but also have to import more than half of their needs.

The consumption of copper is likely to grow appreciably in the foreseeable future, particularly because of its role as the most efficient conductor of electricity. Britain's electrical exports, depending upon the use of copper, have been running at about £360 million per year.

Leading Producers of Copper ('000 metric tons)[2]
(mine production — content of ore)

Country	1961	1962	1963	1964	1965
U.S.A.	1,057	1,114	1,101	1,131	1,229
Soviet Union	540	560	600	675	700
Zambia	575	562	588	632	696
Chile	547	586	601	622	583
Canada	398	415	416	442	463
Congo Republic (Katanga)	295	297	271	277	289
WORLD TOTAL	4,382	4,504	4,613	4,810	5,021

The largest deposits of lead in the world are around Broken Hill, **Lead** New South Wales: it is found there alongside zinc. The same conjunction occurs in British Columbia and in a number of other Commonwealth sources. Galena is the chief source of lead and it often contains silver also. In industry, base lead is often alloyed with antimony or tin.

The production figures of lead are interesting, American output having fallen by almost a third between 1953 and 1962. However, the significance of such a drop in production is not necessarily what it may seem. A cut-back in output may be undertaken quite

Non-ferrous Minerals and Metals

deliberately, in the light of low world prices. After 1963, American output recovered, but Australia is easily the most important non-Communist producer.

Lead has faced competition from substitute materials, including plastics, in the making of pipes, but there is an important demand from motor-car-battery manufacturers. For many years lead has been used for sheathing electric cables, but, especially in the United States, substitutes have again become serious competitors.

While the U.S.S.R., since the late 1950s, has been mining more lead than the Americans (the ratio now is almost 2 : 1), consumption of refined leads shows the positions reversed.

Zinc

There is more zinc than lead in the earth's crust, but the two minerals often occur together. This is so at Broken Hill in New South Wales, and the same conjunction occurs in the great Sullivan mine at Kimberley, British Columbia, the ores of which are processed in one of the world's largest smelters, at Trail.

The increase in world production of zinc is partly a result of the stepping-up of demand by the motor industry, particularly in the United States, where zinc is now used in castings as well as in the making of galvanized steel sheet.[3] The British motor industry consumes more than half the zinc castings made in this country.[4]

Looking at the patterns of lead production and consumption, there is an interesting contrast between the U.S.A. and the Soviet Union. But for zinc the picture is not quite so striking. The U.S.A. consumes considerably more than twice the Soviet total of zinc purchases, while Soviet mine production is now approaching the American figure. The high American consumption of zinc is in part caused by the importance of the motor industry in her economy; it takes 35 per cent of all zinc produced there (as compared with 44 per cent of all lead).[5] Sudden increases in demand by the motor-car and engineering industries may produce a very considerable shift in price over a short period, with consequent effect upon production. Between the beginning of 1963 and mid-1964 the price of zinc more than doubled.[6]

Antimony

Antimony is used in alloy form with lead, tin, or copper. It is needed in the making of ammunition and also of pots and pans. The most important deposits are in China, in Hunan province; at Leydsdorp,

90

in the Transvaal; in Bolivia; and in Mexico. The Soviet Union's deposits are exploited mostly around Frunze and Radzolinsk.

Antimony

Tin

The tin industry of the Western world is strikingly dependent upon mining operations in the tropics and the Southern Hemisphere, and this is one of the few minerals of which the United States is very short. The chief tin deposits are at Kinta and Larnt in Malaya and at Bangka and Billiton Islands between Sumatra and Borneo. Other important producing areas are in Nigeria and Bolivia. The Soviet Union has made great efforts to prospect for and develop those minerals in which it lagged behind until quite recently. The chief Soviet sources of tin are near Chita in Eastern Siberia.

In Malaya it is notable that approximately half the tin ore is produced by dredging and a further two-fifths from gravel pumping. In Thailand alluvial deposits contribute 90 per cent of output, but in Bolivia most production comes from lodes (veins in the rock).[7] In Britain in 1961, 44 per cent of tin consumption was attributable to the tin-plate industry.

Much of the tin smelting (30 per cent in 1964) of the non-Communist world is still carried out in Western Europe. But the percentage has been falling fast. In 1958 it had stood at 50 per cent. Nigeria, the second most important Commonwealth producer and the fifth in the world, decided in 1961 to smelt her own ore, at Makeri. Indonesia, the third world producer, intends also to refine 'the greater part of her tin concentrate at home'.[8]

Uranium

The strategic implications of the distribution of uranium mining need no stressing. Leading world producers are: Canada, Katanga, the U.S.S.R., the U.S.A., and Czechoslovakia. Statistics are not always easy to obtain, but some have been published. Canada's total output of uranium in 1961 was 19,281 thousand lb., and in 1962, 16,862 thousand lb. Inevitably production has been linked to the making of atomic and nuclear weapons, and Canadian output fell, after a peak in 1959, owing to the decision of the United States to cease purchases after the current contracts had been met. So we find that a number of Ontario mines closed in 1960–61. Their total labour force was nearly 4,000. One mine was kept open as a copper-producer; but now a greatly increased demand is coming from nuclear power stations.

Many countries possess uranium in small quantities (it occurs in the earth's crust in the proportion of about 4 parts per million),[9] but extraction is slow and costly. In South Africa it has proved a profitable additional product of gold-mining, being extracted from the spoil-heap residues left from the cyanide leaching of gold ore. In Canada and Katanga it occurs in pitchblende.

Grainger[10] has made a comprehensive assessment of the Western world's uranium resources. The main concentrations are:

1. Blind River, Ontario: 200,000 tons of ore of 'workable grade' (containing about 0·1 per cent of mineral content); Bancroft, Ontario, and Beaverlodges, Saskatchewan.
2. The Colorado Plateau of the U.S.A., including parts of Colorado, New Mexico, Utah, and Arizona: 75,000–150,000 tons of ore.
3. South Africa: uranium-ore reserves, chiefly uraninite, amounting to about 100,000 tons are estimated to exist alongside gold deposits in the Transvaal and Orange Free State. South African production of uranium oxide reached 9 million lb. in 1964.
4. France: reserves of around 20,000 tons; principally in the Auvergne, Haute-Vienne, Forez, Maconnais, and Vendée.
5. Katanga: where the uranium–radium ores from the Shinkolobwe mine are concentrated locally before export to major industrial Powers of the Western world.

Mercury

The strange properties of quicksilver have long been famous. It has only relatively recently become important as an element in the manufacture of explosives. Some of the chief deposits are at Almadén in Spain and New Almaden in California. There are also important deposits in Tuscany, in the Istrian Peninsula, and in the Ukraine. The Mexican deposits are available to the United States, but most of the world's supplies come from the Eastern Hemisphere. Mercury boilers may become an important field of development. The world's first mercury-steam turbine power plant is now in operation at Portsmouth, New Hampshire.

Bauxite is named after Les Baux in south-east France, but the biggest yields in the world today come from countries of the Caribbean. In 1956 a huge additional supply was found at Weipa in the Cape York Peninsula of Queensland. Other major Australian deposits are at Gove, in the Northern Territory, and near Perth, in Western Australia.

Bauxite is the main base of aluminium, which because of its weight/strength ratio has been vitally important for airframe construction, but it is possible that titanium, because of its extreme resistance to heat, may supplant aluminium in the space-craft industries. The aluminium industry is interesting as it requires extremely high operating temperatures, which it is most practicable to obtain by the use of hydro-electric power. In the primary manufacturing process, bauxite is refined to produce alumina, which is then smelted to make aluminium. The demand for aluminium, and so for bauxite, has continued to rise: British consumption increased by a third between 1955 and 1961, the rise being particularly notable in the electrical industry. Research in the non-metals field is intense and continuous, comparisons of utility being constantly made and re-checked. There has been some tendency for aluminium to oust tin, as a raw material for containers, in the U.S.A., while, on the other hand, aluminium is assailed by new metals in domestic utensil manufacture.

Many aluminium installations are noted for their extraordinary size: Kitimat in British Columbia for instance, which at the beginning of 1964 was working to its full installed capacity of 212,000 tons per annum. The site possesses the power and raw-material bases for expansion by a further 100,000 tons of annual capacity.[11] Canada also has Arvida, another world-class plant, standing on the Saguenay River, where bauxite from the Guianas is unloaded at Port Alfred. Arvida possessed locational advantages over units in the southern United States in the procurement from Greenland of the cryolite used in converting alumina into aluminium, but such advantages were shared with other large plants in the St. Lawrence zone, which are near to hydro-electric power. Recently the supply position has been altered by the development of an artificial cryolite. The United States consumes half of the aluminium produced in the non-Communist world, and the biggest world manufacturer is the Aluminium Company of America (Alcoa). The order of production of aluminium in Europe is: (1) West Germany; (2) France; (3) Norway; (4) the United Kingdom. The spectacular discoveries of bauxite in Australia have already made her a major supplier of industry in the U.S.A., Japan, and Canada. The Gladstone, Queensland, plant will have twice the capacity of Kitimat, and from 1967 onwards 200,000 tons of alumina per annum is due to be supplied to the U.S.A. from the Kwinina refinery in Western Australia.[12]

Bauxite and the Manufacture of Aluminium

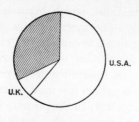

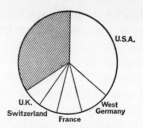

WORLD TOTAL, 1953: $U.S. 36,250

WORLD TOTAL, JUNE 1964: $U.S. 42,905

WORLD GOLD
HOLDINGS
(figs. in millions
of dollars)

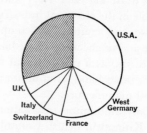

WORLD TOTAL, JUNE 1965: $U.S. 43,030

FIG. 8.1   World gold holdings

The U.S.A. is still the largest holder, but it no longer hoards
most of the world's supply.

Precious
Minerals

The precious minerals that impelled the early explorers to great
feats of endurance are still sought after today. Nations still seek to
accumulate *gold*, the chief hoard having for many years resided in
the United States — most of it closely guarded in Fort Knox. In
1953 the U.S.A. had over nine times the amount of gold held in
Britain (Fig. 8.1); but in 1964 she held only four times as much as
this country. The Americans have been concerned about the
deterioration that has occurred in their position, especially since
1959. The main reason for the loss seems to have been the huge
amounts of aid provided by the Americans to other countries: this
has upset the U.S.A.'s normally favourable balance of trade. Gold
is always news, and the increase of production in the Soviet Union,
although the Soviets themselves have been reticent, shows in the
continued heavy shipments to London and Switzerland. In 1963–64
these were used to finance massive purchases abroad of wheat and
other important items deficient at that time in the Soviet Union.

South African gold production, with a remarkable development in the Orange Free State, has continued to increase — reaching 30·5 million oz. in 1965. The Russians have reported the discovery of an important new field on the Kolyma River in Siberia, and American sources at one time estimated Soviet production at 10–12½ million oz., though this figure was halved in later estimates.[13]

The old primacy of the New World in *silver* supplies is still strongly evident, with the United States and Mexico still in the lead. Thoman stresses the commercial contrast between the leading precious minerals. When all of them except gold — silver, platinum metals and diamonds — are added together, the total value of their production is only about half that of gold.[14] The Spaniards found a great wealth of silver in Mexico, and that country still produces between a quarter and a fifth of the world's supply.

The romance of *diamonds* seldom fails to excite the imagination which has been stirred in recent times by the exploits of the exceedingly successful Williamson company in Tanganyika, originally a one-man venture, which later became linked with the South African De Beers.

One of the more interesting developments elsewhere has been the discovery of diamonds in recoverable quantity off the coast of South-West Africa. The demand for industrial diamonds has increased spectacularly; and this despite the fact that they lack the intrinsic interest of gemstones. The African continent maintains a remarkable lead in both categories, producing, by weight, 80 per cent of all the world's diamonds, and by value 70 per cent. In recent years, as in the case of gold, the Soviet Union has become a significant producer. The Republic of South Africa, in 1960–62, produced 20 per cent by value of total world output; and, of South African production, two-fifths came from the single Premier mine in the Transvaal.[15] Most gemstones are cut in either Belgium, Israel, or the United States, the two chief cutting centres being Antwerp and Tel-Aviv.

The main consumers of *platinum* today are the catalytic plants of oil refineries. A decade ago the main world platinum producers were the Transvaal and Ontario, but increased supplies now come from the Urals, and the Soviet Union is about equal in importance to the other world-class producers. Platinum is also consumed in the manufacture of chemical fertilizers, glass, and explosives. Platinum is even more expensive than gold, and most of the world output finds its way to the United States.

There is a constant industrial demand for fireproofing material, and consequently for *asbestos*, for which there is no general substitute. The mineral occurs usually as chrysotile asbestos, associated with igneous rocks such as serpentine. Very few countries possess abundant supplies. Forty per cent of total world output comes from the Eastern Townships mines in Quebec; but since 1962 Soviet output, mainly from Bazhenovo in the Urals, has almost equalled Canadian production.

Mica is a strategic mineral, important in the manufacture of electric lamps and of materials required to withstand high voltages and great heat. Eighty per cent of world output comes from India. The other important producers are the Malagasy Republic and Brazil.[16]

Sulphur is vitally important as the source of sulphuric acid, and is remarkable for its occurrence in a wide variety of forms. In the past, the most prolific has been the mineral 'caps' of salt domes, as for instance in the Gulf Coast region of the United States. Sulphur is also obtained as a by-product in the processing of natural gas, as for instance at Lacq, in south-west France. Until 1960 half of the world's sulphur output came from the U.S.A. Since then the American share has fallen slightly, with the big rises in output from the U.S.S.R., France, and Canada.[17]

Graphite occurs as a mineral in nature; it can also be manufactured from petroleum coke and pitch coke. The manufactured product, being far purer than natural graphite, is in demand as a moderator in the reactors of atomic power stations, a single reactor needing as much as 2,000 tons. By far the biggest producers of natural graphite are the Soviet Union, North Korea, and China.[18]

Before the end of the 1950s new thinking on stockpiling metals in the United States had been produced by: (i) technological advance, in the discovery of synthetic substances and new alloys; (ii) alterations in the supply requirements of the defence industries, called forth by the discovery of new materials and by the needs of new weapons; (iii) the achievements of friends or adversaries of the United States; (iv) changes in the whole pattern of defence planning. 'Originally built up to meet the requirements of a five-year war, the stockpiles became outdated in 1958, when the basic assumption was changed to a three-year war'.[19] One item of specific interest, in the changed conditions, is the eventual likelihood of a diminished military role for aircraft. There has been some uncertainty as to the demand by the defence industries for aluminium, almost 2 million tons of which had accumulated in the American stockpile by 1962.[20] The scale of American stockpiling is illustrated further by the position of lead and zinc holdings, which in 1963 stood at 1 million tons of lead and 1·5 million tons of zinc.[21]

American non-ferrous mineral production has often been studied alongside that of the Soviet Union, but there has been some difficulty in finding a common basis of comparison in all cases. Various estimates have been made; most of them showing the Soviet Union well ahead in manganese, chromite, nickel, and tungsten and the United States even further ahead in molybdenum and vanadium. The Americans also lead in copper and the Russians in lead. In zinc they are about level; both countries are short of tin.

The example of tin shows how the stockpile can serve as a balancing reservoir, with important effects upon price and, therefore, directly upon world production. The United States, and she alone, is responsible for the price of supplies released from the reserve. Vigorous exchanges took place, in 1963–64, upon the matter of price, between the International Tin Council and the U.S. General Services Administration. The G.S.A. is responsible for the control and administration of stockpiles. Releases from stock may act to prevent what would otherwise be a severe price rise, with consequent effects for consumers of tin. In 1963 consumption of tin in the non-Communist world was estimated at 160,500 tons; mine production at only 141,200 tons. Stockpile releases were logical in these circumstances. The different authorities were agreed that for 1964 a similar deficit of around 20,000 tons was to be expected. This was the amount that the G.S.A. had decided to release during that year.[22] In fact, when prices continued to rise, partly because of political conditions in the Far East, G.S.A. released a further 12,000 tons.

The volume of stockpiling, superfluous to even strategic needs, is illustrated by the case of nickel. Stocks held by the U.S. Government at the end of 1963 stood at 204,000 tons — as much as 159,000 tons 'surplus to the desired maximum objective of the stockpile'.[23]

American Stockpiling

Ores and metals make up almost 9 per cent of total U.K. imports. The United States spends large sums of money on the purchase of bauxite and alumina, copper, lead, nickel, tin, zinc, and other

From Mineral to Metal

97

strategic minerals that are 'not listed'. The result of demand, on the contemporary scale, for ores and base metals is, of course, to produce a dependence upon sometimes uncertain foreign sources of supply. In comparing copper production and consumption, one notices the happy position of Canada, the deficits of West Germany and the United States, and the supremacy as producer–exporters of Africa and South America (principally Chile).

Levels of consumption convey information about the general state of industry in the countries concerned and about their strategic preparedness. Above all, mineral consumption reflects upon the disparity between the rich and the poor nations. Minerals are exploited, necessarily, where they occur in nature. They are consumed, primarily, by the wealthy. Whereas a large part of the world's copper is found south of the Equator (over 40 per cent in 1960), nearly all of it is consumed in the Northern Hemisphere. This has been put in different ways: 'it is estimated that North America, Western Europe and Japan account for 87 per cent of the free world's final consumption of copper', and from the same source: 'more than four-fifths of the free world's copper is eventually consumed by three-tenths of its population'.[24] Elsewhere we read, narrowing down the picture still more: 'sixteen per cent of the world's population uses practically all the world's manufactured copper'.[25]

Mining Regions

I. Katanga–Zambia

Of the world's mining complexes, one of the most important is Katanga–Zambia, the mineral riches of which straddle a frontier. The Congo portion of the region is notable, among other reasons, for the fact that production is entirely in the hands of a single company — the former Union Minière du Haut-Katanga. This giant concern produces about two-thirds of the world's cobalt, as well as zinc, cadmium, germanium, radium, and uranium. But the chief wealth of Katanga lies in its copper — deep-mined or open-cast — which puts the Congo sixth in world production (Fig. 8.2). Zambia is even more important for copper, producing nearly twice as much as Katanga. Over 500,000 tons come annually from the mines that lie between Bancroft and Ndola.

There are intimate connections between the mines and the European countries that still supply the bulk of capital and management: Belgium in the case of Katanga; Britain in the case of Zambia.

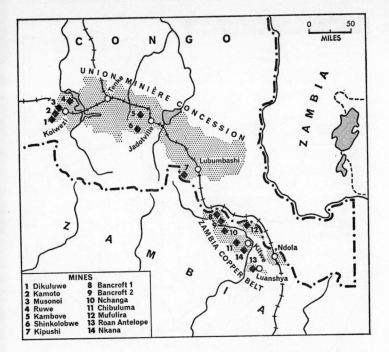

FIG. 8.2   Mining areas of Katanga and Zambia

The copperbelts of Central Africa have been notable for their exploitation by foreign companies. A recent development has been the expropriation of the Union Minière holdings: the Katangese mines are now owned 60 per cent by the Société Générale Congolese des Minerais (GECOMIN), but their copper is still marketed by the parent company of the Belgian Union Minière.

In 1963, a single company, Anglo-American, produced 345,000 tons of copper from its three mines of Nchanga, Rhokana, and Bancroft. Their competitors, Rhodesian Selection Trust (R.S.T.), produced over 220,000 tons from the three mines of Mufulira, Roan Antelope and Chibuluma. The enterprises in both countries have faced threats of nationalization by independent African governments.

Zambia has no coastline and has to rely largely upon rail communication with the sea via Portuguese territory (Fig. 8.3). The two producing regions are partly interdependent in power supplies, vital transmission lines crossing the border near Musoshi, but Zambia now draws most of her energy from the Kariba Dam on the

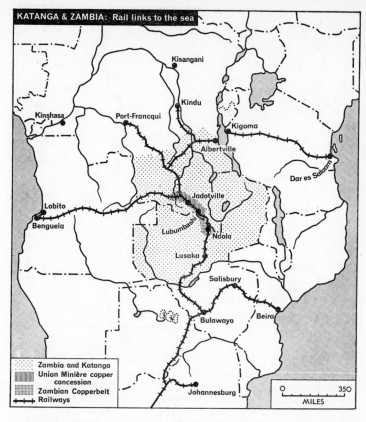

FIG. 8.3   Rail links to the sea from mining areas of
Katanga and Zambia
Both copperbelts have rail connections to the sea only through
foreign territory.

Rhodesian border — a matter of great concern to the copper
companies during the Rhodesian crisis of 1965–66.

II. *Sudbury*

The foremost mining region in Canada, and one of the most
notable in the world, is Ontario's Sudbury Basin, which in 1962
produced 45 per cent of Canada's vast mineral output. From
Sudbury comes most of the world's nickel and most of Canada's
copper. From the Sudbury ores (Fig. 8.4) comes all of the Canadian
output of the platinum group of minerals, as well as iron, silver,

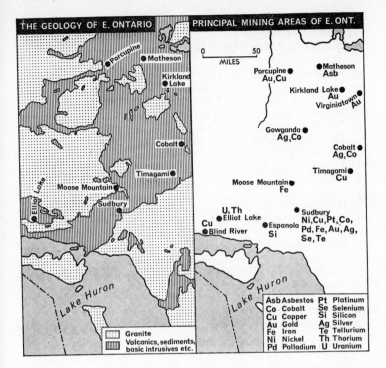

THE GEOLOGY OF E. ONTARIO | PRINCIPAL MINING AREAS OF E. ONT.

Mining Regions

Porcupine
● Matheson

Kirkland
● Lake

Cobalt ●

Timagami ●

● Moose Mountain

Sudbury

Lake Huron

Elliot Lake

Granite
Volcanics, sediments, basic intrusives etc.

0   50
MILES

Porcupine ●
Au,Cu

● Matheson
Asb

Kirkland Lake ●
Au
Virginiatown ●
Au

Gowganda ●
Ag,Co

Cobalt ●
Ag,Co

Timagami ●
Cu

Moose Mountain ●
Fe

U,Th
● Elliot Lake
Cu
● Blind River   ● Espanola
Si

● Sudbury
Ni,Cu,Pt,Co,
Pd,Fe,Au,Ag,
Se,Te

Lake Huron

Asb Asbestos   Pt Platinum
Co . Cobalt   Se Selenium
Cu Copper   Si Silicon
Au Gold   Ag Silver
Fe Iron   Te Tellurium
Ni Nickel   Th Thorium
Pd Palladium   U Uranium

FIG. 8.4 Sudbury and the mining region of eastern
Ontario

Eastern Ontario, with the neighbouring areas of Quebec, is one
of the most varied and valuable mineral storehouses in the world.

cobalt, and gold. Most of the nickel production is in the hands of
one of the world's largest mining corporations, the International
Nickel Company of Canada, known as INCO. In most countries
nickel is mined open-cast, but at Sudbury the ore is obtained mostly
from deep mines, such as Creighton, where the main production is
from the 4,600-foot level. But at the new Clarabelle pit the ore is
mined by surface digging.

1. Barclays Bank, Intelligence Dept., March 1962.
2. Metalgesellschaft A.G., Frankfurt-am-Main.
3. Barclays Bank, Intelligence Dept., April 1963.
4. Ibid.

NOTES

**Non-ferrous
Minerals and
Metals**

5. Thoman, *The Geography of Economic Activity*, p. 490.
6. *Guardian*, 14 July 1964.
7. Barclays Bank, Intelligence Dept., Dec. 1961.
8. *The Times*, 29 Sept. 1964.
9. See *Metal Statistics, 1965* (American Metal Market), p. 143.
10. L. Grainger, *Uranium and Thorium* (Newnes, 1958).
11. Aluminium Ltd., *Annual Report*, March 1964.
12. *Financial Times* supplement on 'Australia', 13 Sept. 1965.
13. *The Times*, 31 Aug. 1965; ibid., 23 Dec. 1965.
14. Thoman, *The Geography of Economic Activity*, p. 432.
15. Commonwealth Economic Committee, *Non-Metallic Minerals* (H.M.S.O., 1964), p. 188.
16. Ibid., p. 168.
17. Ibid.
18. Ibid., pp. 151–3.
19. *Financial Times*, 7 Dec. 1962.
20. Ibid.
21. Barclays Bank, Intelligence Dept., April 1963.
22. London Tin Corporation, *Annual Report*, 12 July 1965.
23. Commonwealth Economic Committee, *Iron and Steel and Alloying Metals*, p. 159.
24. Sir Ronald Prain, 'Attractive and Versatile Metal', *The Times* supplement on 'Copper', 27 Jan. 1964.
25. Sir Charles Darwin, reported in *The Times Review of Industry* (Dec. 1962), p. 61.

Engineering and Allied Industries   Chapter 9

Engineering is a main constituent of the technological revolution that has transformed and is transforming our age. The machine is a criterion of progress, distinguishing the primitive from the civilized; our machines are more complex and more ingenious than any known before, being grouped particularly around an invention — the internal combustion engine — that is perhaps the most significant of modern times. The economy depends upon transport and trade. Ships are now speedier, more complicated; mechanized agriculture depends upon the tractor; urban life is organized around the motor-car; and in the skies we see the start of supersonic travel. The civil engineer has found ways of building more quickly, and techniques of prefabrication can be particulariy significant for countries suffering from housing shortages. Mechanization has invaded the home, supplying a vast array of amenities for our pleasure and comfort. Engineering as an employer is increasing rather than diminishing in importance. In Britain the labour force in the engineering–shipbuilding group of industries numbers 4,500,000. In Sweden almost half the workers in manufacturing and mining are engaged in metals and engineering.

The importance of the engineer in Britain is illustrated by the sum of £250 million[1] spent by the steel industry alone, during the period 1945–62, on capital construction undertaken by civil engineering contractors. Second to constructional work, as reckoned by consumption of steel, is general engineering, followed by the car industry.

THE ENGINEER-ING INDUSTRY

Engineering is a skilled trade and the engineer one of the elite of industry. The poorer, undeveloped countries have been desperately short of the engineers to undertake the tasks of construction involved in modernizing and expanding their inadequate economies. They have lacked the roads and the railways to bring succour and progress to their villages.

Engineering and Allied Industries

The underdeveloped — but rapidly expanding — economies of South-East Asia, Africa, and South America have lacked the capital and the engineers to build, in concrete and steel, the power stations and pipelines that they need. So we find that engineering contractors have come from Europe, from Britain, Italy or West Germany, from the Soviet Union or the United States, and are supported perhaps by funds from the World Bank or by loans from the wealthier States.

SHIP-BUILDING

Unlike the newest industries, shipbuilding has not shown a common pattern of progress. The shipyards — British far more than American — were hit, more than almost any other business, by the slump of

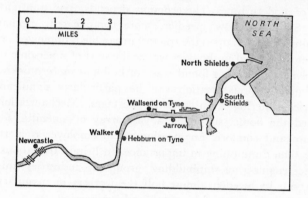

FIG. 9.1   Shipbuilding on the Tyne
Tyneside has long been a world-class shipbuilding centre.

the early 1930s. Britain's shipbuilding industry, in common with that of other countries, is circumscribed by physical conditions, being still concentrated on the rivers where it thrived half a century ago — on the Clyde, the Tyne–Wear–Tees, the Mersey and the Lagan, and in Furness. Modern yards, such as those at Barrow, may be heavily dependent upon naval orders. England's North-East Coast, with 29 per cent of the total U.K. shipbuilding and ship repairing labour force in 1965, has a great variety of facilities to offer to customers (Fig. 9.1). The Tyne yards alone have 23 per cent of the total U.K. workers in the industry. A number of yards, as on the Clyde and the Tees and in Northern Ireland, have won

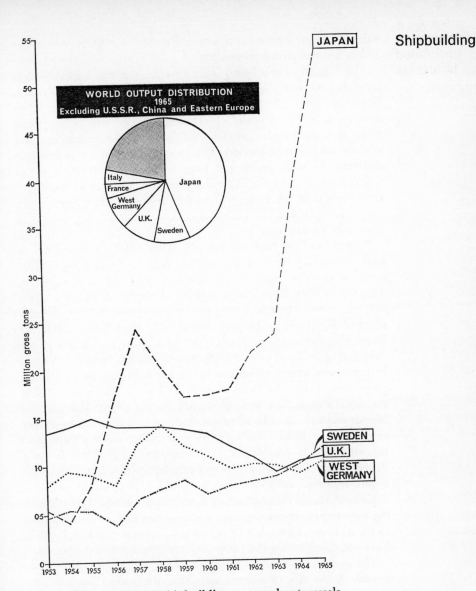

FIG. 9.2 World shipbuilding — merchant vessels
launched

Japan continues her remarkable success. Sweden's achievement,
too, is notable.

105

Engineering and Allied Industries valuable orders for the construction of drilling-rigs to be used in the North Sea search for oil and gas.

The biggest vessels being built now are tankers, and there has recently been some sign of an increase in the size of liners. France, Germany, the United States, and Italy all have large liners more modern than our 'Queens'. In Britain in 1962, out of 1,073,000 gross tons launched, 403,000 tons belonged to oil-tankers and 160,000 tons to bulk carriers. The most spectacular naval building concerns the nuclear-powered *Dreadnought*-type submarines, all of which have so far been allotted to Barrow. The purely passenger liner tends to be much larger than the cargo or the cargo–passenger vessel. The vast majority of British vessels of these last two categories are under 10,000 tons.

Britain has long been accustomed to the idea of competition in engineering and precision industries from Germany and Japan (Fig. 9.2). In 1957 the Japanese produced 2·4 million tons of shipping. This fell to 1·7 million tons in 1959, and rose again by 1962 to 2·1 million. Between then and 1964 production almost doubled. Japan's share of ships built in the world has steadily risen. Before the Great Depression her share was about 6 per cent; in 1937–38 it was 16 per cent and in 1962, 26 per cent. A striking fact has been the drop in Britain's own share, which has kept pace with the rise in Japan's proportion. Before the Depression, Britain was building over half of the world's ships. She was the world's biggest shipbuilder and the biggest carrier. Already in 1933 her share had dropped to 27 per cent. In 1962 Britain built 13 per cent of the world's ships, and exported far less than Japan, West Germany, or Sweden. In 1964 British yards provided only 10 per cent of world output, although orders improved in 1965.

Cairncross and Parkinson drew attention to a considerable drop in the long-term carrying capacity of non-tanker vessels.[2] This was due to the increased time taken to turn round in port and should, by itself, have promoted rather than impeded the demand for new vessels.

The most notable recent technological development has been the growth in the size of tankers and other freighters. The Japanese were to the fore in the construction of the monster ships that are now almost a commonplace at the busiest tanker terminals; but British shipbuilders were not far behind. In 1962 vessels of 100,000 tons were being built in four Japanese yards: Sasebo, Ishikawajima-Harima, Mitsubishi, and Uraga Dock (Fig. 9.3). In 1965, 165,000-ton tankers were on the drawing-board in Japan; in the same year,

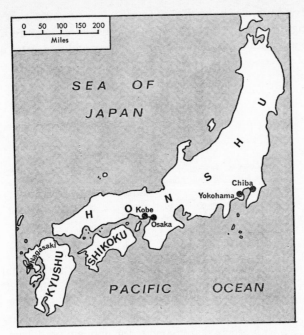

FIG. 9.3 Japan's largest shipyards
The centres shown can build units of 200,000 tons
or more.

a 170,000-ton tanker was laid down at Belfast, and the Japanese and others were thinking in terms of 200,000-ton vessels.

The reasons for Britain's lapse in construction derived not merely from superior advantages possessed by a single country, but from the general industrial and technological progress of the rest of the world. Behind each shipbuilding industry is a formidable organization of marine and general engineering, supported by an iron and steel industry. It may happen that a given producing country is not self-sufficient in all the vital raw materials of steel. In the past Japan had to spend large amounts of foreign currency on imports of ore, as well as of steel and scrap. The Germans also import much of their ore. The Swedes lack coal, but have ample electricity supplies. The world's producers have been driven to design and to build by increasing world trade and the consequent demand for vessels. But with the growth in producing capacity, the struggle for export orders has become more fierce. Tenders for new vessels are open to competition throughout the world, and such factors as

delivery dates can be critical. The efficiency of yards must have a
bearing upon the price tendered. The drive for competitiveness has
led to amalgamations between shipbuilders, and to greater integration of processes, described by Cairncross and Parkinson.[3]
In some cases shipbuilders are also shipowners.

Leading Shipbuilding Nations[4]
(Ship Launchings — 'ooo gross tons)

Country	1962		1963		1964		1965	
	Launch-ing	% of world pro-duction	Launch-ing	% of world pro-duction	Launch-ing	% of world pro-duction	Launch-ing	% of world pro-duction
Japan . .	2,183	26·07	2,367	27·73	4,085	39·80	5,363	43·96
W. Germany	1,009	12·06	971	11·37	890	8·67	1,023	8·39
U.K. . .	1,073	12·81	927	10·86	1,043	10·16	1,073	8·79
Sweden .	841	10·04	888	10·40	1,021	9·94	1,170	9·59

Their building programmes are closely controlled by national trade
figures. In Britain, when exports have flagged, domestic demand
has generally saved the day for the shipyards. There may in the
future be more scope for joint projects by such organizations as
N.A.T.O., with orders shared among the national producers.

One factor in production, which has often been feared and
criticized and, in different circumstances, welcomed, is Government
intervention. Allen attributed the fall, discernible even in the late
1920s, in Britain's share of world production, largely to massive
foreign subsidy.[5] The spectacular Japanese progress was promoted
by organization and sacrifice, but also by the considerable funds for
capital re-equipment made available from the World Bank, that is
primarily from American sources. Britain's government and industry
evidently learnt from this. The recent impressive improvement in
shipbuilding achievement, with increasing production and full order-
books, was partly attributable to the large-scale assistance provided
by government, enabling industry to quote very favourable credit
terms.

THE MOTOR-CAR INDUSTRY

The motor-car industry was the creation of men such as Daimler,
Benz, Panhard, Morris and Austin, some of whom were as much
organizers as inventors. Jones and Darkenwald provide interesting
historical detail of the American industry.[6]

The internal combustion engine has revolutionized human affairs since its rapid development in the period 1865–83. The adaptation of the petrol engine to road vehicles was epoch-making. Such vehicles had existed, slow-moving — dormant, as it were — since Cugnot's steam engine. The motor car as we know it emerged from the conjunction of a number of inventions and developments, such as that of the pneumatic tyre.

Just as a number of trades contributed to the early motor-cars, so today a large variety of concerns supply the car-manufacturer. Such components in Britain notably include tyres, batteries, glass, dynamos, starter motors, carburettors, brake linings, and sparking-plugs. There are other links between the firms that press sheet steel for the car bodies and the concerns that fit these and the other components on to the chassis. But there is no hard-and-fast rule about the processes of car manufacture. This mass industry is a creation of our twentieth century; to this century belong its peculiar features both of specialization and concentration.

The concentration of production has resulted in the creation of giant corporations. This has come about through the amalgamation of smaller concerns or their absorption by one or two leading competitors. The United States is the world's largest producer of automobiles of all kinds. The present degree of concentration there is not new: the Big Three — General Motors, Ford, and Chrysler — were in 1927 already producing 25 per cent of the country's total car output. But they benefited, in relation to their competitors, from the rigours of the unparalleled Depression of the 1930s, which fell with particular severity on this consumer industry. The result was eventually to concentrate national output, by 1962, to the extent of 95 per cent in the Big Three.

The place of the giant car firms in the respective national economies is assured. In 1966 the Ford Motor Company of Britain was thirteenth among British corporations in the order of capital employed. B.M.C. was thirty-sixth. Maxcy and Silberston[7] show 1951–53 as the vital period in which B.M.C. lost ground to Ford of Britain. In the United States, General Motors is the biggest of all the corporations and has been so for some time; the Ford Motor Company is third. American productivity in this industry has far exceeded the British and the relative position of the U.K. has been little altered by the introduction of American capital and methods. The enormous size of the domestic market is the chief factor affecting American production and salesmanship. The comparatively low

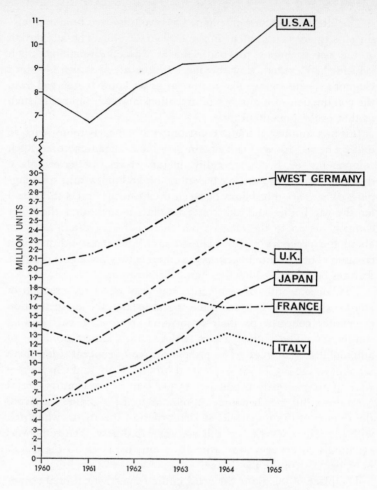

Fig. 9.4 Output of major automobile-producing
countries

The fastest-growing car industry is that of Japan, but America is
still supreme in world production.

density of the rail network in the New World has helped. But
probably the greatest impetus to car production, followed by many
imitators, was the decision of Henry Ford to design and build a
cheap family car.

The motor industry will always be associated with the pioneer
development of the assembly-belt system. The essence of this idea

was to provide maximum efficiency through the optimum application of organization. Efficiency was produced by reducing movement and narrowing the contribution made by each operative. Car components had to be standardized. Often their insertion into the assembly process became a task for the merely semi-skilled. The early assembly lines have since been improved. Time-and-motion studies have reduced still further the individual's part in the whole, and there has been a continuing increase in the advantages to be gained from economy in scale and organization that accrue to the largest concerns. Along with an increase in the size of the manufacturing concerns has gone a standardization of the parts used in making individual cars and in many cases, particularly in the United States, a reduction in the number of models made by the separate corporations. In 1955 the General Motors concern, over its whole range of models, was using only three body shells. In Britain agreement on standardization among the major producers has been reached on the voltage of electrical equipment to be installed, on carburettors, wheels, and tyres.[8]

The
Motor-Car
Industry

The world motor-car trade (Fig. 9.4) has been remarkable for:
(i) the progress shown by the West Germans (total exports of $1\frac{1}{2}$ million in 1964 and in 1965);
(ii) the erratic performance of the U.K. industry, and still more, that of France;
(iii) the recent appearance of Japan as a significant exporter.
In organization and structure, there is a marked contrast in the industry between:
(a) the degree of concentration in the American industry, with one firm providing nearly half of the total native production;
(b) the degree of fragmentation among the main West European producers: over half of the total automobile output is taken up by four concerns — two of them American, none British.

The British car industry was concentrated overwhelmingly, until very recently, in the South Midlands and the London Basin, with great factories at Longbridge, Cowley, Dagenham, and Luton. Coventry had the reputation of the car city, *par excellence*. But the last decade has seen the partial dispersal of production, and the establishment, with governmental sympathy and approval, of very large units in Lancashire and Scotland: most notable are Halewood, near Liverpool, and Linwood, near Paisley. There remain older

The United
Kingdom

producing centres at Crewe and Abingdon, and smaller concerns at Bradford, Warwick, and Malvern. In the United Kingdom commercial-vehicle production is more concentrated than car production. The most important centres are Dunstable, where over one-third of all trucks produced in this country are made, the Leyland–Chorley district of Lancashire, Coventry, and Dagenham. Ford make tractor engines at Basildon, linking with their other factories at Antwerp and in the United States.[9] Many automobile factories and organizations in Britain, as in the United States, were developed out of allied industrial processes, but it is only rarely in Britain today that firms important for cycles and motor-cycles also make cars. The focus of cycle and motor-cycle manufacture lies further north. The chief pedal-cycle firm is in Nottingham. B.S.A., the Birmingham Small Arms Company, produces over three-fifths of the total output of British motor-cycles,[10] catering for a market threatened by imports from Japan.

The motor industry has maintained its recent home-sales figures only because of protective tariffs. Abroad, Britain is faced with duties against her goods, but high levels of exports of motor vehicles have been maintained. Normally, nearly one-half of the private cars made in the U.K. are exported, as well as nearly one-quarter of commercial vehicles, and more than four out of five of all agricultural tractors.

Henry Ford's first car, the Quadricycle, was built in a back-street shed in Detroit in 1896. His Model 'T' sold 15 million between 1908 and 1927. These cars came off the assembly lines of two vast plants outside Detroit: River Rouge and Highland Park. Detroit is still the world's leading centre of car production. The concentration on this city is really remarkable: 30 per cent of all automobile workers in the U.S.A. are to be found there.[11] The 'satellites' of Detroit include the big cities of Chicago, Milwaukee, Indianapolis, Buffalo, and Cleveland, as well as Flint, Michigan, which is second only to Detroit in the scale of its car industries. Further afield there are important concerns in Kansas City, St. Louis, Los Angeles, Philadelphia, and New York. The American automobile industry is a barometer of the country's prosperity, and an important factor in the total demand for iron and steel. An increasingly affluent society will consume more cars, more tyres, more gasoline. The enormous strength of the American passenger market — in comparison with the

112

Russian — is seen in their 1960 figures of production of passenger cars: U.S.A., 6,675,000; U.S.S.R., 139,000. In 1963 the U.S.A. produced 7·6 million cars, in 1964 9·3 million and in 1965 a record 11 million.

American farming provides a huge market for tractors and for many other types of commercial vehicles. International Harvester is the world's largest producer of heavy tractors. British producers have, however, made important inroads into the American market with light tractors.

The West German industry has been remarkable for its rate of growth and for the volume of its exports. Total production of passenger cars in 1960 was $1\frac{3}{4}$ million; in 1965, $2\frac{3}{4}$ million. Since 1960 West Germany has been the largest overseas supplier of the American market. During the decade ending in 1964, West German car exports showed a remarkable advance (Fig. 9.5). In 1962–64 sales abroad almost equalled the combined totals of her two main rivals. The biggest share of this success belonged to Volkswagen. Since 1961 this firm has been producing at Wolfsburg more than a million cars each year: in 1955 they sold 55,000 to the United States; in 1963, 300,000 (out of total overseas sales of 800,000). The Wolfsburg factories plan to raise their annual output to $2\frac{1}{2}$ million by 1970.[12] Opel's achievement, from its factory at Russelheim, has been second only to Volkswagen. Opel, the West German subsidiary of the American General Motors, was by 1963 producing over half a million cars per year, and has been capturing a growing share of the domestic market.

The Japanese record in automobile production has been different from West Germany's, resembling in fact more the experience of the Soviet Union. Both Japanese and Russians have concentrated more in the past on the production of commercial vehicles. But both have also had the know-how and the organizational ability to undertake a greatly accelerated flow of passenger vehicles from their factories (which owe much, in both countries, to American inspiration). But since 1963 the Japanese have been devoting a markedly increased effort to the passenger side of the industry, with a view to export as well as to home sales. Car output, only 78,000 as recently as 1959, had reached 166,000 by 1960; 408,000 by 1963; and 696,000 in 1965.[13] Two producers, Toyota (at Toyota City) and Nissan,

E   H.G.P.

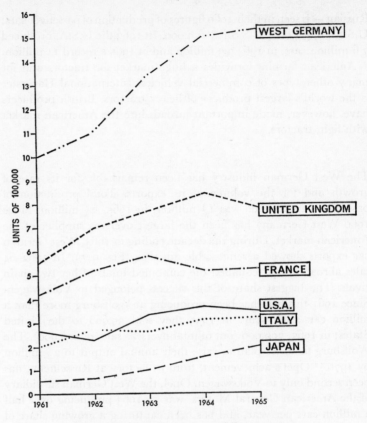

FIG. 9.5   Leading automobile exporters
West Germany, represented mainly by the single firm of Volkswagen, is by far the biggest exporter.

provide 65 per cent of total national output.[14] One of the outstanding Japanese achievements has been in the manufacture and export of
motor-cycles, mopeds, and three-wheelers. In 1963 production of
motor-cycles of over 51 c.c. capacity amounted to 1,148,000 units, the
leading makers being Honda, Suzuki, and Yamaka.[15] Japanese three-
wheelers are starting to replace the pedicabs of South-East Asia.[16]

France   The French motor-vehicle industry achieved a high rate of expansion in the period 1950–58. In this respect it shared in a trend that
was common to the countries of Western Europe, and differentiated

them from the Communist countries of the East. The output of cars in France increased from 257,000 in 1950 to 924,000 in 1958, and to a peak of 1,521,000 in 1963. Production fell by 7 per cent in 1964. The French industry is notable in several respects: (i) it has been penetrated, in part, commercially by the Americans: the important firm of Simca is a subsidiary of the American General Motors; (ii) the four largest producers are supreme; (iii) a large part — 40 per cent — of car production is exported.

France — Automobile Production, 1964[17]

Renault	. .	437,084
Citroën	. .	368,601
Simca	. .	264,316
Peugeot	. .	227,585
Panhard	. .	29,460
Facel	. .	302

1,327,348

The French industry shows a very strong regional concentration. Two-thirds of the car producers' resources are to be found in the statistical Région parisienne.[18]

The Italian industry is noted for the degree of near-monopoly **Italy** asserted by the firm of Fiat, which produces nearly four-fifths of all Italian motor vehicles. Its main factory — Mirafiori, near Turin — has 35,000 workers and 3,500 office staff. For some years between a quarter and a third of Fiat output has been exported. In 1966, one of the biggest commercial contracts ever signed provided for Fiat to build 600,000 cars annually in the Soviet Union. Inside Italy itself there is a vehicle-population ratio of only 1 : 13, as compared with 1 : 6 in Britain and 1 : 2·5 in the United States.

The aircraft industry involves engineering techniques that have **THE** some common ground with the trades of motor-car manufacture **AIRCRAFT** and shipbuilding. So we find that there are big corporations making **INDUSTRY** both cars and aeroplanes or planes as well as ships.

Engineering and Allied Industries

Large-scale car production had begun in America before the First World War. The aeroplane industry as we know it came hastily into being during the course of that struggle, when nearly 16,000 planes were produced in the United States.[19] The Second World War produced a new demand for aircraft of all types. The fight for survival among the industrial nations, including all the major aircraft producers — the United States, Britain, Germany, Japan, France, and Italy — meant a frantic search by engineers and designers for better machines and faster engines. The result was inevitably to produce much superior, more sophisticated craft. The Russian industry survived, in 1941–42, largely through evacuation to the east.

The United Kingdom

Technological development all over the world since 1944 has been very largely concerned with the introduction of jet and turbo-prop machines. Britain has not lagged behind in this progress. In the U.K., there is a notable concentration of production upon a few very large factories and upon still fewer producers. In 1965, 258,000 people were employed in the industry: of these, 43,000 belonged to Hawker Siddeley; 37,000 to Rolls-Royce, including 12,000 in Scotland; and 36,700 to the British Aircraft Corporation. The largest factories were those of Rolls-Royce at Derby, and of Hawker Siddeley at Bristol, each with over 22,000 employees.

A few locations are near well-known motor-car centres — for instance, Coventry and Luton. More often, the aircraft works are in older engineering districts such as Wolverhampton, Manchester, or Preston. Elsewhere, they are found on or near the coast, for instance, at Portsmouth, Christchurch, Cowes, or Belfast. The Northern Ireland company, with a work-force of 8,000, is linked with Harland Wolff, the big-scale shipbuilder; Rolls-Royce are also one of the world's leading car manufacturers, as well as being concerned with the supply of nuclear propulsion units for the *Dreadnought*-class submarines.

A number of the aircraft firms have airfields of their own, or have arrangements to use municipal and other airfields, as at Luton and Prestwick. This is one of the considerations that took aircraft manufacturers to what is now Outer London — to Kingston-upon-Thames for instance — and, beyond, to Reading and to Hatfield New Town.

Some of the largest individual units belong to builders, not of entire aircraft, but of engines. More people are employed in Bristol

116

in making engines than in constructing the planes into which they will go. One of the largest plants in the industry is the Rolls-Royce engine works at Blantyre, in Scotland. Many nations fly American planes powered by British engines.

The whole industry has been affected by the uncertainties of defence spending, and very large installations — as at Weybridge — have been dependent upon outsize single projects.

The Aircraft Industry

The Americans, secure during the Second World War from aerial attack, were able to work up to a production of nearly 100,000 aircraft in the single pre-victory year of 1944.[20] The post-war reaction brought a decline to the aircraft centres. The American industry had developed a much wider geographical spread than its older companion, the car trade. Before 1940 the leading centres of production had been in Baltimore, Buffalo, and Los Angeles.[21]

The United States

A deliberate dispersal policy, undertaken by the U.S. Government early in the war, was motivated only partly by security reasons. There existed a large and versatile labour force in such 'new' states as Texas and Kansas, where cost of transport of the raw materials required for airframe assembly was not a decisive factor. There remains today important concentrations of aircraft engine and propeller manufacture in 'old' areas such as Rochester and the 'automobile states' of Michigan, Ohio, and Indiana. But a significant climatic control over the location of airframe and final assembly has been discerned by Estall, Buchanan, and others: these activities are said to be located mainly where sunshine levels are extremely high, permitting round-the-year flying, storage of components out of doors, and a reduction of the winter costs inseparable from operations in the Great Lakes region.[22]

The interior centres of the industry in the U.S.A. include Fort Worth, Kansas City, and Omaha (the headquarters of the Strategic Air Command). Since 1950 and the Korean War there has been a pronounced up-trend in the industry. There are weaknesses: the possible saturation of civilian airlines due to over-purchase, and the over-dependence of some major concerns, such as Douglas and Boeing, upon government contracts.

The American aircraft industry is much larger than Britain's, enjoying a vastly superior native geographical area in which to experiment and operate, and buttressed by a huge domestic market. The American industry has on several important occasions been

Engineering and Allied Industries

successfully protected by a sympathetic government against foreign competition inside the boundaries of the United States. This has been the experience of important British exporters. At the same time, aggressive sales tactics, backed by successful experience inside the American market, have enabled the Americans to sell great numbers of both civilian (mainly Boeing) and military craft abroad.

The Soviet Union

The Soviet, like the American aircraft industry, has the advantage of a vast field of operation. Much has been heard of West European and North American experiment in supersonic commercial aircraft. Less has been published of the Soviet effort, but the Russians are demonstrably technically as far advanced as the Americans in subsonic operations. They conduct, for instance, regular continental flights from Moscow, via Tashkent and Kabul, to New Delhi, as well as the still longer route via Irkutsk, to the Far Eastern provinces. Experience as long ago as the 1930s showed the feasibility of trans-Polar communication with the United States. Aeroflot, the State airline, and the biggest such operator in the world, provides a growing market for Soviet industry, concentrated particularly in the great western cities and in the Urals. There is a very large demand, as in the United States, for military aircraft, including helicopters, of all types.

France

The French aircraft industry has been one of the most enterprising in recent years — this in a field subject to fierce competition. It has been successful in technical accomplishment as well as in sales. In 1961 France was fourth in the world in output, after the U.S.A., the U.S.S.R., and the U.K. It is also fourth in exports. Caravelle commercial aircraft are found in many airlines. Sud-Aviation, based upon Toulouse, produces and exports the Alouette helicopter and, with British companies, is building the controversial Concord supersonic airliner. Nord-Aviation has achieved a very large production of missiles for N.A.T.O.

NOTES

1. M. H. D. McAlpine, 'Building a Steelworks', *Financial Times* supplement on 'Civil Engineering', 12 Nov. 1962.
2. A. K. Cairncross and J. R. Parkinson, 'The Shipbuilding Industry' in *The Structure of British Industry*, ed. D. Burn (Cambridge U.P., 1958), vol. ii, p. 96.

3. Ibid., pp. 105, 110.
4. Chamber of Shipping of the U.K., *Annual Report*, 1965–66, p. 213.
5. G. C. Allen, *British Industries and their Organisation*, 4th ed. (Longmans, 1959), pp. 25, 112.
6. Jones and Darkenwald, *Economic Geography*, p. 481.
7. G. Maxcy and A. Silberston, *The Motor Industry*, Cambridge Studies in Industry (Cambridge U.P., 1957), p. 117.
8. A. Silberston, 'The Motor Industry', in *The Structure of British Industry*, ed. Burn, vol. ii, pp. 16–20.
9. *Financial Times*, 17 Sept. 1965.
10. Allen, *British Industries and their Organisation*, pp. 188–9.
11. R. C. Estall and R. O. Buchanan, *Industrial Activity and Economic Geography* (Hutchinson, 1961), p. 198.
12. G. Turner, *The Car Makers*, 2nd ed. (Penguin Books, 1964), p. 209.
13. *U.N. Monthly Bulletin of Statistics*, April, 1966, p. 75.
14. *The Times*, 29 Sept. 1964.
15. Yoshio Sakurai, 'Motor Output Developing on a Western Scale', *Financial Times* supplement, 'Focus on Japan', 21 Sept. 1964.
16. Ibid.
17. *Annuaire Statistique de la France, 1965* (Paris, 1965), p. 254.
18. Ibid., p. 253.
19. Jones and Darkenwald, *Economic Geography*, p. 485.
20. Ibid.
21. N. A. Bengtson and W. Van Royen, *Fundamentals of Economic Geography*, 4th ed. (Constable, 1956), p. 545.
22. Estall and Buchanan, *Industrial Activity and Economic Geography*, p. 157.

Chapter 10   The Older Textiles

Britain's textile industry has undergone a number of crises. Two centuries ago, producers demanded and obtained protection from cottons originating in Asia. Subsequently, a great manufacturing industry developed in south Lancashire, while wool, with rising living standards, also prospered. In the last half-century cotton has faced still fiercer attacks from low-cost producers in South and South-East Asia. Since the Second World War the biggest test has come from the technological challenge of man-made fibres. This, cotton has been unable to defeat.

The picture in the U.K. now is of big producers, some of them even controlled from outside the industry — principally by I.C.I. The new pattern of production is being shaped by mergers between old units and by the increasing domination of the industry by companies interested in man-made fibres.[1]

COTTON
The United
Kingdom

Catastrophe came to Britain's cotton in the 1930s, as to shipbuilding and other activities dependent for their prosperity upon the level of exports. Economic difficulties at home were enormously aggravated by the development of production in existing or new areas abroad. The most important of these competitors today are Japan, Hong Kong, India, and Pakistan. Faced with the hot breath of competition from Asia, Britain's share of the world market has dropped to a fraction of what it once was. (Before the First World War she was supplying two-thirds of the world trade in cotton piece goods.) The total demand from the poorer countries has increased, but Britain's contribution has fallen. Total exports today of cotton piece goods from Britain are less than a third of what they were, even in 1949. Under the terms of Commonwealth preference, goods from the former colonies and from Hong Kong land in Britain free of duty, whereas competing goods from Japan or from the Common Market have been liable to an import duty of 17 per cent.[2] The answer of the British cotton industry has been to demand limitation of imports of cloth from Asia, while recognizing that home production would have to be reduced.

The industry has long sought to use its special expertise in making quality goods for export as well as for consumption at home, but one of the most striking features of the recession since 1952 has been the decline in the sale of the quality cottons: 'a high proportion of this trade has been lost to competitors in Western Europe and the United States'.[3] Cotton consumption has decreased faster than that of wool.

In Lancashire severe measures of retrenchment have involved the concentration of production in the largest and most efficient mills. The main objective has been *integration* — a term long associated with the industry. *Horizontal* integration refers to linking the same or similar processes, undertaken originally by different concerns; *vertical* integration to the streamlining of the whole or most of the processes of production from spinning, through weaving, to dyeing and finishing. Vertical integration can also now entail control of both the cotton and man-made fibre components of the finished, blended cloth. A notable feature of the industry's transformation during the post-war recession has been the growth in vertical arrangements: in 1961, out of 776 firms in spinning, doubling, weaving, and finishing, 36 'accounted for half of the total number employed, and 26 of the 36 were substantially vertical'.[4] 'Artificial' and 'synthetic' producers, such as Courtaulds and Viyella, have intervened, to become controlling factors in the entire industry.

Government money, channelled through the Board of Trade, has been provided for those firms undertaking retrenchment and re-equipment. Employment in cotton has continued to drop — it fell by a third between 1960 and 1965. (During the same period, employment in Indian mills increased by a third.) Local authorities and the Lancashire and Merseyside Industrial Development Association have striven to encourage diversification. Today far less than a tenth of south Lancashire's people are employed in cotton.

An important difference in the experiences of the American and British cotton industries arose from the volume of emigration to the New World. The continuous flow of migrants, skilled, semi-skilled, or unskilled, from Europe, produced a profound effect upon the labour market in New England. Another difference between the two countries concerned industrial location. The foci of production in Britain have been remarkably constant, but the distribution pattern of American cotton manufacture is very different today from the picture of the 1830s. Today far more cotton is consumed and manufactured in the cotton-growing states — especially in the Carolinas, Georgia, and Alabama — than in New England, although most narrow cotton fabrics are manufactured in southern New England or in neighbouring New York, Pennsylvania, and New Jersey. The decisive factor in the dispersal of the American cotton industry has been the wide availability of different forms of power, the newest of which is electricity.

Japan

The Japanese continue to be one of the world's leading creators of textiles, and despite recent advances in woollen manufactures and synthetics, cotton is still the foremost textile material. Taken together, cotton yarn, cotton goods, rayon, and rayon spun goods represent nearly half of Japan's textile exports. Textile sales are still worth more than any other class of product. This is so despite the fact that textiles have declined as a proportion of total Japanese exports — from over half in 1938 to only a quarter in 1964–65.

India

Indian post-war progress in cotton manufacture has been considerable — if less spectacular than that of Pakistan. The industry existing in the subcontinent at its partition in 1947 was almost wholly centred in the Indian portion. Pakistan's cotton industry has developed very fast, but from very small beginnings; India's cotton textile industry was already massive.

India: Cotton Textile Output[5]

	Cotton yarn (million lb.)	Cotton cloth (million yd.)
1960	1,737	5,048
1961	1,901	5,141
1962	1,898	4,988
1963	1,974	4,836
1964	2,127	5,091
1965	2,072	5,036

Most of India's production, and by far the greater part of the increase intended in her Third Five-Year Plan, is destined for internal consumption by a population at present increasing at the rate of 9 million a year. There are as many operatives employed in India's mills as in those of her principal competitors — the United States, Japan, and Britain — combined. **Cotton**

The growth of cotton manufacturing in Pakistan since the end of the Second World War, and more particularly since partition (the division of former British India), shows a rate of increase that is one of the fastest of any major world industry. **Pakistan**

The period of speedy growth coincided with the Korean War and the temporary world boom in commodities. There existed a basis for factory expansion: first, in the shape of the traditional Indian domestic handloom industry; and secondly in the determination of a new government, which was able and willing to use measures of protection and such devices as depreciation allowances to aid the textile manufacturers. Cotton textile exports from Pakistan have occupied a bigger place in world trade, although piece goods exports in 1963–64 were only a third those of India.

Production of cotton goods in Pakistan is concentrated overwhelmingly in the districts of Karachi, Lyallpur, Dacca, Multan, and Hyderabad. Before partition, the people of the subcontinent had been supplied — to the extent of over 90 per cent — by the mills of Bombay, Ahmedabad, and the other Indian centres.[7]

Pakistan: Production of Cotton Yarn and Cloth[6]
(million yards)

Year	Yarn	Cloth
1960	411	641
1961	413	699
1962	432	725
1963	472	731
1964	507	758

Cotton is only one of the flourishing branches of the textile and clothing industries of Hong Kong. Her cotton spinning mills contain about a quarter the number of Pakistan's spindles, but production of yarn, during the period 1961–64, was consistently about half, **Hong Kong**

123

The Older Textiles

and of piece goods nearly three-quarters, that of Pakistan. Cotton textiles formed the main element of the voluntary Textile Undertaking made to Britain by the Hong Kong Government in 1959: this declared: 'Exports of cotton piece-goods to the United Kingdom for retention there shall not exceed a ceiling figure of 115 million square yards in each year for a period of three years only from a date in 1959 to be appointed by the Hong Kong Government'. Exempt from this agreement were made-up cotton goods as well as yarn. Also, the undertaking did not apply to textiles brought into the United Kingdom for re-export: these have been considerable.

WOOL
The United Kingdom

The employment situation in Britain has been more stable for wool than for cotton — the 1951 figures showed a fall of less than 5 per cent as compared with 1937 — but there is some similarity in the production patterns of the two industries in Britain.

United Kingdom Textiles: Woven Fabric Production[8]

	Cotton mill. metres	Wool mill. sq. metres
1960	99	25·6
1961	94	24·5
1962	80	22·9
1963	77	22·7
1964	79[9]	22·7
1965	77	22·5

In Britain, the weaving of wool, much more than its spinning, has a very high degree of regional concentration. Over 75 per cent of total British workers in wool are to be found in Yorkshire, mainly in the West Riding; and there is a strong local specialization inside the main wool-worsted region: Bradford is by far the biggest worsted centre. But only half the woollen spinning frames employed in Britain are to be found in Yorkshire and the adjacent districts of Lancashire.

There are notable differences in the organization of the industries: the average woollen or worsted mill is smaller than its cotton counterpart. The ratio is striking: 'whereas in cotton a mill with 100,000 spindles may be regarded as typical, in worsted spinning the normal size is in the range of 10,000 to 20,000 spindles'.[10] Also, there is a much less pronounced tendency to vertical integration in the worsted than there is in the cotton industry; in other words, spinning and weaving are usually kept separate. **Wool**

About half of Britain's wool imports come from Australia and a quarter from New Zealand; and most of her home-grown wool is of 'non-apparel' type: that is, it is not suitable to be made up normally in clothing.

The export trade in woollen goods has kept up well, compared with the position in the late 1940s. But compared with the pre-war period, Britain's share of the world market has fallen by about a third. There has been fierce competition from Italy, France, and Germany, with resultant losses in sales to a European market fenced in by protectionist duties. As against this, the home market benefited from the levy (of $7\frac{1}{2}$ per cent *ad valorem* on yarn and $17\frac{1}{2}$ per cent on fabrics) imposed on imports.[11] Cotton has had no such shield.

Wool is regarded as a strategic item. It is therefore subject to stockpiling and is influenced by changes in demand directly following upon international developments. The Korean War of 1950–53 produced a huge increase in the demand for wool from the United States, and prices advanced 300 per cent.[12] The best tribute to the recent resilience of the industry lies in the continued resistance of the smaller firms to closure or amalgamation.

The north-east of the United States has retained its primacy in American wool manufacture. Over a fifth of American workers in wool-weaving are in the single state of Massachusetts.[13] New York, New Jersey, and Pennsylvania are much more important for wool than for cotton. There is often a close organizational and technical relationship between the man-made fibres and the older textiles; there is a corresponding division, in the synthetics industry, between New England and the New York region, on the one hand, and the Piedmont region of the Carolinas on the other. **The United States**

During the First and Second Five-Year Plans, some progress was made in the dispersal of the woollen industry from the old-established centres of Moscow and Ivanovo. The new trend was towards the North Caucasus, Central Asia, and Eastern Siberia. Since then there have been further developments in Eastern Siberia and in the Caucasian Republic of Georgia. The statistics of production **The Soviet Union**

in 1960 show the primacy of the manufacturing region of central
European Russia (the R.S.F.S.R.).

Soviet Union — Woollen Textile Production
Leading Districts[14]
(million running metres)

R.S.F.S.R.		271·8
Centre		194·3
Volga		26·2
North-West		16·2
North Caucasus		12·2
Ukraine		19·1
Donetz–Dnieper		10·8
Byelorussia		15·2
U.S.S.R.		341·8

Unlike most of the major industrial countries, the U.S.S.R. has
adequate raw wool supplies. Production rose, in the period 1955–58,
from 235 to 321 thousand metric tons, but the 1965 Plan — set at
548 thousand metric tons — was seriously underfulfilled. Woollen
manufacture has continued to do better than some branches of
consumer industry in the Soviet Union: a 4 per cent rise in woollen
output, in the period 1960–61, was followed in the next season by
an increase almost as large, but the main Soviet textile effort is
dependent on the success of the "chemical" (synthetic) fibre industry.

Japan Japan has been second only to the U.K. as an importer of Australian
wool. Total Japanese imports of wool have continued to rise in
recent years, despite the vast investment in man-made fibres. The
value of wool imports rose as follows: 1959, $212 million; 1960, $265
million; 1961, $345 million. In 1965 Japan was fourth in the world
in the production of woollen cloth, although output had fallen from
a peak in 1963.

**West
Germany** Much of the German woollen industry was located, before the
Second World War, in Saxony. The market for the manufactures of
this region included at least part of the area of the present Federal
German Republic. The redeployment of industry after 1945 led to
an increased concentration of woollen production in the older

126

centres of Rhenish-Westphalia, such as Wuppertal and München-   **Wool**
Gladbach. The mills are in the Elberfeld section of Wuppertal.
Other production is mainly to the west of the Rhine, in Rheydt,
Enskirchen, and Geilenkirchen.[15]

Most of France's woollen manufacture comes from her northern   **France**
region. The Roubaix–Tourcoing–Fourmies area encompasses 80 per
cent of the country's spinning output, but only 30 per cent of her
weaving. France is a good customer of Australia and New Zealand,
which together supply almost three-quarters of her imports of raw
wool.

1. See *The Times*, 'Fibres Ease out Old King Cotton', 28 July 1964.   **NOTES**
2. *Financial Times*, 11 Jan. 1963.
3. K. L. Wallwork, 'The Cotton Industry in North West England:
1941–61', *Geography*, vol. xlvii, pt. 3, no. 21b (July 1962), p. 243.
4. Lord Rochdale, 'A Critical Year for the Cotton Industry', *Financial
Times* Annual Review, 9 July 1962.
5. The Cotton Board.
6. Ibid.
7. *Report of Textile Enquiry Commission* (Ministry of Industries, Karachi,
1960).
8. U.N. *Monthly Bulletin of Statistics* (April, 1966) pp. 45, 49.
9. Year of fifty-three weeks.
10. Allen, *British Industries and their Organisation*, p. 259.
11. Ibid., p. 277.
12. G. F. Rainnie, 'The Woollen and Worsted Industry', in *The Structure
of British Industry*, ed. Burn, vol. ii, p. 254.
13. Thoman, *The Geography of Economic Activity*, p. 541.
14. Lydolph, *Geography of the U.S.S.R.*, p. 375.
15. See J. Dollfuss, *Atlas of Western Europe* (Murray, 1963), p. 26.

Chapter 11 New Industries – New Processes

The first Industrial Revolution ushered in the Machine Age, and automation is but the latest stage in the transformation that Watt and the mechanical engineers began. Automated processes promise spectacular increases in production, achieved by fewer workers and with smaller applications of effort.

The newest activities are industries of affluence, producing for the wealthiest and most sophisticated societies. The establishment of these branches of manufacture requires very large capital expenditure. Some of their products — the interplanetary rockets, for instance — may be as tall as a skyscraper, and as expensive; but the plastic and fibre materials of the other new growth industries can furnish rich and poor alike with inexpensive material for living. We have come to realize that the natural world provides, in the most basic and prolific minerals, sources of wealth and comfort beyond what has yet been known.

**CHEMICALS
The United
Kingdom**

The chemical industry, as known in Britain, is very largely a product of the twentieth century. The chief determining factor in the initial location of the industry — proximity to deposits of common salt — still has some validity, and the largest undertakings are to be found in the North-East, especially on the Tees, and in the Cheshire–South Lancashire Plain. The industry covers a very wide range of items. The heavy chemicals include sulphuric acid, ammonia salts, and alkalis. These are generally the oldest-established of the chemical branches in Britain, being founded upon native products. The basic sodium chloride gave rise to a number of manufacturing processes and, as existing chemicals became more and more in demand in industry, other outlets were developed. The requirements of war in 1914–18 produced a tremendous growth, which was to be repeated a generation later. Agricultural needs led to the creation of a vast artificial fertilizer industry. As in all the other leading industries,

comparable and parallel developments were proceeding elsewhere. **Chemicals**
Sometimes commercial links crossed over political frontiers, and
these international, almost supranational, groupings of the major
concerns remain a feature of the chemical industry.

The needs of armament industries in 1915 produced the new
explosive of T.N.T. (trinitrotoluene). Such influences were at work
in Germany, in the United States, and also in Britain, where the
eventual result was an amalgamation of the four largest chemical
firms — Brunner Mond & Co., Nobel Industries Ltd., the United
Alkali Co., and British Dyestuffs Corporation Ltd. — into one giant,
Imperial Chemical Industries, with a capital of £65,000,000. In
1962, I.C.I.'s employed capital stood at over £1,000 million (net
profits alone in 1962 were 48 per cent of the issued capital of 1926).
I.C.I. is by far the largest chemical concern in Britain, and one of
the biggest corporations in the world.

In Britain, in recent years, there has been a marked difference
between the growth performance of the different sectors of the
chemical industry. During 1963 soap and detergents fell back, while
there were striking advances in organic chemicals, plastics, and dyestuffs. Over the period 1954–62, plastics was the fastest-growing
major British industry.

The growth rate of the American chemical industry, between 1947 **The United**
and 1959, was second only to that of electronics.[1] The U.S.A. is far **States**
ahead of any other producer in the output of sulphuric acid. There
is a noticeably greater geographical spread of the American chemical
industry than in the case, say, of steel or automobiles, but a significant recent trend has been towards the South, with its notable
advantages, in the Texas–Oklahoma region, for the development of
petro-chemicals. The Gulf area also has an advantage in its resources of mineral sulphur. There is a very marked contrast between
the British chemical industry, dominated by a single concern, and
the American, where production is shared by a huge number of
firms; the six leading American producers (1. Du Pont; 2. Union
Carbide; 3. Procter and Gamble; 4. Monsanto; 5. Dow Chemical
Co.; 6. Allied Chemical Corporation) accounted in 1963 for only
24 per cent of the total national turnover in chemicals.[2] While the
American industry has continued to move ahead, its share of
world chemical production has fallen: from 47·8 per cent in 1953 to
35 per cent, in 1963;[3] but American output is still equal to that

129

of the Common Market countries, the U.S.S.R., and Japan combined.

The United States produces two-thirds of the synthetic rubber manufactured outside the Soviet Union, an effort motivated by American inability — because of the climate — to produce natural rubber, and by the great and sustained demand from the automobile industry. Synthetic rubber output in the U.S.A. doubled between 1955 and 1965. American production of sulphuric acid in 1965 was two and a half times, and of caustic soda five times, that of the Soviet Union.

West Germany

In Germany, amalgamation produced a fantastically large and significant growth in chemicals, exceeding I.C.I.'s achievement in Britain. The monster German firm was I.G. Farbenindustrie. After the Second World War and the Nuremburg Trials, I.G.F. was split into three main parts: Bayer, Farbwerke Hoechst, and Badische Anilin. Farbwerke Hoechst was much older than the parent body, having been started at Frankfurt-am-Main as long ago as 1863. An important chemical concern, Chemische Werke Hüls (C.W.H.), which was once controlled to the extent of 74 per cent by I.G.F., and which commenced the production of buna (synthetic rubber) in 1940, had, despite Allied air attack, achieved an output of 160,000 tons by the end of the Second World War. The main manufacturing centre was at Marl, on the Lippe Canal, where 16,000 people came to be employed in chemicals. By 1960 C.W.H. had become Europe's largest producer of polyvinylchloride and West Germany's largest producer of detergent raw materials. In 1959 buna output from this centre, which recommenced partially in 1951, and fully in 1953, had reached 120,000 tons per annum. Dyestuffs were, classically, an element in the super-rapid growth of German chemical combines, and aniline dyes were the foundation of the original fortunes of Farbwerke Hoechst. Today, Hoechst 'is strong in pharmaceuticals, Badische in fertilizers, insecticides and magnetic tape . . . Bayer in photographic materials'[4] (having merged with Gevaert, the Belgian photographic concern).

East Germany

The post-war division of Germany left a sizeable, though numerically inferior, section of the German chemical industry in the German Democratic Republic. This was founded upon the potash deposits of the Harz and the lignite wealth of the Halle district. Near Halle is the Leuna works, well known for its pre-war hydrogenation of coal, and in 1959 employing 28,500 people. Leuna, using the raw material lignite, is now the largest nitrogen producer in the world.[5] Chemicals represent by far the largest element in East German heavy industry.

In the chemical industry the Japanese have shown the same resourcefulness and willingness to learn from others as they had earlier exhibited in the engineering and allied industries. In total production they are fourth in the world, but they are in the first three in the output of certain basic raw materials of the industry, including sulphuric acid, caustic soda, and carbide. In common with other major world producers, Japan has been notable for the growth rate of her chemicals output. A number of individual chemical items have been expanding in production at an annual rate of between 14 and 20 per cent. But the most remarkable growth — the value of production has increased fifty times, between 1957 and 1961 — has been in petro-chemicals. By 1961 the chemical industry was responsible for almost 10 per cent of the total value of all manufactures. The main areas of concentration of the industry are: (i) the Tokyo Bay region; (ii) near Nagoya; (iii) around Osaka; (iv) on the northern shore of Shikoku. Sumitomo Chemical, based at Osaka and Niihama, is the leading Japanese producer: in 1964 it manufactured 47 per cent of the country's output of ammonium nitrate fertilizer, 38 per cent of its polyethylene, and 28 per cent of all its dyestuffs.[6]

French chemicals production trebled during the period 1952–61, and organic chemicals increased five times. Chemical production is notable for its wide geographical dispersal. Paris has a greater variety than any of the other centres, but notable regional advances are to be found elsewhere: the utilization of the natural gas of Lacq, around which an industrial complex is being built; soda works in the east, near sodium chloride and the production of coal derivatives at Carling; the utilization of hydro-electric power for the making of electro-chemicals in the Alps and Dauphiné; the making of organic and pharmaceutical products at Lyons; and the development of petro-chemicals on the shores of the Étang de Berre, in the south-

New
Industries —
New
Processes
The Soviet
Union

east. At Rouen there are petro-chemicals, dyestuffs, and synthetic rubber.

Chemicals were until recently one of the weakest points of the Soviet economy: this was underlined by the reorientation of target figures for heavy industry in the Seven-Year Plan. Soviet chemicals are based upon very large resources of bituminous coal and lignite and upon an impressive wealth of petroleum and gas. However, the development of heavy chemicals, as well as of the newer derivatives, such as plastics, requires the application of capital and the diversion of resources over a considerable period. The post-Stalin leadership was aware of the chemical deficiencies. Khrushchev stated that two-thirds of the 'basic funds' of the Soviet Union's chemical industry had been built up over the period 1958–63.[7] The positive nature of present trends — set in motion long before the 1963 farming crises, but underlined by it — have been shown by Nove. Chemicals achieved the leading industrial growth rate for the period 1962–63.[8] The accentuated concentration on chemicals, said Khrushchev, was intended almost to double the share of chemicals in the Soviet G.N.P. during the period 1963–70.[9] That an increase even as large as this was feasible is supported by Nove's figure of a 24 per cent increase in investment in chemicals over the period 1962–63.[10] Soviet sulphuric acid production increased by over two-thirds during the period 1959–65.

The Soviet measures were accompanied, in Comecon, by moves towards regional specialization in important items of the chemical industry.[11] Soviet oil supplied by the Kuibyshev–Schwedt pipeline has been paid for by exports from the Leuna chemicals complex. In 1962 the East Germans sold 686,000 tons of potash fertilizer to other Comecon countries.[12]

COAL AND PETRO-CHEMICALS

Petroleum and natural gas are the bases for petro-chemical production, the volume and significance of which has been growing with gathering momentum. During the first half of this century, the production of coal gas and its by-products constituted a major chemical activity. The conversion of simple coke-ovens into by-product units was largely accomplished by the end of the first quarter of the century.[13] Coal tar was used as a base for a wide

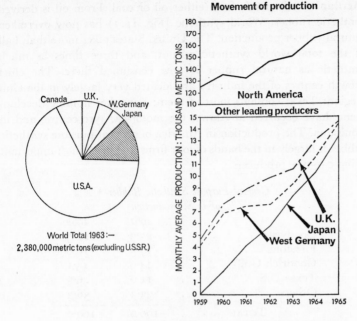

Movement of production

World Total 1963:—
2,380,000 metric tons (excluding U.S.S.R.)

FIG. II.I   Synthetic rubber — distribution of
production

More synthetic than natural rubber is now produced. Most
of the world synthetic production is in the U.S.A., which
manufactures 75 per cent of her total rubber needs.

variety of soap and pharmaceutical products, and it is still important
in this field. Coal has been used — expensively — by I.C.I. at
Billingham, to make oil. More recently, but still in costly fashion,
low-grade coal from Scotland and the West Midlands has been
converted into town gas by the Lurgi process at Westfield in Fife,
and at Coleshill in Warwickshire. Now Coleshill operates within
sight of a much cheaper gas-from-oil installation.

Petro-chemicals are now receiving more investment money than
all the remaining portions of the chemical industry. It involves a
whole series of processes to do with the refining and distillation of
petroleum elements. A huge complex of plants has been opened in
South Wales at Baglan Bay: six different firms have installations
there, for the production of polyurethane raw materials from oil.
Also from oil come the elements of synthetic fibres: terylene depends
wholly upon petroleum for its manufacture; Nylon, 'Courtelle', and

'Acrilan' can be made from either oil or coal. From oil is derived synthetic rubber. World synthetic (Fig. 11.1) has now overtaken natural rubber production. The United States takes more than half of the total world synthetic output, and three times as much synthetic as natural rubber is now consumed there. The chief growth centres of the industry are located very largely in the Gulf Region: Texas contains most of them; but other notable developments have occurred at Akron, the motor-car tyre centre, and in Louisiana. The production in America of general-purpose synthetic rubber is largely in the hands of four firms, the three most important being car-tyre producers.

General-Purpose Synthetic Rubber[14]
(*% of U.S. production*)

	1961	1962
Goodyear . . .	23·3	22·3
Firestone . . .	17·5	16·8
Goodrich Gulf . .	14·9	15·1
Texas U.S. . . .	11·0	9·5
Others . . .	33·3	36·3
TOTAL . .	100·0	100·0

British production of synthetic rubber is concentrated at two centres: Hythe, on Southampton Water, and Grangemouth in Scotland. Both plants are conveniently near to refining points for imported oil, their location being similar to that of the petro-chemical complex at Baglan Bay. The rate of growth of petro-chemical production has drawn comment from a number of sources, one of which[15] emphasizes the contrast between the small dimensions of the original raw material (only about 2 per cent of petroleum feedstock) as compared with the significance of the finished product. Oil has become more important, but it is necessary to remember the key role still played by coal. At Carling in Lorraine the mines, producing over 14 million tons of coal per year, feed integrated collieries, power stations, and chemical plants.[16]

Where oil replaces lignite a much greater saving in transport costs of bulk raw material is possible than if oil replaces bituminous coal. The first stage of operation of the Schwedt-an-der-Oder refinery, involving the production of 4 million tons of oil annually, is intended to provide for the chemical industry of East Germany the equivalent of 60 million tons of lignite.[17] The refinery began operations in 1964.

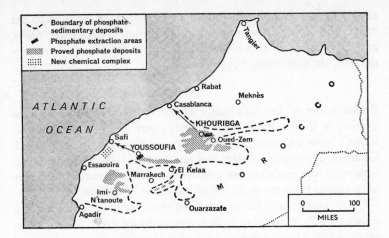

FIG. 11.2 Moroccan phosphates and associated chemical developments

Foreign capital has been needed to exploit the minerals and build the Safi chemical complex.

A Chemical Complex

Many of the raw materials of the world's chemical industry lie in economically relatively underdeveloped areas. The oil of the Middle East is exploited in an environment the social and political elements of which, in many cases, are exceedingly backward and where great extremes of wealth and poverty exist side by side. In Morocco, the vast natural wealth in phosphate minerals has, for some time, been transforming the industrial and commercial outlook of that country (Fig. 11·2). In 1964 phosphate exports made up a quarter of foreign earnings. Now, a chemical complex built at Safi, south-west of Casablanca, will become a fertilizer producer of world class, fed by the world's largest phosphatic supply, from Khouribga, east of Safi. The installations, constructed by French and German engineers, have a supply of cooling water pumped to them from the Atlantic.[18]

MAN-MADE FIBRES

The textile scene today would look strange if deprived of rayon or nylon, let alone the polyesters and acrylics which help to fill our shops. These are all creations of the industrial chemists like Crosse, Bevan, and Beadle, who produced viscose (the base material of

135

rayon) from woodpulp. Rayon, in 1958, accounted for over 80 per cent of the rapidly increasing world production of man-made fibres, and in 1964 rayon provided 65 per cent of man-made fibre production; the synthetics, 35 per cent.

Rayon

Rayon is one of Britain's major industries. Nearly all rayon production is in the hands of a single, giant firm — Courtaulds — formed from an amalgamation between Courtaulds and British Celanese. The combined firm had net assets in 1966 of £300 million, making it the sixth-biggest corporation in the country. Celanese have always been the main British producer of acetate.

Great quantities of timber are needed to manufacture rayon, as a little over 1 lb. of wood is, in fact, consumed for every 1 lb. of rayon produced.[19] About 200,000 tons of sulphuric acid are also used annually. It is not difficult to see, therefore, why such fibre manufacturers have been impelled to construct their own sulphuric-acid works, or why the merger with I.C.I., one of the world's leading acid manufacturers, should have been projected.

The bleached sulphite woodpulp used by the rayon factories is derived mainly from spruce trees from Canada and Scandinavia. More recently, the cellulose has been derived from eucalyptus trees grown in South Africa, where the South African Industrial Cellulose Corporation produces wood pulp in Natal. Caustic soda, one of the chief chemical raw materials of rayon, is derived from Cheshire's salt deposits, although it can also be made from soda ash. The carbon bisulphide required can be made from a variety of base materials: sulphur, coal, charcoal, or methane gas. As in the case of many of the world's relatively new industries, the raw materials of rayon are in very plentiful supply. But great technological refinements are required and vast chemical plants are needed.

Among the most important factors deciding the location of rayon factories are: plentiful power supplies, abundant water,[20] access to imported raw materials (e.g. woodpulp, sulphur) and to domestic chemical production, and proximity to important markets, including the textile plants, carpet factories (viscose accounts for about 40 per cent of the carpet pile used in this country), and motor-car works (viscose has been found to be far more suitable than cotton as a material for tyre-cord fabric, especially when this is made with synthetic rubber).

World rayon production shows the continuing supremacy of the

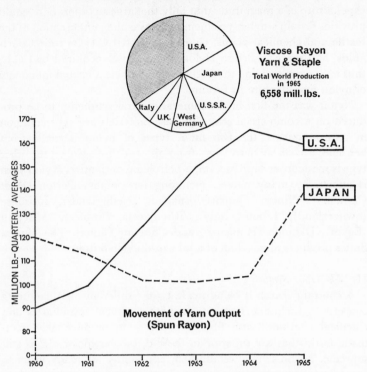

FIG. 11.3 Patterns in world rayon production

The advanced countries lead the world in the production of
sophisticated industrial fibres.

U.S.A. The Americans and the Japanese are well ahead of production in Western Europe and the Soviet Union (Fig. 11.3).

I. *Nylon*

The name 'synthetic', like 'artificial', suggests a substitute or **Synthetics**
replacement. Nylon, the first synthetic fibre, was a substitute for
silk. (Its most notable early use, apart from the manufacture of
parachutes in the Second World War, was as a raw material for
hosiery.) Nylon was invented in the United States, where it was
first produced by Du Pont in 1938. In Britain it was first made
under licence in 1941. War-time shortages, and the rupture of the
normal channels for the import of natural silk from the Far East,

137

encouraged the growth of a new industry that demanded capital expenditure of a magnitude that only the largest corporations could provide. Britain's nylon-producing unit was the joint creation of the textile and chemical giants, Courtaulds and I.C.I. In 1964 Courtaulds' half share in British Nylon Spinners was acquired by I.C.I., thus temporarily giving the Billingham combine a virtual monopoly of nylon manufacture in Britain.

Nylon was the first of the mineral-derived synthetics to be produced on a commercial scale. Its base materials are very common in nature: one of the two main types of nylon is made from benzene, a coal-tar derivative, from air, and from water; the other type is made from caprolactam, a petroleum derivative. Nylon yarn is known by many names, including for instance Perlon (West Germany), Niplon (Japan), Enkalon (Netherlands), Nylsuisse (Switzerland), Lilion (Italy), Rhodiacéta (France), Misrylon (Egypt), Danulon (Hungary), and Chinlon (China). The United States produces almost half of total world nylon output.

II. *The Other Synthetics*

A constant search is being made by the different manufacturing concerns — including textile firms with chemical subsidiaries and chemical combines with fibre divisions — to produce new man-made fibres that are superior to the old, but 'artificial silk' is still supreme. Nylon is now established, apparently for many years to come, but vast sums of money have been expended on research into other promising lines: for instance 'Courtelle', which was the first British acrylic fibre — based upon acrilonitrile, a product derived either from coal carbonization or from petroleum and developed in Courtaulds' laboratories. Commercial production began in 1959 by 'a unique process . . . believed to be the lowest cost (synthetic) process in the world'.[21]

Nylon had been the triumph of the American chemist Carothers in the 1930s; Terylene, a polyester fibre, of the British chemists, Whinfield and Dickson, working in the laboratories of the Calico Printers' Association. Terylene is now made, under licence, by I.C.I.

Man-made fibres are still moving ahead, relative to the older, natural materials. United Kingdom home consumption of man-made fibres in 1962 was 480 million lb. Consumption of raw cotton in that year was 485 million lb., and of raw wool 460 million lb.

138

Moreover, a sizeable proportion of the output of man-made fibres goes to the older industries. For example, of man-made staple fibre in 1962, about one-third went to the cotton and one-quarter to the woollen industries.[22] (All man-made fibres are manufactured by extrusion as threads or filaments. To make staple yarn, the filaments are cut into short lengths, combed, drawn, and spun into yarn in a way similar to the cotton-spinning process.)

The merger between I.C.I. and Courtaulds that was recently contemplated would have made the combined undertaking by far the largest industrial concern in Britain. The vertical integration envisaged by I.C.I., as following from the projected merger, was justified by them on the grounds that they could compete more successfully for a growing market 'against fully integrated companies such as the Du Pont Company in the U.S.A. (whose output of fibres, other than rayon, is three or four times that of the total U.K. production) and the Franco-Italian Rhône–Poulenc–Rhodiacéta Group'.[23] The American Chemstrand, with factories and affiliates in Scotland and Northern Ireland, is the second-largest producer of synthetic fibre in the world. Third is Britain's I.C.I. Fibres, the successor to British Nylon Spinners.

The level of man-made fibre production is linked to the general performance of the textile industry and also related closely to developments in chemicals. Soviet industry for a long time lagged behind in the production of what the Russians call the chemical fibres, and it is significant that this was a period during which the Russian chemical industry as a whole was sluggish. Nevertheless, the Soviet production of sulphuric acid, one of the key ingredients of rayon, was already in 1948 second in the world.[24] In world output, the Americans are first in both man-made fibres and chemicals.

World production of rayon and acetate yarn and staple increased by 120 per cent between 1946–50 and 1962; but this advance was much less than the achievement of the non-cellulosic man-made fibre, the world production of which trebled between 1957 and 1962. The increase in synthetics is still accelerating. For instance, in 1964 British consumption of synthetics was, for the first time, greater than that of wool.[25]

In 1963 British consumption of rayon fibre exceeded that of British-spun cotton (not taking account of imported cotton yarn). In 1964, 30 per cent more rayon than cotton was used.[26]

New Industries — New Processes

Rayon production in Britain has always been located mainly in the Midlands and in Lancashire. One of the earliest developments was at Spondon, in the Derbyshire section of the Trent Valley. Production is related more to the needs of the consumers of rayon than to the entry points of imports of woodpulp or cotton linters. Spondon is on the edge of the 'knitwear province' that extends into Nottinghamshire, Leicestershire, and part of Warwickshire. In this region, in the southern part of the Lancashire cotton area, and in Halifax, Keighley, Huddersfield, and Macclesfield, there is a textile tradition to explain the presence of rayon or other man-made fibres. Newer centres are at Lancaster and Wrexham, and there is a large rayon factory at Greenfield, in North Wales. One of the main regional concentrations of the British chemical industry is in the Cheshire–South Lancashire Plain. Courtaulds manufactures its own sulphuric acid at Trafford Park in Manchester, and at Greenfield.

One characteristic of the textile industry, as it existed in North-West Europe in the last century, was its strong regional bias. A characteristic of the man-made fibre industries is their tendency to produce international offshoots. For instance, I.C.I. Fibres is building a large plant at Oestringen, south of Heidelberg, in West Germany. Courtaulds, in 1964, was producing in Britain at the rate of 350 million lb. of rayon staple per year. Courtaulds' subsidiary in the United States was, at the same time, producing at the rate of 200 million lb. The British firm also has a big holding (£19 million) in the Italian Snia Viscosa.

Nylon is produced in the coal-mining centres of Pontypool and Doncaster, at Gloucester, Spondon, and Aintree. British Enkalon has a plant in Antrim, and Chemstrand is to make nylon at Dundonald in Ayrshire. 'Terylene' is made by I.C.I. at Wilton in Yorkshire; 'Courtelle' at Grimsby; and 'Acrilan' at Coleraine, in Northern Ireland.

The United States

American man-made fibre production, like the rest of its textile industry, is concentrated overwhelmingly in the eastern states. The most important area for rayon staple fibre and filament yarn production is in the southern Appalachians. In the synthetic industry, likewise, there is a concentration, at least so far as the largest and most modern mills are concerned, in the western part of the Carolinas.

Jones and Darkenwald[27] show more than nine-tenths of American rayon output — including the output of Courtaulds' subsidiary in

Alabama — as concentrated in the southern Appalachian and mid-Atlantic states. The essential sulphuric-acid plants are distributed especially around New York and Baltimore. In American synthetics production, locational factors are: the proximity of coal supplies (necessary for nylon), and of oil and natural gas (needed for the other fibres). Most nylon output comes from three super plants at Seaford, Delaware; Chattanooga, Tennessee; and Martinsville, Virginia; and nearly a third of it is now going to make tyre cord and fabric.

Man-Made Fibres

The Soviet Union began slowly in man-made fibre production, her average output of rayon and acetate staple fibre for 1946–50 being only 1·5 per cent of the world total. During the same period, the share of the U.K. was 10·6 per cent, and of the U.S.A., 23·5 per cent. But at that time Soviet consumer industries were recovering only slowly from war and in the next decade output was stepped up to 3·2 per cent of the world total. Rayon production was well ahead of synthetics: even as late as 1961, the ratio was 5 : 1 in favour of rayon. Since that time synthetic has gained on rayon production. In 1963 one report[28] went so far as to forecast that, between 1965 and 1970, the Soviet Union was likely to overtake both the U.S.A. and Japan in man-made fibres; another, that by 1970 the Russians would have 40 per cent of world output.[29]

The Soviet Union

Japan, like Germany, was devastated by war, but a considerable part of her industrial base was able speedily to recommence operations, assisted in re-equipment by copious aid from the United States. Since 1961 Japanese rayon has supplied a sixth of world production. In that year they produced more chemical — like the Russians, the Japanese refer to man-made as chemical fibres — than natural-fibre yarn. The ratio was 559,000 to 551,500 tons. These results were backed by a chemical industry of world significance: the Japanese are third in the world, after the United States and the Soviet Union, in output of sulphuric acid and equal second, with the Soviet Union, in the manufacture of caustic soda.

Japan

In Italy, as in Japan, we see a parallel development of the man-made fibre and chemical industries. The Italians were to the forefront in the large-scale production of rayon during the 1920s. Both

Italy

old and new centres of Italian textile production are in the north in the traditional centres of Lombardy and Piedmont; the new rayon and synthetic factories are at Turin in Piedmont, and further to the east. At Varedo are made rayon and the synthetic Lilion. At Torviscosa, built on former marshes in the Venetian Lowlands, there is a textile-chemical town, constructed by the biggest Italian textile group, Snia Viscosa.

France The French industry, more than in Britain, is to be found in old and famous textile centres — in Lyons, Colmar, St. Quentin, and Troyes. The Rhône–Poulenc–Rhodiacéta group, one of the leading world man-made fibre producers, was formed under the umbrella of the Common Market. This combine is typical of the international man-made fibre operators, with branches in four of the E.E.C. countries, in Spain, Sweden, Switzerland, Argentina, and Brazil and with large investments in British chemicals.

PLASTICS The plastics industry is notable for its rate of growth — leading producers have expanded their output recently by as much as 10–15 per cent per annum — as well as for its still only partially realized potential as a substitute for metals, wood, and glass.

One of the oldest plastics in general use is Bakelite. The plants that manufacture it now make Melamine — phenolic resin — as well. Other thermosetting plastics are polyurethane and urea formaldehyde (UF). As opposed to thermosetting are the thermo-plastics: nitrocellulose, less dangerous than it sounds, though highly inflammable, which is used for making table-tennis balls; cellulose acetate; polypropylene; and polyethylene ('polythene'). Polythene is a pre-1939 achievement of the industry. A near relative of poly-thene is polytetrafluoroethylene (PTFE). Highly important also are polyvinyl chloride (PVC) and polystyrene. One of the most valuable of all thermoplastics is a type of nylon called nylon 6.6, with a melting-point of 264° C. (507° F.).

World production of plastics in 1962 was 8·5 million tons — 10 per cent more than in 1961 — most of the output coming from oil derivatives. The American share of world production has fallen very considerably since 1950 (Fig. 11.6).

Industries that have benefited from plastics' lightness, consistency,

rust-proof properties, flexibility, and cheapness are: domestic **Plastics**
appliances and hollow-ware; the car industry and chemical engineering; building and electrical undertakings (more and more pipes,
for instance, are being made from PVC and polyethylene). As
packaging material, the potential of plastics is far from exhausted.
The textile industry itself uses plastic materials — nylon 6.6 and
terylene. Electronics, plastics' only rival as a growth industry, would
be unthinkable in its present form without plastic components for
radios, television, and telephones.

Dunning and Thomas refer to the growth in total production of
the British plastics industry: 28,000 tons in 1938; 158,000 tons in
1950; 575,000 tons in 1960. But this is a comparison merely
by weight: 'when specific gravity is taken into account, for
example, their present volume exceeds that of all the non-ferrous
metals'.[30]

The British industry has shared in the general prosperity of **The United**
chemicals. In the period 1962–63 the industries having the steepest **Kingdom**
growth rates in the United Kingdom were: organic chemicals,
plastics materials, and dyestuffs, in that order. Demand for plastics
in Britain has been rising by the impressive amount of 10–15 per
cent annually. The table of British plastics production shows the
increasing significance of thermoplastics.

U.K. Plastics Materials Output[31]
(1958 = 100)

Category	1959	1960	1961	1962	1963 (estimated)
Thermosetting	116	121	116	125	129
Thermoplastic	123	148	156	165	197
TOTAL	120	136	139	148	168

The American plastics industry is most important in the North-East, **The United**
particularly to the north and west of the New York conurbation: **States**
polyesters are manufactured especially in the state of New Jersey;
polystyrene especially in New York City and in the state of Massachusetts. Other centres are: Ohio–Michigan; the oil region of
Texas–Oklahoma; and the West Coast, especially near Los Angeles,
San Francisco, and Seattle. Despite the huge growth in American
plastics production, her share of total world output has continued

to fall. American output of plastics and resins increased by a third between 1962 and 1965, but during the same period West German production grew by almost two-thirds. Nevertheless, American production in this field in 1965 was equal to the combined output of Japan — by then the second world producer — West Germany, and Britain.

West Germany

In the inter-war period, and during the Second World War, I.G. Farbenindustrie was the leading world producer of plastics. By 1961 I.G.F.'s successors had brought West German plastics production to a higher per-capita level than that of the United States and 50 per cent higher than Britain's.[32] West German plastics output, only 125,000 tons in 1950, had risen to nearly 1·5 million tons in 1963, out of a world total of around 10 million tons.[33] The German industry is concentrated in the Ruhr, with its great coal resources, and elsewhere in the Rhine Valley. At Marl, north of Recklinghausen, Chemische Werke Hüls (C.W.H.) now has a plastics output more important than the synthetic rubber that it was originally created to manufacture. Hoechst plastics, another large producer, is located at Frankfurt-am-Main.

The Soviet Union

In the Soviet Union, decisions have been taken to invest huge sums in an attempt to make up some of the leeway in plastics production. Planned developments provide for an expansion from the output of 605,000 tons in 1961 to 1,660,000 tons in 1965 and 5,300,000 tons in 1970. Much of the equipment with which the Russian industry started was German. There are ample supplies of the raw materials — coal, petroleum, and natural gas — and there is a comparison with Britain in the emphasis placed upon thermoplastics, as against thermosetting plastics. In 1962–63 production actually increased by 24 per cent. This compared with an increase in production in the chemical industry as a whole of 16 per cent, and in gross industrial production of 8·5 per cent.[34]

Japan

The Japanese industry has expanded spectacularly, and plastics production is heavily concentrated in the Tokyo and Osaka districts. The biggest factories for polyethylene are located at Niihama, on the Shikoku shore of the Inland Sea, at Yokkaichi, and Kawasaki (Fig.

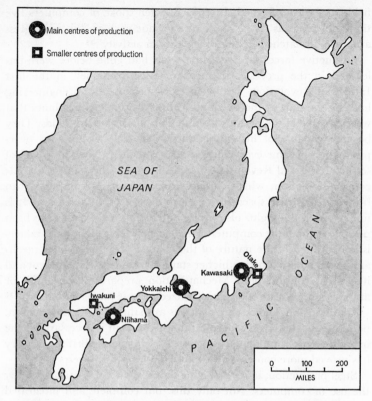

Main centres of production

Smaller centres of production

SEA OF
JAPAN

Kawasaki

Otake

Yokkaichi

Iwakuni

Niihama

PACIFIC OCEAN

0   100   200
MILES

FIG. 11.4   Japan — location of polyethylene manufacture
Japan's share of world plastics production has trebled in a decade.

11.4). In 1957 Japan had been fourth — well behind Britain — in
world production. In 1963 the Japanese were making almost twice
as many plastics and plastic materials (excluding synthetic rubber
and man-made fibres) as the British, and by mid-1964 had caught
up with the West Germans.

At the centre of the modern electronics industry is the computer, a
machine that can, in various degrees, collect, assimilate, memorize,
analyse, deduce, organize, direct, and command. It can do the work
of many men, and more quickly. Through the effectual conquest of
time achieved by the computer, human achievement in the material

**AUTO-
MATION
AND THE
ELEC-
TRONICS
INDUSTRY**

F   H.G.P.

145

field can be transformed. In 1962 Bowden spoke of computers five thousand times as fast as those of a decade earlier: 'this is progress at a rate unmatched in any other human activity'.[35]

Productive forces far exceeding what had gone before were unleashed in the processes of mechanization contained in the first Industrial Revolution. The sciences of mechanics and engineering had, by the start of the twentieth century, produced machines that were capable of taking most production out of human hands. They became capable of increasing output at such a rate that overproduction became everywhere a serious danger. Now, in a kind of second Industrial Revolution superseding mere mechanization, has come automation, which through the medium of computers can bring an immense speed-up of the processes of organization. It is unlikely that the flights of sputniks and astronauts would have been possible without the computer. The Russians have made a characteristic definition of the nature of the change: 'compared with mechanization, automation is a higher stage of technical development and its logical continuation. Mechanization prepares the ground for automation, because only a mechanized process can be automated'.[36]

Dunning and Thomas are cautious as to the scope for automation, pointing out that a very large capital investment is necessary for the introduction of automated processes.[37] In general, British industry has proved more conservative than American in this respect.

Steel production, in several of its processes, is being automated by the use of computers. Not only this, but complete and integrated control is envisaged, comprising a boss computer with subsidiaries in charge of the contributory departments.[38] Complete automation is only an aim and not yet an achievement, but present trends, and the increasing tempo of activity in a number of countries, point towards the realization of schemes for total control by man-made machines. The Russians state confidently: 'We are already entering the realm of complete automation of production, where not only the monitoring, protection and control of the technological process but all the operations of starting and stopping the machinery are automated'.[39]

It is in connection with air- and spacecraft that some of the most spectacular developments in electronics can be expected. Two of the main advances in the aviation sector have been air-traffic control and automatic landing. Such systems need to be accurate to an extreme degree: the British Air Registration Board will only allow a liability to error of less than 1 in 10 million.[40] Of the huge total expenditure on the American moon exploration programmes, it has

146

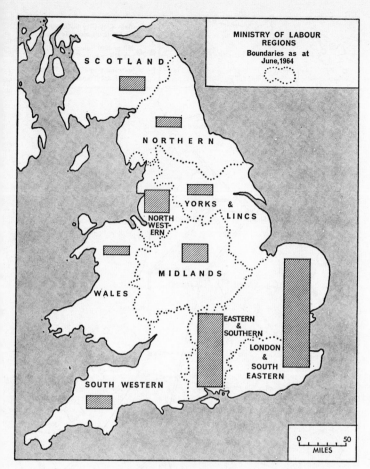

SCOTLAND

NORTHERN

YORKS &
LINCS

NORTH
WEST-
ERN

MIDLANDS

WALES

EASTERN
&
SOUTHERN

LONDON
&
SOUTH
EASTERN

SOUTH WESTERN

0   50
MILES

FIG. 11.5   U.K. electronics industry — regional distribution of employment
The industry is heavily concentrated in the south-east.

been estimated that £500 million will go towards guidance and
control systems.[41] It seems likely also that the use of computers may
produce a significant advance in long-range weather forecasting.
Miniaturization is especially important in the production of transistors for the radio-television industry, for aircraft, rockets, and
spacecraft.

The British electronics industry is concentrated especially in the
South-East region (Fig. 11.5).

**The United
Kingdom**

147

Main City-City both-way links
for 625-line Colour Television.

960 or 1800 Telephone Circuits
per Microwave Carrier.

Spur links to 625-line Television
Broadcast Transmitters.

FIG. 11.6   Radio links in Britain

Further developments include: (i) the extension of two-way colour
television links between (*a*) Birmingham and Norwich, (*b*) Ply-
mouth and Goonhilly; (ii) the replacement of the Aberdeen–
Inverness colour television link by a spur link to broadcast
transmitters; (iii) the installation of telephone circuits between
Belfast and Dublin per microwave carrier.

Britain's chief native computer producers are: (i) International Computers and Tabulators (I.C.T.), a group that embraces the related departments of Ferranti, Electrical and Musical Industries (E.M.I.), and the General Electric Company (G.E.C.); and (ii) English-Electric-Leo, incorporating Marconi and Elliott-Automation. Each unit of these corporations is very large. Most have made their mark previously in the neighbouring fields of electrical engineering. Internationally and nationally, there exists for the automators a market of enormous proportions. It is not surprising that there are interlocking relationships between the electronics corporations of North America and Western Europe.

Britain's television industry has grown with the development of more sophisticated apparatus. Colour television, using 625-line equipment, will soon be established in Britain, as in other countries of Western Europe. City-to-city links are being established, beamed from the massive G.P.O. towers in London and Birmingham; and at Goonhilly Downs, in Cornwall, a satellite ground station receives transmissions from the United States (Fig. 11.6).

Automation and the Electronics Industry

In the U.S.A., in the period 1963–64, the computer market is said to have been expanding annually at the rate of £1,200 million: the world picture shows the dominance of the United States. The American industry is still more remarkable for possessing, in International Business Machines (I.B.M.), a concern that has built more than half of the total world computer installations. I.B.M. is a major force in the British market, as also in the markets of the rest of the non-Communist world. It is conceivable, even, that some exports may begin to flow from the West to selected areas of the Communist East. However, the principal sales field continues to be inside the United States, where the electronics revolution first occurred and where automation is more advanced than anywhere in the West. There are working in the U.S.A. about two-thirds of the world total of computers.

The United States

The Japanese have been to the forefront in electronics generally, and in the development of transistors in particular. In 1963 the Japanese made 17 million radio and nearly 5 million TV sets. The electrical industry employs around a quarter of a million people; and its annual rate of production growth, in the period 1958–63,

Japan

149

New Industries — New Processes

France

was 25 per cent.[42] Indeed, a greater percentage of Japanese than British homes has television receivers.

The French electrical and electronics industries combined are expanding at the rate of 10 per cent per annum. Electronics manufacturers are concentrated especially around Paris. Two of their leading lines are television and radio-beam equipment. The French compete with the United States and with Britain's Decca Company to provide radar equipment for the airports of the world, but in computers, over two-thirds of the French market is covered by American-controlled organizations.

NOTES

1. Thoman, *The Geography of Economic Activity*, p. 514.
2. *Chemische Industrie International* (Düsseldorf, July 1964), p. 60.
3. Ibid. (June 1965), p. 60.
4. *The Times*, 9 Feb. 1965.
5. G. W. Hemy, *The East European Chemical Industry*, no. 3: *East Germany* (Joseph Crosfield, Warrington, 1959), p. 53.
6. Sumitomo Chemical, *Annual Report* (1965).
7. *Soviet Weekly*, 12 Dec. 1963.
8. A. Nove, 'Soviet Economy's Uneven Development', *The Times*, 7 Feb. 1964.
9. *The Times*, 10 Dec. 1963.
10. A. Nove, op. cit.
11. 'Chemical Drive by Comecon', *The Times*, 26 Nov. 1963.
12. Ibid.
13. Stamp and Beaver, *The British Isles*, p. 325.
14. *Competition in the Synthetic Rubber Industry*, Eighth Report of the Attorney-General (U.S. Govt. Printing Office, Washington, D.C., 1963), p. 10.
15. J. H. Dunning and C. J. Thomas, *British Industry: Change and Development in the Twentieth Century* (Hutchinson, 1961), p. 150.
16. *The Times*, 11 Nov. 1963.
17. *G.D.R. Review*, May 1964.
18. *The Times*, 29 June 1965.
19. D. C. Hague, 'The Man-Made Fibres Industry' in *The Structure of British Industry*, ed. Burn, vol. ii, p. 203.
20. N. M Mitchell states that 150–200 gallons of water are required to produce 1 lb. of viscose rayon, and 1,000 gallons to produce 1 lb. of acetate: 'The Textile Industry', in *The Economic Geography of Industrial Materials*, ed. Albert S. Carlson (Chapman & Hall, 1956), p. 371.
21. Courtaulds Ltd., *Financial Statement*, July 1962.
22. *Financial Times*, 11 Feb. 1963.

23. I.C.I. statement, 8 Feb. 1962.

24. I. Svennilson, *Growth and Stagnation in the European Economy* (United Nations, Geneva, 1954), p. 287.

25. *Guardian* supplement on 'Man-Made Fibres', 31 March 1965.

26. *The Times*, 8 Feb. 1965.

27. Jones and Darkenwald, *Economic Geography*, p. 528.

28. *The Times Review of Industry* (Feb. 1963), p. 51.

29. *Financial Times*, 19 March 1963.

30. Dunning and Thomas, *British Industry: Change and Development in the Twentieth Century*, p. 160.

31. 'Petro-chemicals: the Barometer of Growth', *The Times Review of Industry and Technology* (April 1964), p. 21.

32. *Guardian*, 7 Sept. 1963.

33. *The Times*, 15 Oct. 1963.

34. *Chemische Industrie International* (March 1964), p. 79.

35. B. V. Bowden, 'Electronics and Automation: Growing Impact on Society', *Financial Times*, 17 Dec. 1962.

36. A. A. Uskov *et al.*, *Technical Progress in the U.S.S.R.* (For. Lang. Publ. House, Moscow, 1965), p. 15.

37. Dunning and Thomas, *British Industry: Change and Development in the Twentieth Century*, p. 178.

38. Sir Leon Bagrit, 'The Spencer Works: A Major Advance in Automation', *Financial Times*, 26 Oct. 1962. See also P. J. Shipp, 'The Computer Takes Over' [the steel industry], *The Times Weekly Review*, 14 Nov. 1963.

39. Uskov *et al.*, op. cit., p. 24.

40. Sir Leon Bagrit, 'The Electronics Revolution', *Financial Times*, 3 Sept. 1962. See also *Financial Times* supplement on 'Computers', 6 Sept. 1965.

41. *Financial Times*, 17 Sept. 1962.

42. Fumio Iwashita, 'Economic Olympics in Electronic Goods', *Financial Times* supplement, 'Focus on Japan', 21 Sept. 1964. See also *Financial Times*, 3 June 1964; *Sunday Times*, 21 June 1964.

Chapter 12   The Organization of Production

Modern industry relies upon enormously varied sources for its raw materials, which are in turn worked upon by a labour force that may be numbered in tens of thousands, and contains several layers of skill, from the labourer through the artisan to the engineer.

Industry now often demands long years of training for production, for management, and for the conduct of labour and public relations. A producing organization may contain a large number of units of different size or may, on the other hand, be located at a single mammoth factory. 'Industry', it should be said, properly involves all that contributes to the increase of wealth — not only mining and manufacturing, but also trade, transport and agriculture. What is sometimes known as 'industrial' organization, therefore, involves only part of the industrial process.

The increasing prosperity of our mechanized civilization is due primarily to the sheer volume of output, but production could not have prospered without the ability to dispose of the ever-increasing flow of manufactures. Distribution is usually markedly separate from production and, in our own economy, it is rare for the two aspects to be under a unified control. However, there are notable exceptions: the electrical supply industry also distributes and sells current. Coal is mined by the nationalized Coal Board, and distributed mainly by the nationalized Railways Board, but road and sea transport are mostly in private hands. The sale of coal is conducted by a huge number of small and by a small number of very large urban concerns.

Size and Monopoly In sheer size of operation, the very biggest American corporations (the fifteen with sales of over $2,000 million, in 1963) have only three rivals in Europe — Unilever, Nestlé, and Philips.[1] There are special economic and geographical circumstances operating in the U.S.A.: five of the leading fifteen are oil firms; three are motor-car manufacturers. Of the ten British leaders,[2] reckoned according to their capital assets, three also are oil companies. One oil firm — Esso — is American; one — British Petroleum — is 40 per cent State-owned. The parent company — Royal Dutch Shell — of the third is 60 per cent Dutch-owned. Of the seven remaining British leaders, two are tobacco companies, British-American Tobacco and British Imperial Tobacco. B.A.T. is the formerly American firm, now wholly British-owned, that entered the market before 1914; B.I.T., the British combine that was formed to combat it. The two eventually reached a working arrangement to protect their spheres of influence.[3]

The large producer benefits from the "economies of scale", which a large firm can realize. Research facilities are likely to be better in a huge organization, with its ample funds. Big corporations are able to afford to pay well for the services of men of the highest technical grade; they are in a position to compete successfully for highly skilled men. Giants, such as I.C.I. and Courtaulds and pharmaceutical firms such as Boots, can make experiments and take expensive risks for the benefit of their organizations.

At the present time, we are at the beginning of an automation era, which is likely to work still further to the advantage of the big operators. These have sufficient reserves to induce confidence on the part of investors, and can, in case of need, withstand losses that would break a smaller competitor.

In certain branches of private industry, advertising, because of the nature of the product concerned, has been able to achieve a vast increase in sales, but a consequence has been the necessity to maintain this volume of advertising in order to meet competition from comparable rivals. This has been true particularly of the industries producing detergents, pharmaceutical and toilet requisites, packaged foods, domestic appliances, drink, tobacco, and confectionery.

The concentration of production to the degree of real or virtual monopoly has posed considerable problems for Western society. The elimination of competition may obviously be contrary to the public interest, so that in the United States anti-trust legislation has been invoked by administrations committed to upholding private enterprise. In Britain, public monopoly in the shape of the nationalized industries is subjected to annual supervision by Parliament, to which their governing boards are responsible.

In Communist society, national monopolies thrive on a scale that dwarfs the British Coal Board or Railways Board. The Soviet power

The Organization of Production and steel industries, their chemical and consumer trades, machinery, car and textile industries are all State-owned and State-run. These are super-monopolies. The Communist claim, of course, is that all is done in the public interest, subject to scrutiny by representatives of public institutions. Ideas of rationalization have led to new thinking in the Eastern world. There have been reports from the U.S.S.R. of 'a grouping of factories producing articles of the same type, under the direction of the staff of the largest factory of the group, which becomes the "leading factory".'[4]

In the West, government intervention in economic affairs has been promoted by the need for increased defence expenditure, by the complexity of recent developments in defence technology, and by the rapid expansion of atomic and nuclear facilities. In Britain, two very different organizations are concerned with nuclear power: the Central Electricity Generating Board and the Atomic Energy Authority.

The strategic implications of nuclear energy are such as to compel government interest in its manufacture. The undertaking by private companies of highly secret work, such as that involved in the *Dreadnought* and similar submarines in Britain, may lead to both government surveillance and the dependence of that company on defence contracts. In certain cases, for instance the Polaris-type weapons of Britain, a country may become at least partially dependent on governments other than her own.

The Far East contains, in the Japanese Zaibatsu, outstanding examples of the working of industrial monopoly, the creation of which was encouraged by friendly administrations in Tokyo in the latter part of the nineteenth century. The Zaibatsu corporations, the largest of which were Mitsubishi, Mitsui, Sumitomo, and Yasuda, embraced before 1939 over four-fifths of Japanese trust business. These four leaders controlled half of Japan's coal industry, 69 per cent of her railways, 60 per cent of her shipping, and nearly half of her machine-tool industry. At least one source has credited their post-war derivatives with very large competitive and social advantages: modernity; flexibility; encouragement of innovation and invention; the promotion of welfare.[5] The Japanese have for many years shown themselves alive to the demands both of technology and of the market.

In Britain, as in Western Europe, it has been made clear that large-scale operations encourage the development of automative techniques. This has been found true also at the Sochaux plant of the Peugeot motor-car concern, where a labour force of 25,000 produced 259,000 cars in 1962 and 289,000 in 1963. Automation is of growing importance in some of the biggest units of the steel industry — for instance at the Spencer steelworks at Llanwern in South Wales. Here was carried out the first application of such techniques to hot strip-mill processes.[6]

Integration

In the case of manufacturing concerns, the largest producers see, in the working of their departments, the operation of a series of related processes: they are integrated. It does not follow that all the operations of the great employers are so related. Some companies, for instance in the property and distributive trades, have taken over industries far removed from their original nuclei.

For integration to occur, large amounts of capital must be found, but with the advantages to be anticipated, integrated processes are a good investment risk. The resulting reorganization may involve the linked processes of by-product manufacture, or the acquisition of plants that take in the first stages of transformation from the raw material. The development of by-products may work through the association of similar companies in a linked complex, as at Baglan Bay in South Wales, or at Carling in Lorraine. The most complicated developments may involve the collaboration of international concerns, the ultimate bases of which may be thousands of miles apart. A good example of this is Europe's largest petro-chemical complex at Rotterdam–Europoort, where refineries, fibres, plastics, and pharmaceuticals work side by side. In this case, industries have been attracted to oil, while oil companies — for instance Shell — have been encouraged to diversify further into chemicals. While I.C.I. have taken nylon polymer manufacture to Europoort — transporting the necessary basic materials from Wilton, in the U.K. — they have also built their own refinery at home to cater for Billingham's expanded petroleum demand.

The vertical integration, such as is found in some steel and chemical concerns, produces large units carrying a complete or very wide range of processes. The largest car-producers may make their own steel, with the necessary blast furnaces and coke ovens lying alongside assembly and finishing plants, as is the case at Dagenham. The relation of integration to scale of production is well illustrated by the Western world's largest plant, belonging to Ford Motors, at River Rouge, Dearborn, Michigan, where 3,200 tons of steel are smelted daily for the company's car-production lines.

The Organization of Production
The National Arrangement of Production

Patterns of trade are determined largely by the often conflicting policies of independent governments. Serious and determined attempts have been made to reach international accord on tariff reduction, but the area of agreement has been limited. Usually the necessary compromises have been reached between groups of Powers whose interests have been complementary rather than competitive; but on the other hand the impressive progress of the Common Market is significant, containing as it does ancient competitors and protagonists.

The result of a national arrangement of production is that all is tailored to national needs. One aspect of the 'normal' organization is its alignment around State capitals. This, the new supranational planners seek to change. With fully organized regional arrangements, there is likely to be a shift of production in favour of linked units. Common Market developments have increased the importance of the Sambre–Meuse Valley and of Rhenish-Westphalia.

International Companies and Operations Overseas

The national basis of production is consistent with the large-scale operations pursued by the parent or subsidiary companies overseas. A part of primary production, especially in the realm of minerals and certain strategic commodities, is in the hands of huge concerns based in the main industrial consumer countries. Leading examples are furnished in Central and Southern Africa, and in South and Central America. Acute political problems may arise from the operation of foreign corporations in tropical and other areas, for instance in Indonesia. In Zambia it has been thought possible that a newly independent government would seek to buy out one of the two leading copper-producers in Africa. The French companies mining oil and gas in the Sahara may feel that their investment is at risk in independent Algeria.

The largest wholly-British motor company, the British Motor Corporation (B.M.C.), has subsidiaries in the Commonwealth. There are obvious possibilities in this way of exporting 'know-how' while establishing manufacture near the intended market. Similar trends operate in regard to the American motor-car corporations. Fords have built very large plants at Cologne, as well as in Britain at Dagenham and at Halewood on Merseyside. Vauxhall Motors, a G.M.C. affiliate, has plants at Luton and near Liverpool.

In the case of companies engaged in fruit or vegetable processing or sales, where the primary material is of tropical or subtropical origin, some large Western-based corporations — as in chocolate, sugar, or bananas — own plantations in Africa or in Central America, thus deriving very large economies from control of both ends of the supply process. The largest British sugar-processing concern has provided striking evidence of the commercial advantages of participation in the linked processes of such an industry.[7] The sugar-consumer loses when market prices rise: such changes occurred spectacularly in 1962–64, the major alteration being due to the ravages of Hurricane Flora in Cuba and Haiti. During this period the price of sugar per ton varied between £20 and £100; but a concern that also owned plantations stood to lose less than other producers from a rise in primary prices.

Companies dealing in rubber and in vegetable oils also have an interest in the control, by ownership, of the source of supply, and consequently of the price of the tropical raw material: the largest European consumer of vegetable oil is Unilever, an Anglo-Dutch concern. Chemical companies are notable for their international subsidiaries and ramifications. An outstanding example is Du Pont, the Western world's largest chemical operator: in 1958 Du Pont's investment in its European subsidiaries stood at £1·4 million. In December 1963 the estimated figure (referring to companies in the U.K., the Netherlands, Belgium, France, Spain, Sweden, West Germany, Luxembourg, and Switzerland) was £53 million.[8]

International Companies and Operations Overseas

The first Industrial Revolution was built upon coal. There was a very marked correspondence between factory building and the availability of fuel. Most of Britain's big cities are still either near coal, or are on tidewater, and London is able to obtain fuel by sea from Northumberland and Durham, but electrical power acts as an equalizing influence within the nation-State, and there is no longer a rigid dependence on coal. The ability to transmit power ensures that other factors will have a much greater influence. Electrical energy can be passed from the furthest corners of Wales and Scotland to the National Grid, whence it is available in case of need in any region. More spectacularly, power can be transmitted across frontiers and under water: to Vancouver Island from the Canadian mainland; to Denmark from Sweden; and between Britain and France.

Special factors operate to control the location of the power stations themselves. Coal-fired stations are situated in places to which the

Energy as a Factor in the Location of Industry

bulk fuel can be easily brought. This normally involves a choice of location near water, or with a short rail haul from a coalfield. Water is highly important for cooling: for this reason, stations such as Drakelowe and Willington are sited near rivers — in their case, the Trent. London's stations, such as Bankside and Battersea, and the coastal stations of Sussex and Hampshire, get their fuel by sea. In North America, and on the continent of Europe, inland water navigation for bulk commodities is more important than it is in the United Kingdom, and thermal power stations are sited along the Rhine and Meuse as they are along the rivers running west from the Appalachians to the Mississippi.

Hydro-electric power stations are necessarily tied to water supplies. France, on whose power Britain can draw at peak periods through the Dungeness cable, has hydro resources on her south-central rivers. Large installations are to be found on the Dordogne, the Durance, and the Rhône at Génissiat and Donzère–Mondragon, and on the Rhine.

Since the end of the Second World War, the effect of the availability of liquid fuel supplies has been to promote the appeal of coastal and estuarine sites for power stations. Nuclear-generated power requires vast quantities of water and nearly all the stations are in fact on tidewater.

The rapid rise in the proportion of energy consumption devoted to oil products — petroleum, diesel oil, paraffin, and lubricants — has helped to promote the establishment of new industries in new areas. There is little difference in the price of petrol between different regions of Britain. Unlike coal, which is transported mainly by either rail or collier, oil is carried chiefly by road, although there are important pipelines providing a distribution service from unloading points such as those in South Wales, on Southampton Water, and on the Thames estuary.

Another equalizing factor is gas, supplies of which are controlled ultimately by the Gas Council. Prices are fixed by Area Gas Boards, so that where demand is constant and healthy tariffs may be favourable, but there is not likely to be a decisive regional variation.

The significance of energy as a localizing factor may depend on the proportion that it contributes to the final cost. In the Soviet Union, Probst gives examples of energy-intensive industries: synthetic rubber and fibres, ammonia, aluminium, and nickel. Electricity makes up a considerable part of the final cost of aluminium, the manufacture of which is located today in regions such as

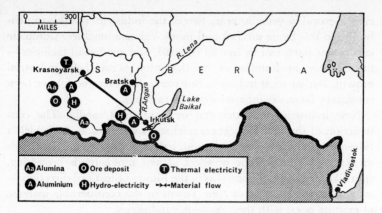

Energy as a
Factor in the
Location of
Industry

FIG. 12.1   Aluminium in Siberia — an example of
industrial location

The aluminium industry of eastern Siberia is founded upon local
raw materials and plentiful supplies of energy.

Eastern Siberia (Fig. 12.1) and the Caucasus, where current is
cheap. Synthetic rubber is produced from calcium carbide at
Yerevan, in Soviet Armenia, where there is hydro-electric power.
The easily-mined natural gas of Bokhara is expected to produce
a greatly accelerated rate of industrialization in that part of Central
Asia.[9]

The cost of transport is an important factor in the location of manufacture of bulky and weighty raw materials. Bulk is more important
than weight. Water facilities are all-important, bulk commodities
being most cheaply transported by sea, river, or canal. The size of
the units of cargo means that handlers can afford to instal specialized
and expensive machinery. For some items, such as liquids and
mineral ores, mechanical handling may be essential. Advantages
accrue to ports specializing in certain cargoes or, at least, dealing
with very large and regular consignments: one sees the operation
of competitive factors favouring in turn the Continental ports of
Antwerp, Rotterdam, Hamburg, and Bremen.

Many problems arise from bulk transport by road and rail, but
the Railways Board has endeavoured to extend its bulk-handling
facilities for such diverse commodities as coal, oil, iron, cement,
fertilizer, milk, and beer. The total amount of traffic carried by road

**Bulk Raw
Materials**

The Organization of Production

rises inexorably year by year, two of the industries notably contributing to this being aircraft and motor-car manufacture. Complete cars or car parts can be moved by road, and good road facilities — for instance to London or Southampton — can help industrial growth. But for most industries our roads, however good, have been subsidiary factors compared with the railways.

New industries may demand new transport media. The construction of the first Dungeness nuclear power station, for which a tidewater site was deemed essential, led to an improvement of roads on Romney Marsh. The prospect of new motor-roads projecting, spur-like, around London — as in the Bishop's Stortford direction — may assist the creation of New Towns or the considerable increase of existing ones, with their consumer industries.

Labour Supply

Labour is an essential ingredient of all industry, but changes in the demand for labour may be irremediable: they may stem from long-term alterations in the balance of advantage between producing regions or competing industries. The cotton industry in England is a case in point. The decline of production in Lancashire is not new, having proceeded almost unchecked for more than a generation. The cause has lain in the superior facilities possessed by competitors in the Far East. The story of industry in Lancashire has not been one of unrelieved gloom. New trends have appeared in Bolton and Blackburn, in Rochdale and Oldham. Manchester, with Salford, has long been fully diversified, and now we read of a second industrial revolution in cotton: 'Engineers have designed and constructed a whole range of new labour-saving machinery, precision-built and capable of greatly increased speeds, which has rendered obsolete much of what had gone before'. Smalley has shown in the same article how a typical mill producing 670 lb. per hour of combed cotton yarn needed 207 operatives in 1950; by 1964 this has been reduced to 60.[10] The new mills, with fewer but bigger machines, are more efficient. Labour productivity has grown: there was a 15 per cent increase in this respect in the cotton industry between 1959 and 1963.[11] With higher productivity has come also higher wages. It is noteworthy, though, that cotton and its allied trades have clung to Lancashire. Nylon is different: it is a chemical process, owing nothing to the traditional imports of textile fibres. Cotton remains firmly linked to the arteries joining Liverpool with Manchester, and these two cities to the factories. At the same time, newly diversified

South Lancashire has demolished some of its old mills or, elsewhere, uses them to accommodate wholly new trades.

The division of labour on a world-wide scale was made possible by advances in transport technology; these improvements in turn being called forth by urgent new consumer needs. The products of the tropical and subtropical lands demanded payment, which came from the sale of industrial products. The market was no longer local but world-wide; it was not a single group of consumers, but a multitude of opportunities.

There has been a general increase in the importance of the market factor. This has occurred for a number of reasons: changes in the character of industry; improvements in transport; industrialization of former backward areas; the redistribution of population and growing urbanization. The twentieth century, particularly in the last twenty-five years, has seen the steady growth of the consumer industries. Greater affluence has induced much higher spending on domestic appliances. This social development has been stimulated by intensive advertising, especially since the advent of commercial television. There has been a very striking development of such consumer industries in and around London. Manufacturing is only a part of the changing economic picture, and the manufacturing element of industry has diminished as efficiency has improved. Higher standards of living and more leisure have produced more travel, entertainment, and personal services. Changes in the character of industry have gone hand in hand with the increasing urbanization of our civilization. Young people and young industries tend to congregate in towns.

Manufacturing industry itself demands services, which grow with prosperity, but transport media may clog our big cities. Roads become more and more congested, and commuter traffic has, in places, had to move underground. The increasing difficulty of movement between London's railway terminals, lacking a link line such as the Parisian 'Ceinture', has long been apparent. Now, overhead lines and monorails are suggested as palliatives to the acute traffic problems that impede industrial growth.

It is possible to exaggerate the significance of the market factor, even in the conditions operating in South-East England. The South-East Survey, published in 1964, accepted the certainty of population and industrial growth in this part of Britain. There have been many pointers to a development and strengthening of the links between this part of the country and the Continent. On the other hand, the expansion of trade with E.E.C. members does not necessarily confer decisive advantages upon concerns located in the South-East, as compared with those in other parts of the British Isles. This consideration has been emphasized by Chisholm.[12] The establishment of new transport forms between London and the other parts of Britain is likely to confer all-round advantages, which will not be confined to firms operating from factories in or near the metropolis.

NOTES

1. *Financial Times*, 11 Sept. 1964.
2. *The Times*, 'Britain's Largest Business Groups', 21 June 1965.
3. R. Evely and I. M. D. Little, *Concentration in British Industry: An Empirical Study of the Structure of Industrial Production, 1935–51* (Cambridge U.P., 1960), p. 118.
4. 'The Soviet Scene: New Forms o. Economic Organisation', *Financial Times*, 22 Feb. 1963.
5. 'The Japanese Zaibatsu: Monopoly and Efficiency', *Financial Times*, 20 Sept. 1962.
6. *The Times* supplement on 'The Spencer Steelworks', 26 Oct. 1962.
7. Tate and Lyle Ltd., *Annual Report*, March 1964.
8. 'Du Pont in Europe', *The Times Review of Industry and Technology* (March 1964), pp. 20–23.
9. Probst, in *The Location of Communist Industry*, ed. Hemy, p. 84.
10. E. G. Smalley, 'Automation for the Spinner', *Guardian* supplement on 'Lancashire's Textiles', 24 March 1964.
11. G. H. Jolly, 'Revolution in Spinning', ibid.
12. Michael Chisholm, 'Must We All Live in South East England?' *Geography*, vol. xlix, pt. 1, no. 222 (Jan. 1964), pp. 13–14.

Planning and Government Intervention

Today many countries possess their national plans. Some are comprehensive, embracing all branches of economic activity; others refer only to certain sectors of production. Britain possesses a 'mixed economy', part privately-owned and operated, part nationalized and responsible to Parliament; but government intervention may extend, for instance through the control of credit, to all spheres of economic life.

Soviet experience has been a powerful example to planners in other countries with far different circumstances from those to be found in the single-party Soviet State. The State Planning Committee organizes its work on the basis of planning periods, which have varied between five and seven years. Only very occasionally have plans been altered or superseded during the period of their operation. Investment is directed and funds made available through the State Banks.

Planning — Eastern and Western

Soviet planning is very different from the Western brand. In Britain, government intervention is now tolerated but is far from being always welcome. Nevertheless, there is general acceptance that the State is not to be regarded as an inevitable enemy. The ravages of boom and slump, particularly the British and American experiences of the 1930s, were sufficient to induce an acceptance of government policies designed to avoid widespread economic disruption. There is now at least an indirect control of the total volume of demand, through the medium of taxation and revenue duties such as purchase tax. Supply is affected by central direction of credit facilities, and governments are in a position to deter or to encourage spending, to dampen or to prime production.

Overcrowding in British cities, particularly in the London region, but also in the Midlands, Lancashire, the North-East, South Wales, and Central Scotland, has been partially met by the creation of New Towns (Fig. 13.1), many of them containing important growth industries.

NEW TOWNS

Estimated populations 31st.Dec.1964

● Over 50,000
◉ 25,000–50,000
○ Under 25,000

The date against each town name
represents the year of designation
as a 'New Town'

+ North Buckinghamshire New Town
'draft designated'

Glenrothes 1948 ○

1955 ○
Cumbernauld ○ 1962
◉ Livingston
1947
East
Kilbride

Washington 1964 ○
Peterlee 1948 ○
Newton Aycliffe 1947

Skelmersdale
○ 1961

◉ Runcorn 1964

Dawley
○ 1963   Corby
                          ◉ 1950
Redditch
1964 ◉

                    +   Stevenage
                          1946
                          ●
            Welwyn Garden City 1948 ●   Harlow
Cwmbran   Hemel Hempstead 1947 ●   ● 1947
1949 ◉   ○
                    Hatfield 1948 ●
                              1949 ●
                    Bracknell ◉ Basildon
                    1949

                          ● Crawley
                          1947

0 | | | | | 50
        MILES

FIG. 13.1   U.K. — 'New Towns'

The New Towns, especially numerous around London, are an
attempt to dissipate some of the results of overcrowding.

More direct intervention is possible. The most obvious means is via the acquisition of industry by the State. The existing pattern of State control in the U.K. was initiated by the Labour Government of 1945–50, which nationalized coal, electricity, gas, and inland water transport. The coal companies, of which there were many, had their properties expropriated, and received compensation in the form of government stock. They were replaced by the National Coal Board, a body responsible to Parliament, with a chairman appointed by the Minister of Fuel and Power. The electricity and gas companies, likewise, were replaced by Councils reporting annually to Parliament. Measured by assets, electricity is the leading nationalized industry. Nationalization does not involve responsibility to a particular government. The day-to-day working of nationalized industry is in the hands, not of a Minister, but of independent administrators and technicians. It is possible, in theory, though in practice it has appeared improbable, for their policies and actions to be at variance with the general intentions of the government. National Boards and Councils are required to pay their way; they are affected by the general climate of economic activity; and indirectly they are subject to government control in the scale and timing of their borrowing.

Nationalization

War-time emergencies led to special interventions by Western governments. These included the direction of both labour and industry, the purpose being to fortify those strategic manufactures that were suddenly needed much more than in time of peace. Controls were necessary to switch men, materials, and money from inessential production. 'Inessential' trades were those that catered largely for private domestic consumption and for exports. The two world wars introduced rigid controls of shipping in Britain — essential for a nation depending on sea communications. A corollary of emergency control of production was the regulation of demand, effected through rationing. Such measures were restricted in Britain to the period of actual war and its immediate aftermath. They have been paralleled elsewhere, even in times of peace, when shortages of food and consumer goods have made a free choice unrealistic: such has been the experience of the Soviet Union, of Eastern Europe, of China, and of Cuba.

Direction and Control

Planning and Government Intervention Farming and a National Plan

Soviet planning has not been nearly so successful with agriculture as with industry. To some extent this may have resulted from the advantages that industrial planners enjoy in a context of increasing mechanization. Farmers and workers on the land have often resisted controls, and production has been erratic.

Western intervention in farming matters has usually taken the form of encouragement rather than direction. Agriculture has to some extent been treated as a vulnerable part of the economy, to be protected and cushioned against foreign competition. British farming employs a smaller and smaller labour force, but its prestige is still strong. Agriculture was a crucial factor in the abortive negotiations between Britain and the Six in 1962. French farmers have been important in deciding the policy of their government, even of a powerful administration like that of de Gaulle.

Regional Problems

Governments have a duty to sustain the interests of their subjects. In various parts of Western Europe there has been considerable concern because of the uneven rates of economic progress between the different sectors of separate nation-States. Britain has seen a steady drift of new industry and of young manpower to certain parts of the Midlands and the South. A falling-off in demand has hit particularly the coastal and estuarine cities of the coalfields and of Northern Ireland. The resulting periods of recession — not desperate enough to equal the Depression of the 1930s — have led to government intervention. This has taken the form of advice, encouragement, and firm support for industries contemplating new bases in the North.

In the shipbuilding industry, government support could not have been more direct — the placing of orders for expensive vessels in Barrow, Birkenhead, and the Tyne, the Clyde, and Belfast. In Scotland, foreign investment and enterprise, especially from the United States, have provided a moderate anchor against recession; but some of the industries thus set up, being closely tied to domestic consumption, have themselves been affected by the general climate of trade. In 1965, the government became the chief shareholder in a shipbuilding enterprise on the Clyde.

Government Intervention and Spending

The government is Britain's largest spender. Some industries such as shipbuilding may, at least in some areas, be largely dependent on government orders. The most expensive item in the national budget

166

is defence, part of which is equipped from government ordnance factories. The Civil Service and the administrative machine, both national and local, are still growing. It is now a familiar fact that many of our most prominent scientists are engaged, directly or indirectly, on defence or other government work. Government spending helps to create employment. The building of airfields and the construction of radar stations provide work both in this country and abroad. In some instances intervention arouses or is perhaps the answer to intense local controversy. An example was the case of the Malta Dockyard, first sold to private enterprise and then re-requisitioned in 1963. It is natural to seek some political pattern in public spending, since this is obviously controlled by the party in power at Westminster. In this connection it is interesting to see the dimensions of public expenditure, expressed as a percentage of the Gross National Product (G.N.P.), and recorded for the decade 1952–62. At the start of this period there was a decline in public spending, relative to the growth of the rest of the economy; but after 1958 the downward trend was strikingly reversed.

Government Intervention and Spending

One of the main areas of government interference has been in the location of industry. The method of intervention may be either direct or indirect. During the inter-war years, considerations of defence rendered the London region officially 'exceptionally vulnerable' and the Midlands 'unsafe'.[1] Similar reasons impelled the war-time American administration to promote the development of defence industries — especially aircraft manufacture — in interior locations. This contrasts with the extreme emphasis upon Southern California exerted by the space industry in the post-war period.

Development Areas

In Britain, government pressure in favour of the Development Areas has taken the form of promotion, not direction. Official interest dates from the Special Areas Act of 1934, and was carried a stage further by the Distribution of Industry Act of 1945. The main positive incentive to factory building in Development Areas is, of course, financial — the making available of loans at specially low rates of interest and the remission of taxation.[2] Government policy dictates the distribution of Industrial Development Certificates (I.D.C.s), required before any industrial building of 'significant size' can be embarked upon.[3] However, small success has attended some recent efforts of this kind. The director of the Lancashire and Merseyside Industrial Development Association has agreed that the

1945 Act 'made practically no impression on the overall industrial structure of the north-western region up to 1951 and made even less impression in the period 1951–60'.[4] The Development Areas in England and Wales are:

1. West Cumberland.
2. The North-East.
3. North-East Lancashire.
4. South Lancashire.
5. Merseyside.
6. Wrexham and district.
7. South Wales and Monmouthshire.

There are similar areas, of considerable size, in Scotland. Six 'major growth areas' were identified by the Toothill Committee's Report[5]: the new towns of East Kilbride, Cumbernauld, Livingstone, and Glenrothes, plus Irvine and the Grangemouth–Falkirk district. North Lanarkshire, central Fife, the Lothians, and the Vale of Leven in Dunbartonshire were termed 'growth areas'. Scotland has benefited, both in achievement and in promise, from the development or initiation north of the Tweed of notable growth industries: cars, electronics, chemicals, man-made fibres, and synthetic rubber. Planners have realized, in the contexts of both Scotland and North-East England, that road-transport improvements are essential to prevent the hardening of industrial arteries. The Forth Road Bridge is being followed by a parallel thrust across the Tay. The list of Scottish developments is impressive enough to suggest that government intervention might be superfluous; but the older Scottish trades continue to decline: Q4 is going ahead on the Clyde — with the indispensable help of a massive Whitehall loan — but in other shipyards anxieties persist. On Scotland's east coast the jute trade of Dundee continues to endure difficulties of competition with low-cost foreign production.

A number of studies have drawn attention to the seriousness of the present problem of an expanding economy in one part of the country and a declining economy in the rest. A thoughtful survey has calculated that the areas 'at risk' might well lose half of their present population — that is, 11 out of 22 million — before equilibrium was reached. The prosperous zone, or 'congestion area', as it has been called, would soon become far more congested, as it was forced to accommodate four-fifths of the country's population.[6]

The State may be a very deliberate employer. There have been numerous instances of governments undertaking important public works, specifically to provide employment. This was done in Hitler's Germany, when a formidable level of unemployment was hidden by a government's preparations for war. In the United States, President Franklin Roosevelt organized the Public Works Administration, the P.W.A., to bring some hope to distressed communities. In this country it has been suggested that the State may have to go further into production, to bring industry to development areas, if normal commercial processes do not suffice. Considerable doubts about the future remain, even after the impressive White Papers of 1963 on the North-East and Scotland,[7] and the National Plan of 1965. Investigations may have been over-sophisticated in seeking to show that the North-East was a region 'not in decline but in transformation'. The White Papers envisaged — but as 'neither predictions nor proposals ' — that by 1981, there could be:

1. In both regions, an impressive new network of motor and trunk roads.

2. A rise of population, in the North-East, from 2,875,000 to 3,300,000. On Scotland, the White Paper was more cautious: 'there are limits, however, to what this policy by itself can do'. There is, unfortunately, a considerable history of emigration out of Scotland.

3. The creation of New Towns or the expansion of similar existing centres. In the North-East, there are already to be found Peterlee and Aycliffe. In addition, Washington (intended population 70,000 to 80,000) and Cramlington (48,000) would relieve the pressure on central Tyneside, ten miles away.

4. The whole of the North-East, from Cramlington to south of Darlington, would become a Growth Zone.

5. These proposals would be buttressed by financial measures. Exchequer grants to local authorities and tax incentives to industry would be supported by increased public spending in the designated areas.

One of the most significant economic developments of the 1960s has been the creation of the National Economic Development Council (N.E.D.C.), based on 'new and more effective machinery for the co-ordination of plans and forecasts for the main sectors of the economy. There is a need to study centrally the plans and prospects of our main industries, to correlate them with each other and with the government's plans for the public sector, and to see how in aggregate they contribute to, and fit in with, the prospects for the economy as a whole, including the vital external balance of payments'.[8]

The eventual membership of the N.E.D.C. included the Chancellor of the Exchequer, the President of the Board of Trade, the Minister of Labour, representatives of major private industries and labour, and the Chairmen of the British Transport Commission and of the National Coal Board. Separate bodies subordinate to N.E.D.C. ('Little Neddies') were set up for leading industries, including electrical engineering, electronics, machine-tools, and mechanical engineering. There followed 'Little Neddies' for a number of consumer trades. A 4 per cent per annum rise in the Gross National Product (G.N.P.) was envisaged in 1963, by N.E.D.C. and by the government, as a reasonable target for the next few years.[9] This was considerably greater than the annual increase in the G.N.P. for the period 1956–61, which had been only 2·7 per cent. The Labour Administration that took office in October 1964 accepted the original N.E.D.C. target, but growth fell short of government expectation.

Official intervention has in the past been directed primarily by the Treasury. This situation arose out of Treasury control of national spending, including the financing of nationalization. The Treasury was reconstructed in July 1962 under three 'functional' groupings. One of these had the task of co-ordinating economic policy, and was to concern itself 'with the balance of the national economy as a whole, dealing with short-term economic trends, long-term reviews of resources, problems of economic growth and incomes policy'.[10] The main Treasury effort of 1961–64 was supplemented by the assignation of the Board of Trade to undertake the preparation of a series of regional programmes. These collectively were capable of exerting a considerable impact upon national economic development. It was through the Board of Trade that there proceeded major plans for increased public spending in the North-East and in Scotland.

The Labour Administration produced a more drastic reorganisation, with the creation of a Department of Economic Affairs, as well as of a Ministry of Technology. The new Department of Economic Affairs took over the Board of Trade's responsibilities for regional planning, besides acting as 'co-ordinating centre' for the work of other related departments,[11] including Transport, Aviation, Power and — another new creation — the Ministry of Overseas Development. The Ministry of Technology was enlarged in scope in 1966, to include most of what Aviation had done before.

Early in 1965 British Railways published, in connection with their major scheme for railway modernization (the 'Second Beeching Plan'), estimates of the 'assumed changes' in the British economy that would accompany growth rates of (i) 3 per cent; (ii) 4 per cent. They accepted the statistical risks involved in the formulation of a plan that had coincided with a change of government at Westminster, but thought it not unrealistic to anticipate transport requirements 20 years ahead. The Machinery of Control

Later the same year the Department of Economic Affairs produced its National Plan, based upon estimates of their growth rates that were made by individual industries. The Plan spelt out expectations in detail. Growth rates of 8 per cent and over were predicted for oil refining, and for the gas, electricity, and chemicals industries. (These, of course, did not take into account the possibility of success in the search for North Sea gas and oil.) The big increase forecast for engineering was linked to expected export performance and so, directly, to world conditions. But the whole Plan, with its reliance upon an annual growth rate of 4 per cent, was unsupported by subsequent achievement.

Materially, France has suffered far more than Britain in the twentieth century. Disastrous losses in manpower in the First World War were followed by calamitous defeat in the Second. Her economic recovery has been as remarkable as that of Germany. The results of French planning have been to elevate the reputation of her civil servants as well as of President de Gaulle. France's Modernization Plans have run: (1) 1947–53; (2) 1954–57; (3) 1958–61; (4) 1962–65; (5) 1966–70. They have been the work of the General Planning Commissariat. Planning in France

There are interesting comparisons between the mixed economies of France and Britain. In France, coal, electricity, and gas were nationalized, as in the United Kingdom. In addition, there was established a public sector in oil, which started with the creation, in 1945, of the Bureau de la Récherche de Pétrole (B.R.P.), to organize the search for oil in metropolitan France.[12] Domestic supplies of gas have become more and more important, with the development of the Lacq gas field. The discovery and exploitation of oil and gas in the Algerian Sahara, by B.R.P. and by the international oil companies, have had momentous consequences for independent Algeria and considerable significance for France. The

Planning and
Government
Intervention

State has a majority holding in the major natural-gas concern, the Compagnie Nationale des Pétroles d'Aquitaine.
France's railways were nationalized in 1936, as were Britain's in 1946. The State has a majority holding in the share capital of the two largest shipping companies, and the State airline — Air France — corresponds to our B.O.A.C.–B.E.A. As is the case in Britain, the most significant aspect of French planning is its application to a mixed economy; but there are industries, such as motor-cars, that contain a public element in France, while in Britain they are completely under private ownership.

One feature of government planning is the capacity of State management to take decisions that might be unpopular or impossible for others to contemplate. Thus new industries can be sited in relatively remote regions. Old industries can be ruthlessly pruned of surplus production. France's coal-mines produced, in 1959, nearly 60 million tons. Output was reduced deliberately, by government order, and has since levelled out at about 53 million tons.

France resembles Britain in the State control of most domestic energy production. Equally important is the supervision of investment, and its concentration on the items deemed to be nationally vital. The French Fourth Plan provided for a steep rise in investment in natural gas and in thermal power stations and the construction of two oil refineries in the Strasbourg region. But the eventual effect of State intervention may be far from revolutionary. In fact French practice 'may largely amount to planning by cartels, with the officials participating by helping to set targets for production and the like.'[13] If this be the case, planning will serve only to confirm the trends that were apparent before the present policies were undertaken.

NOTES

1. Estall and Buchanan, *Industrial Activity and Economic Geography*, p. 126.
2. Ibid.
3. Ibid.
4. *The Times*, 14 Nov. 1963.
5. Scottish Development Dept., *Central Scotland: A Programme for Development and Growth*, Cmnd. 2188 (H.M.S.O., 1963).
6. W. F. Luttrell, 'Britain's Regional Problem', *The Times*, 2 Jan. 1964.
7. Cmnd. 2188, 2206.
8. Letter dated 28 Sept. 1961, from the Chancellor of the Exchequer to T.U.C., Federation of British Industries, etc.

9. N.E.D.C., *Growth of the United Kingdom Economy to 1966* (H.M.S.O., Feb. 1963); *Conditions Favourable to Faster Growth* (H.M.S.O., April 1963).

10. Treasury Press release, 30 July 1962.

11. *The Times*, 12 Nov. 1964.

12. John and Anne-Marie Hackett, *Economic Planning in France* (Allen & Unwin, 1963), p. 71.

13. Thomas Wilson, *Planning and Growth* (Macmillan, 1964), pp. 41–42.

Chapter 14 Energy

Nations are commonly divided into Great Powers and Small. They may be distinguished economically by their differing abilities to transform resources into industrial wealth. Nowhere is this more clearly seen than in the production of energy. The pattern of world output has changed, and is changing, to Britain's detriment; and, to some extent, the standing of the entire Western world has suffered by comparison with the very real achievements of Russia and China. Russia has for some time led in bituminous coal production, in which China must also now be considered a world figure. In petroleum, America still leads, but Soviet progress has been spectacular.

Most power wealth exists in the form of fossil energy, which can be consumed but not renewed: thus the curve of coal production (Fig. 14.1) shows that a critical point is approaching (as it is, also, for petroleum). There remains considerable room for manœuvre, however, in the extent to which improved technology can utilize limited resources. In petroleum, the North American heavy crude and tar-sands deposits could transform the world situation — and not only for oil.

The chief sources of energy in many of the underdeveloped regions of the world are human and animal muscle, and in many industrialized areas the main primary source is still coal. But present British estimates predict that, in 1970, petroleum will be supplying more than half as much energy as coal, compared with only one-third a decade earlier.

The total demand for energy has mounted in spectacular fashion in recent years. The electrical supply industry is only a part — if a major part — of energy production, but in the years 1960–62 electricity growth was more than three times that of industry in general. Increased demand for energy has arisen notably from expanding industries such as electronics, petro-chemicals, and metallurgy.[1] Similar progress in sales has recently been made by the gas industry.

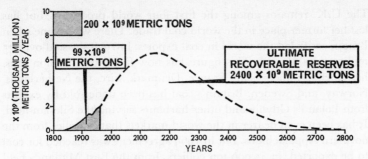

FIG. 14.1 Coal — ultimate world production

Output will reach a peak in nearly two centuries' time, provided coal is not supplanted by cheaper fuels. (After M. King Hubbert.)

U.K. Energy Consumption[2]
(per cent)

	1960	1961	1962	1963	1964	1965
Coal . . .	74·2	71·9	69·9	68·3	65·4	62·2
Natural gas .	—	—	—	0·1	0·1	0·4
Petroleum . .	24·8	26·9	28·8	30·1	32·7	34·6
Nuclear electricity .	0·3	0·4	0·5	0·9	1·1	2·0
Hydro-electricity .	0·7	0·8	0·8	0·6	0·7	0·8
TOTAL .	100·0	100·0	100·0	100·0	100·0	100·0

There was a marked resemblance between the patterns of energy consumption in 1960 in the U.K. and West Germany and similarities, too, in expectations for 1970, when it has been forecast that coal will supply only half of total U.K. power consumption.

Federal German Republic — Energy Supplies[3]
(per cent)

	1960	1970 (estimate)
Coal	59·7	45·0
Lignite	14·6	11·2
Petroleum	22·2	37·6
Hydro-electric power, natural gas, and atomic power .	3·5	6·2
TOTAL .	100·0	100·0

In France, the energy position is rather different. There, petroleum passed coal as a source of energy during 1965–66.

The U.K. remains among the first four world producers, but has lost her former place in the world coal trade. There was a time when Britain easily led the world in coal exports: in 1938 she sold over 35 million tons abroad. This figure has now fallen to 5 million tons, her chief customers being France, Denmark, Eire, the Netherlands, Norway, and Sweden. Britain's coal has been undersold by exports from Poland's Gdynia and other harbours serving the Silesian field. It has been even dearer in the world markets than supplies from the northern Appalachians. But in 1965 agreement was reached for coal to be exported, in 45,000-ton colliers, from the East Midlands field and the port of Immingham to Italy — re-opening an old Mediterranean market to British fuel.

Output per man-shift in Britain's mines has shown a striking improvement. The labour force in mining is still diminishing: it fell by 28 per cent between 1955 and 1964.

U.K. Coal Output per Man-Shift (Coal Face)[4]
(tons)

1947	1955	1961	1962	1963	1964	1965	1966 (27 wks. Jan.– June)
2·86	3·28	4·18	4·55	4·95	5·12	5·38	5·67

Many of the older seams, in the long-established collieries, have or will soon have reached the limit of usefulness, in the sense that the coal there is economic to obtain. In fact the newer mining areas, and those where seams are thicker and perhaps less faulted, have long had to 'carry' the areas losing money. The largest producer now is the East Midlands Division, covering the North Derby, Nottinghamshire, South Derby, and Leicestershire coalfields. In 1965 this Division produced 45 million tons, very profitably. Extremely high figures of output per man-shift have been reached in the same Division: the mid-1966 figure for face-workers was 170 cwt.

There has been a spectacular increase in mechanization at the coal face since the Second World War, and especially in the last decade. In 1947 only about 2·5 per cent of total annual output was produced from 'fully mechanized faces', by power-loading machines, which both cut the coal — usually on long-wall faces, where machines are most economical — and also load it on to conveyor

176

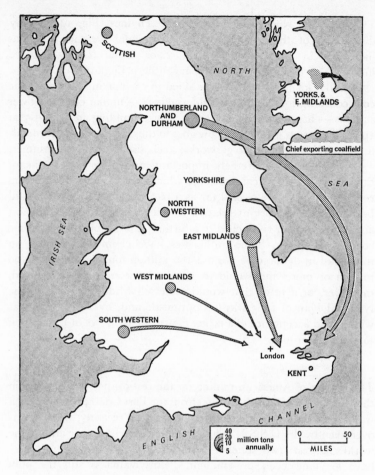

FIG. 14.2   U.K. — coal movements

London's energy-producers still depend upon the transport of coal: (*a*) by sea from the north-east; (*b*) by rail from the East Midlands.

belts. In 1954, 8 per cent of total output was fully mechanized. By 1960 the figure had risen to 38 per cent; and by 1965 to 75 per cent. Rationalization has mainly taken the form of the closure of un-economic pits. The social consequences have been especially severe in Scotland and in Durham.

Railways are essential to the movement of coal, but by far the most important single transport route is the sea journey from the

G   H.G.P.

177

Tyne and the North-East coast to the Thames (Fig. 14.2). Any dislocation of this movement by exceptional weather, such as happened in 1947, can produce chaos in electrically-powered industry, particularly that based in southern England.

Coal has for long been closely allied to gas-making, although the coal consumption of the gas undertakings — unlike electric power stations — has decreased in recent years, standing in 1964–65 at 19·7 million tons. More coal now goes to the coke ovens of the metallurgical industries than to gasworks; steel, also, is a major consumer.

By-products are extremely important, and there are significant links with the chemical industry, which have arisen chiefly from research into the use of coal tar as a base material. But coal is still becoming less important relative to other power forms, and most authorities appear reconciled to a further appreciable drop in home coal consumption. Some authorities have claimed that after an initial fall in demand to around 160 million tons, an eventual 200 million or more tons would be required per annum — produced, moreover, at a price that would undersell Middle East oil.[5] The National Plan of 1965 was less optimistic and, by 1966, there was widespread acceptance of a target figure, for 1969–70, of 170 million to 180 million tons.

The United States The impact of American mining on the rest of the world is seen in the massive exports of cheap coal from the East Coast ports. America was first in the world in coal production until recently, when it was overtaken by the U.S.S.R. The Appalachian deposits are among the world's largest: two states — Pennsylvania and West Virginia — have for long been pre-eminent. Pennsylvania is still the only anthracite producer in the U.S.A., but output has fallen drastically — from 100 million tons in 1917, to 59 million in the Second World War, 21 million in 1958, and 17 million in 1961–62. The leading states in bituminous production are now: (1) West Virginia; (2) Kentucky; (3) Pennsylvania; (4) Illinois.

The Soviet Union Despite the degree of industrialization in Soviet Russia, the most important mining region is still the Donetz, which continues to supply more than a quarter of all Soviet coal production. But its total reserves are less than 3 per cent of the national figure. On the other hand, southern Siberia, including the Kuznetsk field, has deposits containing nearly one-quarter of the total energy potential of Russia's coal. The Urals, one of the key industrial areas of all Russia, has little bituminous coal, but quantities of lignite, which is used by very large power stations. **Coal**

After the devastation of war, coal output in West Germany recovered. reaching a peak in 1956 at 150 million metric tons. Production levelled out for a time; declined (1959, 140 million tons); then appeared almost to level out again (1960, 141 million; 1961, 141 million; 1962, 140 million; 1963, 141 million; 1964, 140 million; 1965, 135 million tons). **Germany — West and East**

Competition from oil has been severe and is growing, with refineries opening on the sea coast, on the River Rhine, and under construction in Bavaria, the latter connected by transalpine pipeline with Italian terminals on the Mediterranean.

Lignite production is important in West as in East Germany; but the leading world producer is East Germany. Her resources have provided the chief source of fuel for the Spreewald power stations of East Berlin. Expectations in West Germany are that the proportion of total energy derived from oil will increase greatly during the 1960s. West Germany, like Britain, will be deeply affected by developments in the North Sea, as she has been already by the gas discoveries in the Netherlands and the construction of pipelines from Groningen into Rhenish-Westphalia.

The Carling complex in Lorraine is an example of new techniques applied to the coal industry. As in Britain, the industry has become the base of a considerable chemical production. Since the Second World War the use of coal as a primary fuel has steadily decreased, most of it now being processed for by-products, but production has remained rather more stable than in Britain. **France**

Chinese Communist statistics of coal production are difficult to interpret. A British work on the Chinese coal industry reported in 1961, without comment, the official claim: 1958, 271 million tons; 1959, 348 million; 1960, 425 million.[6] American estimates are different, K. P. Wang reporting that there have not been any official claims 'since 1960, when many figures apparently were **China**

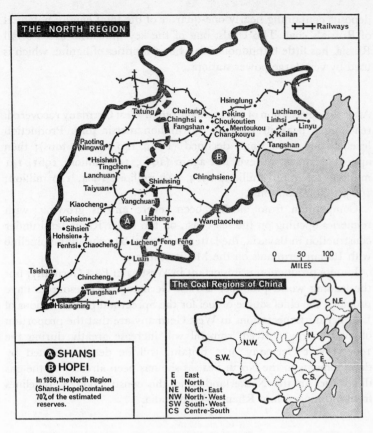

FIG. 14.3 The Chinese coal industry — the northern region

Chinese coal reserves are heavily concentrated in two provinces bordered by the Hwang Ho and the Yellow Sea.

grossly exaggerated'. He goes on to quote the estimates of the U.S. Bureau of Mines: 1961, 223 million tons; 1962, 223 million; 1963, 241 million.[7] The location of Chinese production (Fig. 14.3) is not open to dispute.

PETROL-
EUM

Nearly all of the world's petroleum is now mined north of the Tropic of Cancer. The years since 1954 have seen oil production in the Middle East more than doubled, to equal output in the United

States. During the same period the Soviet output of oil, which a decade ago was only a sixth, is now more than a half of America's. North African production has increased impressively since 1959.

The U.S.A. still leads the world, and inside America Texas produces about as much as the next three states — Louisiana, California, and Oklahoma — combined. Intensive prospecting has brought results; in the decade 1951–61 proved reserves inside the U.S.A. went up from 3,645 million tons to 4,210 million tons. There is not a limitless amount of oil in the New World: for some years it was possible to achieve approximate parity between output and discovery, and during the period 1951–61, while production increased by 17 per cent, the ratio of reserves to production remained constant at 12 : 1; but during the period 1961–63 proved reserves decreased. This change occurred in both North America and the Soviet Union, although the decline could have been temporary, and such pessimism as it engendered premature. Nevertheless, the figures for all reserves of fossil fuels must level out eventually,[8] and production decline.

Oil can be extremely expensive to mine, but costs differ according to location. They are greater, as regards labour cost, in California than they are in Kuwait; but in the Middle East, British and American companies have to pay high royalties — usually around 50 per cent — to the local governments. North Sea oil would provide the British Treasury with valuable revenue.

Kuwait, Saudi Arabia, and Libya are examples from the Middle East of recent notable progress in petroleum production. The Saudi Arabian oil industry dates from 1936; production by 1965 had reached 99 million tons; but production in Kuwait, which started only in 1946, had risen to 107 million tons. The chief foreign capital for the industry of this region is provided by the Americans, followed by the British and the French; but the Japanese, as well as many smaller companies from the West, have appeared on the scene since the Second World War. More spectacular even than Middle East progress have been the events in Libya where, from nil production in 1960 and less than 1 million tons in 1961, output leapt to 40 million tons in 1964 and 58 million in 1965.

World petroleum output continues to rise, year by year, having doubled between 1950 and 1960. It is likely to double again by 1970. World production topped 1,000 million tons for the first time in 1960 and is now running at over 1,500 million. In the United Kingdom, demand for petroleum rose over two and a half times in

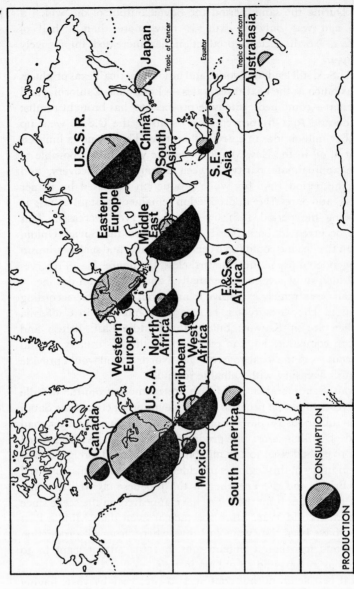

FIG. 14.4   World oil supply and demand, 1965

The world petroleum map shows the heavy dependence of some highly developed industrial regions on supplies from the sub-tropics.

FIG. 14.5 Athabasca oil sands — storehouse of energy

The oil sands provide an enormous potential for future world needs. At present, though accessible, they are virtually untapped.

the period 1952–62. Britain, like Japan and Australasia, has to import almost all of the oil she needs (Fig. 14.4).

The progressive exhaustion of the world's mineral wealth, including petroleum, has produced an ever more intense search for the reserves that remain, but a realistic assessment of them awaits agreement on the utilization of the 'heavy crudes' of the U.S.A. and Venezuela and of the Athabasca tar sands in Alberta (Fig. 14.5). Reserves of heavy crudes in the U.S.A. have been said to equal 'the volume of power reserves of conventional crudes';[9] Venezuelan heavy crudes to exceed — at an estimated recovery rate of 10 per cent — the 'present published estimates of proven reserves';[10] and the Athabasca tar sands deposits — again at a 10 per cent recovery

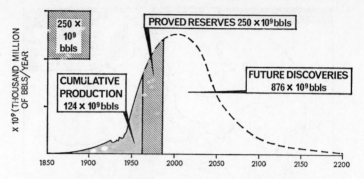

FIG. 14.6 Crude oil — ultimate world production

One of the most interesting features of the graph is the great volume of expected future discoveries.

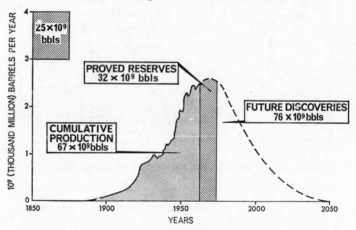

FIG. 14.7 U.S. crude oil — ultimate production

The graph (after M. King Hubbert) shows the severe decline in U.S. production expected to occur well before the end of this century.

rate — to exceed by '50 per cent . . . the total reserves of the Free World',[11] but an important later opinion has gone so far as to assert that the same tar sands of Alberta, along with the shales of Colorado–Utah–Wyoming, contain 'with today's techniques . . . more than five times the world's proved reserves of oil',[12] which had been estimated, in 1962, at $1,250 \times 10^9$ barrels.[13]

Hubbert's estimates for the future of both the world (Fig. 14.6) and United States (Fig. 14.7) petroleum production and reserves were also made in 1962. They did not take account of the tar sands, **Petroleum** and predicted culmination, for the U.S.A., by 'the late 1960s'. Over most of the world, petroleum becomes a still greater factor in fuel supplies. While oil has been increasing its share in the U.K., to occupy nearly a third of total energy consumption, in the Soviet Union it has grown in importance to supply, in 1964, a half of Russian fuel needs.[14]

The earliest important pipeline in Europe ran from Baku to Batum **Pipelines** on the Black Sea. Today, there are lines from Kirkuk in Iraq to Tripoli in the Lebanon and Banias in Syria.

The Trans-Arabian Pipeline system (T.A.P. line) runs from the Saudi Arabian fields to Saida (Sidon) in the Lebanon. Each major line requires pumping stations to keep the oil moving, and there are ten such stations on the T.A.P. line inside Saudi Arabia.

There are important lines, for both oil and gas, from the southern and south-central fields of the U.S.A. to the industrial conurbations north of Ohio. From the Albertan fields, lines run south and east and west. From Kuibyshev on Russia's Volga River runs the 2,900-mile 'Friendship Pipeline' to Schwedt-an-der-Oder, in East Germany, with branches to Warsaw, Budapest, and Prague; completed in 1964, the planned ultimate throughput capacity is 40–50 million tons per year.[15]

Even in the United Kingdom, with its limited area, there is scope for economy in the movement of crude oil from terminal to refinery, perhaps involving a coast-to-coast route, and in the throughput of fuel from refinery to central distribution point or to the industrial — especially petro-chemical — consumer. The completed lines, involving the movement of crude oil from deep tidewater to refinery, are:
  (i) Finnart, on Loch Long, to Grangemouth (Central Scotland).
  (ii) Angle Bay, on Milford Haven, to Llandarcy (South Wales).

The specialized need of London Airport for aviation fuel has called into being the line from Walton-on-Thames to Heathrow. An additional line will run to London Airport from Fawley, on Southampton Water, as will one from there to the petro-chemical centre at Severnside (Fig. 14.8). By 1970, oil and chemicals pipelines will cross the country from Thames to Mersey, and from Mersey to Tees.

In Western Europe, major lines now cross the Alps and others are projected, for instance from Trieste to Vienna. A pipeline runs north

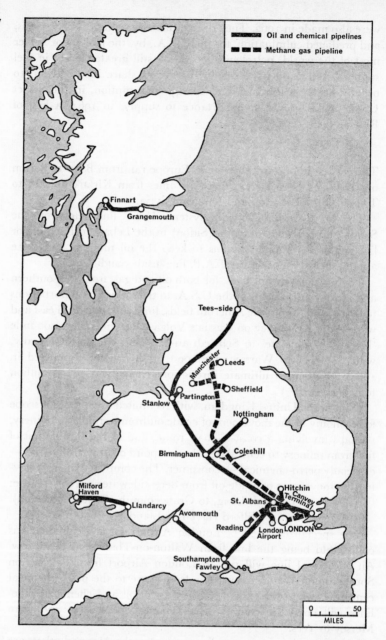

FIG. 14.8 U.K. — oil, methane and chemicals pipelines

Further cross-country links can be expected with the exploitation of North Sea methane.

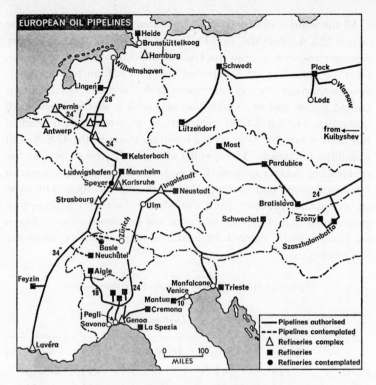

FIG. 14.9   European oil pipelines

The European energy distribution picture is due to change still further, with the completion of a methane link between the Soviet Union and northern Italy.

from the Lavéra refinery, near Marseilles, following the Rhône–Saône Valley to Strasbourg and Karlsruhe (Fig. 14.9). Other lines run south to Cologne and Frankfurt from the North Sea coast.

The steep rise in world demand for oil has produced a corresponding increase in movement by sea. Total movement of oil in 1965 was 747 million tons. In 1951 the figure had been only 204 million tons: this was exactly the amount imported into Western Europe from the Middle East in 1965. Tonnage of vessels has gradually increased, the latest designs being for tankers of as much as 200,000 tons. Where the deep water required by the modern tanker has not been available, long piers have been built, as at Kuwait's Mina al Ahmadi.

Energy Movement by Sea All the main world routes have increased their traffic. In the case of the U.S.A., still the world's largest producer, there is a very extensive movement from the Gulf of Mexico to East Coast ports, but little American oil is exported (only 10 million tons in 1965). From Venezuela run strategic routes to the industrial north-eastern United States and to eastern Canada, with a smaller trade from Colombia. The Caribbean export trade, as a whole, had reached 168 million tons by 1965, with 81 million going to the U.S.A. and 19 million to Canada. The opening of the St. Lawrence Seaway has enabled big tankers to reach Chicago. Caribbean oil movement to Western Europe had reached 43 million tons by 1965. The most massive traffic proceeds from the Middle East and a large and growing volume of exports to Japan has developed. Soviet Russia has fairly recently entered the field as a major exporter, using her Black Sea ports.

Principal Destinations of Middle East Petroleum[16]
(million tons)

Year	Destinations				
	U.S.A.	Canada	W. Europe	Japan	Australia
1961	$17\frac{1}{2}$	$6\frac{3}{4}$	139	$29\frac{1}{2}$	9
1963	$14\frac{1}{2}$	$6\frac{3}{4}$	166	$45\frac{1}{2}$	$11\frac{1}{4}$
1965	$17\frac{1}{4}$	7	$204\frac{1}{4}$	$72\frac{1}{2}$	$14\frac{1}{2}$

The principal sea routes for the oil of the Middle East remain: (i) from the Persian Gulf, via the Suez Canal; (ii) from pipeline terminals in the Lebanon and Syria; but the Suez route has twice been dislocated by Israeli–Egyptian armed conflict.

HYDRO-ELECTRIC POWER Some of the achievements in hydro-electric power production rank as modern wonders of the world. One cannot but be awed by the sheer dimensions of installations such as Kariba, Kuibyshev, or Aswan.

The Grand Coulee dam in the United States has changed the economy of an entire region. It, and the associated projects further north, have become an area of some economic controversy. Tsimlyanskaya and Kuibyshev have transformed the Volga valley.

188

On the Nile, the Aswan High Dam is creating vast new opportunities for Egypt.

The role of hydro-electric power is a matter of some controversy. We are not now completely certain of the significance and proper place of a mode of energy production that seemed, not long ago, to have an assured future. Considerations of cost have intervened; the capital requirements, in Britain, of a hydro-electric station, per unit of power generated, are about four times those of a coal or oil-fired units. Furthermore water power, like the other, older sources of energy, is now faced with the competition from nuclear power plants. In many parts of the world there exist great quantities of potential water power. One of the problems in their exploitation is the need to ensure adequate flow. Where nature does not provide this, pumped storage has sometimes been attempted, to use the same water over and over again. It is easy to exaggerate the significance of hydro-electric power. In Sweden, which has almost no coal but abundant running water, H.E.P. provides no more than 35 per cent of total energy consumed.

The Significance of Hydro-electric Power

The abundance of coal in Britain has put the hydro-electric engineer at a disadvantage. H.E.P. production is not economically feasible, with most large cities within reach of solid fuel or of imported petroleum. But in Scotland and in parts of Wales, there are districts with all the physical requirements for the generation of water power: an estimate by the Board of Trade in 1921 gave the potential for Scotland as $1,900 \times 10^6$ kWh per year. After the Second World War the North of Scotland Hydro-Electric Board estimated the figure at $4,000 \times 10^6$ kWh.[17] The cost factor has led many to question the basis of further development of H.E.P. in the Highlands, or elsewhere in Britain. Quantitative progress there has been, production of H.E.P. by the North of Scotland Board having grown eight times in the period 1949–62. The Loch Awe–Cruachan plant, using pumped storage, and with a capacity, when completed, of 400 mW, came into operation in 1965. The similar installation at Blaenau Ffestiniog, in North Wales, has a capacity of 320 mW. A further pumped-storage scheme is projected for Loch Sloy in Scotland. But the future for hydro-electric power in Britain remains in doubt.

The United Kingdom

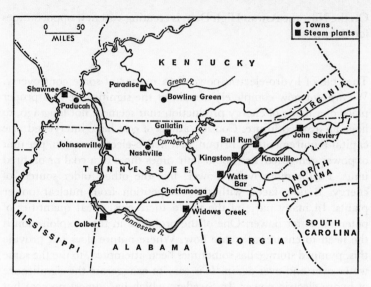

FIG. 14.10   T.V.A. — thermal electricity stations

Very large power stations, operated by the Tennessee Valley
Authority, utilize cheap water-borne coal supplies.

**The United
States**

The main hydro-electric installations of the United States are to be
found: (i) at Niagara; (ii) in the Tennessee Valley; (iii) on the
Columbia River, in the North-West; (iv) on the Colorado River;
(v) on the eastern slopes of the Rocky Mountains, particularly on
the South Platte and Pecos rivers. The largest American dams are
(i) Grand Coulee, on the Columbia River, with an installed capacity
of 1,974 mW, and (ii) Hoover, on the Colorado, with 1,250 mW.
The publicly-owned Tennessee Valley Authority has built or
acquired twenty-seven major dams on the Tennessee River system;
but one point must be noted concerning the sources of T.V.A.
power (Fig. 14.10): its thermal generators contain more than twice
as much capacity as its hydro-electric installations. The biggest
steam plants are Watts Bar, Bull Run, and Paradise. In the east of
the region, six hydro-electric plants belonging to the Aluminium
Company of America are integrated with the T.V.A. power system,
as are five Corps of Engineers H.E.P. dams on the Cumberland
River, in the north.

American hydro-electric production continued to increase during
the period 1960–64, but at a rate slower than that in the Soviet
Union, where output increased by more than half over that period.

190

One of the marvels of the twentieth century has been the harnessing of nuclear energy. Since 1945 there has been a parallel development of commercial and military nuclear projects, and Britain has provided one of the chief programmes of research into the peaceful uses of nuclear energy.

The capital needs of nuclear power stations are huge and these installations, in order to justify their existence, have to be large. They are more expensive to build than thermal stations, expensive to maintain, and more than usual attention has to be paid to safety factors.

The role of nuclear power in a given country depends primarily upon an assessment of the comparative costs involved. A number of questions arise. What is the cost of the nuclear fuel? What are the prospects for cheaper coal? What, if any, are the strategic considerations involved in setting up a relatively new form of production? Will the advent of nuclear power increase or diminish dependence upon imported supplies, whether of raw materials or of processed elements? It is not surprising that different answers have been given by different authorities. In Britain, the Central Electricity Generating Board claimed in 1965 that the advanced gas-cooled reactor (A.G.R.) system, promoted by the Atomic Energy Authority and chosen for the Dungeness 'B' station (due to come into service in 1970), would have an advantage of at least 10 per cent over the most efficient coal-fired station. Dungeness 'B' will cost at least £110 million.

Nuclear Power Stations — Cost of Power [18]

Nuclear power station	Date of commissioning first set	Capacity (MW)	Estimated running cost allowing for capital expenditure (pence per kWh)
Berkeley	1962	275	1·23
Bradwell	1962	300	1·12
Hinkley Point 'A'	1963	500	1·02
Trawsfynydd	1964	500	0·97
Dungeness 'A'	1964	550	0·74
Sizewell	1965	580	0·73
Oldbury	1966	560	0·73

A drastic improvement in the prospect for nuclear power in Britain has been forecast for 1975, by which time the Central Electricity Generating Board anticipates that the nuclear power stations,

FIG. 14.11   U.K. — nuclear generating stations

Nuclear power stations are typically confined to coastal sites well removed from heavily populated areas.

including the second generation — their output 5,000 MW — will undercut the running costs of coal and oil installations.

Other countries, of course, are faced by the same question of cost that so influences decisions about British power policy. With the development of nuclear power, the resultant energy has gradually become cheaper, and each succeeding station is scheduled to produce more cheaply than its predecessor (Fig. 14.11). The first nuclear power stations in Britain were those at Berkeley on the Severn, and Bradwell on the south side of the Blackwater estuary in Essex.

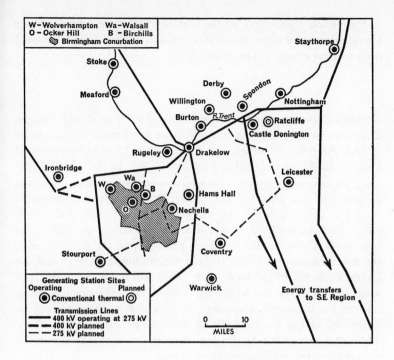

W – Wolverhampton   Wa – Walsall
O – Ocker Hill   B – Birchills
🐚 Birmingham Conurbation

Staythorpe

Generating Station Sites
Operating   Planned
◉ Conventional thermal ◎

Transmission Lines
━━ 400 kV operating at 275 kV
━ ━ 400 kV planned
─ ─ 275 kV planned

Energy transfers
to S.E. Region

0   10
MILES

FIG. 14.12   U.K. — power from the Midlands

Energy is transferred from the middle Trent valley to the huge
market in the London region.

Judged with the larger conventional stations, the nuclear units
have only moderately-sized outputs. The combined output of the
first five nuclear stations to be commissioned will only just top the
achievement of a single 2,000-M.W. coal-burning station.

The C.E.G.B. is not alone in its interest in nuclear power in
Britain. The Windscale installation in Cumberland, with its 28 MW
of power now flowing into the National Grid (small compared with
the 575 MW from Berkeley and Bradwell combined, and the 500
MW from the Hinkley Point 'A' Station), is under the control of the
Atomic Energy Authority (A.E.A.). Other A.E.A. installations are
at Chapelcross, Calder Hall, Capenhurst, and Aldermaston. Calder
Hall and Chapelcross will soon be contributing between them 444
MW each year to the National Grid. In 1965 the chairman of one
of the Electricity Boards was prepared to project trends far enough
to forecast that forty nuclear power stations would need to be built

in the period 1980–2000, at the end of which time nuclear power would contribute more than either coal or the other conventional fuels to total energy consumption.[19]

Britain's electricity supply industry is notable for its steady progress in output, and for the changes that have been made in the choice of fuel. At different times, pessimistic views have been expressed about both the cost of coal and its availability. In the period 1947–50, great difficulties were envisaged in finding sufficient coal supplies to satisfy all the potential consumers, because coal production in 1947 had failed to reach 200 million tons. The result of the difficulties and uncertainties was a decision to transfer partially from coal to oil. However, the emphasis placed upon the need for coal, the special measures taken to help the mining industry, and the increasing tempo of mechanization, produced, not a coal deficit, but a surplus. However, since 1961 the demand for coal by British power stations has increased, as a result of a decision to draw on coal for nearly all of the largest units of the new generation of stations. Three-quarters of the total extra capacity brought into use in the period 1962–65 was dependent upon coal.

C.E.G.B. Actual and Estimated Distribution of Power-Station
Fuel Consumption
(percentage of total output)

	1960–61	*1970–71*
Coal and coke .	84	73
Oil . . .	16	11
Nuclear . .	nil	16

Coal supplies have been the major factor in determining the location of conventional — i.e. non-nuclear — power stations in Britain. Nearness to the market, at least in a country as small as ours, is not a vital factor. Losses there may be in transmission, but the cost of transporting fuel to generating station is more critical than the cost of transmitting the generated power. The comparative cheapness of waterborne transport of fuel has permitted the growth of great installations near to waterborne supplies.

There are major production regions in South Lancashire, in the West Riding, around Birmingham (Fig. 14.12), and in the East

Midlands, particularly in the Trent Valley. Projects which are to be started before 1970 include a third Drakelow station, and 2,000-MW stations in the Trent Valley (Cottam and West Burton 'C' station) and in Yorkshire (Eggborough and Ferrybridge 'C'). The biggest coal-fired station (2,400-MW capacity) is at Longannet, on the Forth.

Power stations can consume fuel that is not suitable for the domestic grate or even for industrial boilers. In Soviet Russia peat is used on a large scale: in 1955 it was much more important than natural gas as fuel for power stations, and not far behind petroleum products.[20] Today it has been overtaken by gas. In Britain the stations make use of the smallest coal and 'slack', which may be an embarrassment elsewhere. The Trent Valley power stations consume about 5 million tons of low-grade coal mined — often mechanically and at low cost — in the East Midlands Division of the N.C.B. The East and West Midlands are now moving large quantities of power to the London region, and this process will be greatly accelerated by 1970. The U.K. representative at the World Power Conference, held at Melbourne in 1962, predicted that although the proportion of coal used would fall, the actual amount of coal consumed by the power stations, owing to the quite steep rise in the demand for electricity, would go up from 58·2 million tons in 1962 to 64·2 million tons in 1965 and 79·2 million tons in 1970.[21]

Electric power in the United Kingdom is distributed by the National Grid, the standard voltages of which are 132 kV and 275 kV (1 kV = 1,000 volts). There are 275-kV links between the London area and the following points: (i) Central Scotland via the upper Trent Valley, Lancashire, and Carlisle; (ii) the North-East coast via the lower Trent Valley and Ferrybridge; (iii) South Wales via Melksham, and Hinkley Point via Melksham; (iv) Lydd via Sittingbourne and Canterbury. The Lydd line continues under the Channel at 200 kV to France, and operates on direct current (D.C.). There are also important cross-country 270-kV links between Ferrybridge and Preston, between Blyth and Carlisle, and between South Lancashire and Blaenau Ffestiniog. A new 'Supergrid' is replacing the former system. This is being done by upgrading the present 275 kV to 400 kV. The generating areas of the Trent Valley and Birmingham are being connected by Supergrid with the other regions of the C.E.G.B. By 1970 Britain should have 2,500 miles of

Electric Power Transmission

Energy   400-kV line. This is far from being the highest world voltage. In
Canada transmission lines carrying 735 kV will connect the Mani-
cougan and other hydro-electric generating stations north of the St.
Lawrence, via Quebec City, with Montreal. The U.S.S.R. has put
into operation a section of 800-kV D.C. line, running from Volgograd to the Donetz Basin. The scale of economy introduced by the
higher-voltage lines is demonstrated by the fact that a 400-kV
circuit 'can usefully carry four times as much power as the 275 kV'.[22]
In the U.S.A., the Bonneville power station in the Rockies is
being connected with the Mississippi Valley by a 1100-kV D.C.
line running east for a thousand miles;[23] and in the U.S.S.R., four
coal-fired stations, all of 3,800 MW, are being built at Ekibastuz,
on the Karaganda coalfield, to transmit power by 1500-kV D.C.
line to Voronezh and the Urals.[24]

NATURAL   Within the past twenty years natural gas has become a power
GAS   material of world importance. The process has been going on for
longer in the United States, which even in 1962 was consuming 93
per cent of the methane used in the non-Communist world. In that
year also, the United States was credited with possessing 38 per cent
of the total world natural-gas reserves.[25]

The position of the North American continent in regard to the
cumulative production–output–reserve ratio for natural gas was
given in 1962 by a Canadian authority, who also supplied a comparison with the Communist countries.

North America's Situation in Natural-Gas Supplies[26]
(10^{12} cu. ft.)

	Cumulative production to 1961	Production in 1961	Reserves at end of 1961
North America . .	242·8	14·6	321·0
Soviet Sphere . .	19·4	2·65	83·4
World Total . .	297·8	20·9	720·7

This would seem to suggest that the U.S.A., with Canada, was
rapidly approaching the half-way point towards exhaustion of
reserves. However, this presupposes that reserves are constant: in
fact, they have tended to grow with production. The explanation

lies in the fact that, as potential is converted to actual, so possible are turned into proved reserves. American natural gas production in 1964 was 5·4 per cent greater than in 1963.

An interesting American work on Soviet power supplies has quoted United States sources to maintain that the finding rate in this unique industry is '2·0 cubic feet per foot of gas withdrawn'.[27] Hodgkins listed Soviet claims for 'known reserves' in 1958 as greater than the 'surveyed industrial reserves' of the United States. Opposed to this was the estimate given by Hume that American reserves in 1961 were almost four times those of the 'Soviet Sphere'; but in 1963–64, the rate of growth of Soviet production was nearly four times the American.[28]

The picture of American gas production shows a considerable increase since 1950 in the importance of Louisiana, though Texas has easily kept its overall lead. There is a greater regional concentration in the gas than in the petroleum industry.

Methane has been found in huge quantities in Alberta. Lines transport this to the coast of British Columbia, to California, and eastwards — via the Trans-Canada 34-inch line — to Winnipeg. From there, a 30-inch line connects with Toronto, and a further 20-inch to Montreal. There are connections south from Winnipeg up the Red River Valley into the United States, and similarly, south by way of Niagara to Buffalo. Canada is now an exporter of gas.

The biggest developments in gas production in the period 1950–60 were made in the Soviet Union. Methane pipelines have been important there since the later part of the Second World War. The first Soviet gas pipeline of note — between Buguruslan and Kuibyshev — was completed in 1943. There has since been a very rapid extension of pipeline building, alongside the accelerated programme of gasfield exploitation.

In Western Europe, a large gasfield was found at Lacq, from where grid lines now supply most of France. In the north of the Netherlands there has been great activity by the international oil companies wishing to exploit the Slochteren field, now known to be one of the biggest, and perhaps the biggest, of all the world's major deposits. Britain has important commercial links with the Algerian methane field at Hassi-R'Mel (Fig. 14.13). Specially-built boats transport the liquefied gas from Arzew, on the Algerian coast, to Canvey Island. From there it is distributed by pipeline to Area Gas Boards. French methane tankers likewise ply between Arzew and Le Havre. It has been suggested that similar boats should

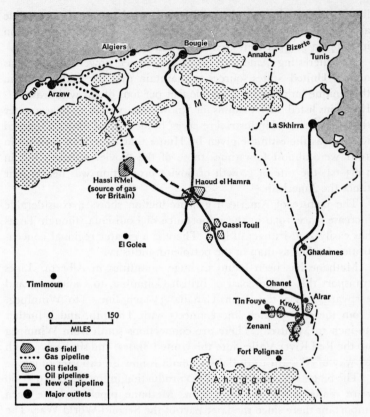

FIG. 14.13   Oil and gas outlets from Algeria
The methane shipped abroad from Arzew supplies the Algerians
with much-needed revenue.

carry methane to Canvey from the Shell-B.P. gas concessions in Nigeria.

In 1964 there came a report that the Dutch had offered to supply half of Britain's total gas requirements, but at a price that, at that time, was not economic to the Gas Council. The Dutch reserves in Groningen are being exploited by Nederlandse Aardolie Maatschappij (N.A.M.) — a joint venture of Royal Dutch Shell and Esso. It is physically possible — and economically attractive, provided that the price is right — for a pipeline to run from the Dutch coast to eastern England — a distance of about 120 miles. The Dutch are already building a pipeline from the Slochteren wells to

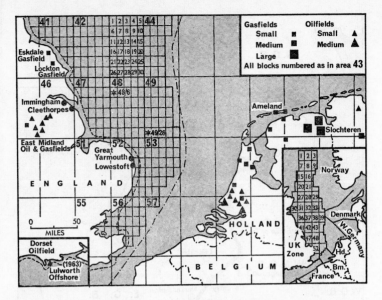

FIG. 14.14 North Sea gasfields

The U.K. section of the North Sea gasfields is divided into areas (1–57) and the areas into block concessions. Thus block 48/6 contains the B.P. well, the first to pump gas ashore to the British coast.

Germany: it will pass under the Rhine to Cologne. Important developments could also occur off the coast of Germany and the Netherlands, perhaps eventually to the west of Denmark. Many firms — Dutch, German, British, American, and international — are concerned in exploration and drilling. The relevant agreement applying to the exploitation of extra-territorial sections of the ocean floor is the Geneva Convention on the Law of the Sea, signed by Britain in 1958 and ratified in 1963. This gives the riparian States sovereign rights over mineral and other natural resources of the continental shelves. Where such shelves meet, it is feasible to parcel out the area by the use of a median line.

Britain's portion of the North Sea continental shelf has now been largely parcelled out (Fig. 14.14), with major concessions to British Petroleum, to Shell–Esso and the leading American oil companies, to Total, the French subsidiary, and to the nationalized Gas Council (in association with oil concerns). The oilmen operate from expensive and massive rigs, many of them built on the Clyde, on

FIG. 14.15   U.K. — methane grid

Recent developments, besides the conveyance to the main methane grid of B.P. gas, include the projected construction of a second feeder main from the Norfolk coast, carrying gas from the Shell well in block 49/26 (see Fig. 14.14).

the North-East coast, or in Northern Ireland. Land bases of the oil-seekers are at points along the east coast between Lowestoft and Sunderland. There will follow a similar division of the Dutch and German waters to the north of Holland and the Frisian Islands.

Oil from the British Petroleum wells reaches the coast by pipeline at Easington (Fig. 14.15).

The large-scale exploitation of the United Kingdom section of the North Sea gasfields will bring very important consequences: the existing methane grid from Canvey will be copied in an even larger network extending west from East Anglia and Lincolnshire; there will be considerable orders for new drilling-rigs, steel pipes, and helicopters and other supply craft. North Sea gas holds out the prospect of an improvement in Britain's trading position, since petroleum is such a significant item in our imports bill. A programme of conversion of existing industrial and domestic installations and appliances is necessary in order to transfer to methane consumption; this has already been done to a large extent in the Netherlands. There are likely to be industrial developments on Britain's East Coast similar to those that have occurred near the Lacq gasfields in France. The British gas industry will be the first to benefit, and all methane pumped to the shore will be sold to the Gas Council, agreement on prices per therm having been reached between the Council and some of the oil companies.

The nationalized gas undertakings in Britain are major consumers of coal — although they need less than they did a decade ago. In 1964–65 coal purchases fell below 20 million tons for the first time in a generation. The Gas Boards also take nearly a third of the gas produced in the coke ovens of private industry. Gas was relegated temporarily to the background by the rapid development of electric lighting, but since 1945 there has been a notable recovery in both the future prospects and the industrial-social image of the gas industry. Increasing amounts have been spent by the gas under-undertakings on capital equipment (£64 million for the period 1963–64) and the producing points have been linked by gas grids and long-distance mains. Large sums have been spent on the development of the Lurgi process for the high-pressure gasification of coal. Plants using this process are now in operation at Westfield, in Scotland, and Coleshill near Birmingham; but since the Lurgi developments started, it has been found more economical to produce gas from petroleum. There is a high concentration of gas production around London (Fig. 14.16). The cheapest process now uses methane, as the result of a long-term agreement between the Gas

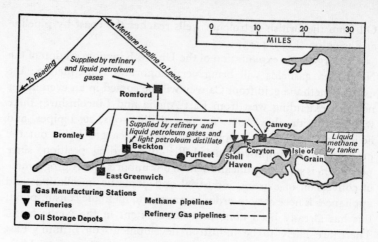

FIG. 14.16   Gas-manufacturing stations of London

London's energy requirements are enormous and expanding. The Thames is a vital channel for the reception of imported fuel supplies.

Board and Algeria, but there are several other possible sources of natural-gas supply.

The picture of U.K. production over the period 1950–60 shows that after 1956 there was a decrease in the percentage of town gas derived from coal-based plants, this having fallen by 1965 to 70 per cent. There have been important technological advances: first, the discovery of ways to manufacture gas from light petroleum distillates, a refinery product; secondly, the development of gas manufacture direct from crude oil. The most recent plants in the North-West are oil-to-gas installations, sited conveniently near petroleum terminals. The cost of such plants, per unit of gas produced, is only one-sixth that of conventional coal plants. A tenth of town gas, in 1965, was being made from Algerian methane. Some of the newest U.K. East Coast plants, for instance at West Hartlepool and on Humberside, will be well placed to receive supplies of methane either from abroad — including the Netherlands, perhaps, by pipeline — or from the North Sea.

1. R. S. Edwards, 'Greater Demand', *The Times* supplement on 'Electric Power in Britain', 6 May 1963.

2. Ministry of Power.

3. *The Times* supplement on 'The Federal German Republic', 24 April 1965.

4. National Coal Board.

5. 'New Optimism on Energy (2)', *The Times*, 21 May 1965.

6. G. W. Hemy, *The Chinese Coal Industry*, pt. i (Joseph Crosfield, Warrington, 1961), p. 3.

7. K. P. Wang, 'Mineral Industry of Mainland China', *U.S. Minerals Yearbook, 1963*, vol. iv (U.S. Bureau of Mines, 1964), p. 1793.

8. See D. Linton, 'The Geography of Energy', *Geography*, vol. l, pt. 3, no. 228 (July 1965), p. 218.

9. Dr. Georg Tugendhat, 'Vast Oil Wealth Locked in Heavy Crudes', *The Times*, 1 Sept. 1964.

10. Ibid.

11. Dr. Georg Tugendhat, 'Athabasca Oil Tar Sands Should Be Exploited', *The Times*, 11 Dec. 1963. See also *A Description and Reserve Estimate of the Oil Sands of Alberta* (Oil and Gas Conservation Board, Province of Alberta, Oct. 1963).

12. 'The New Optimism on Energy in the U.S.', *The Times*, 20–21 March 1965.

13. M. King Hubbert, *Energy Resources: A Report to the Committee on Natural Resources* (National Academy of Sciences and Research Council, Washington, D.C., 1962), p. 74.

14. *The Times*, 13 July 1964.

15. 'Comecon's Growing Pains', *The Times Review of Industry and Technology* (Feb. 1964), p. 72.

16. British Petroleum, *Statistical Review of the World Oil Industry* (annually).

17. J. G. Warnock, 'Water Power: The Unlimited Source', *Financial Times* supplement on 'World Energy', 24 Sept. 1962.

18. *The Times*, 3 July 1963.

19. G. S. Buckingham, reported in *The Times*, 23 Sept. 1965.

20. J. P. Cole and F. C. German, *A Geography of the U.S.S.R.: The Background to a Planned Economy* (Butterworth, 1961), p. 120.

21. *Financial Times*, 22 Oct. 1962, with reference to a paper by A. Parker.

22. *The Times*, 29 Jan. 1964.

23. Dr. Georg Tugendhat, 'Problem of Electricity Distribution Costs', *The Times*, 16 July 1965.

24. *Keesing's Contemporary Archives*, 26837D, 3–10 July 1965.

25. George S. Hume, 'Long Distance Movement of Natural Gas', *Financial Times* supplement on 'World Energy', 24 Sept. 1962.

26. Ibid.

27. Jordan A. Hodgkins, *Soviet Power: Energy, Resources, Production and Potentials* (Prentice-Hall, 1961), p. 134.

28. Commonwealth Economic Committee, *Sources of Energy* (H.M.S.O., 1966), pp. 144–5.

Chapter 15 The United States – The Organization of Abundance

The Steel Industry
American industry is still supreme in the world. This applies to all branches of manufacturing, light and heavy, capital and consumer goods. In the industrial requisites that go to make up a Great Power, the United States is fortunate. Its steel capacity is still well in advance of the Soviet Union, although a graph of production shows Russian achievements steadily overhauling American. United States steel production, unlike that of the Soviet Union, has been liable to violent variations. Occasionally, drastic falls in production have been attributable to prolonged strikes — perhaps in the steel industry itself; but the normal pattern is for output to oscillate in accordance with domestic demand, especially that of the automobile industry. Car production takes between a fifth and a quarter of American steel. Capacity of the steel industry has continued to increase. The leading states of the Union have a production of pig-iron that would be considered respectable in many sovereign countries: in 1964, Pennsylvania produced over 20 million, Ohio over 15 million tons. The steel industry in that year employed 837,000 people. On the other hand, during the Great Depression, output had slumped disastrously to 15 million tons in 1932 and plants were operating at only one-fifth of capacity. It required the National Industrial Recovery Act, the New Deal, defence orders, and a general world recovery to rescue steel from this, the biggest crisis in its history.

American steel is a story of growth, and also of the concentration of production in relatively few hands. The history of the industry's leaders is portrayed by Gertrude Schroeder. Before 1900 American industry in general, and steel in particular, provided a picture of the vigorous competition of a large number of small units: in the case of steel there were more than five hundred.[1] Immediately after the turn of the century, in 1901, the United States Steel Corporation was formed. Capacity and sales by U.S. Steel increased steadily. The greatest number of employees in the first half of this century was reached under war conditions, in 1943, when 340,000 were on the payroll.[2] The other huge companies are Bethlehem Steel and Republic Steel. Bethlehem Steel is notable for its location away from the main controlling factors of Pennsylvania coal and Minnesota ore. It was deliberately created on an East Coast site, dependent upon ore imported from Cuba or from South America.[3] To that extent Bethlehem established a trend that has since been paralleled in Europe: that is, growth near tidewater, using imported ores or scrap.

Production figures for the American steel industry show the continued lead of the Pittsburgh–Youngstown, but also the importance of the Chicago–Gary district. The pull of coal and anthracite in the Appalachian fields is still vital; but American dependence upon imported ore has grown swiftly, particularly in the period 1953–55. Nevertheless, there is a striking difference between America and other major producers, in the extent of dependence upon imports. The U.S.A. is much nearer self-sufficiency than is Japan, West Germany, or even the U.K. It is not surprising to find that the American industry is in the forefront of technological research and advance. One of the comparatively recent developments in steel manufacture is the use of great quantities of oxygen, injected into the molten iron or steel. There has been a notable increase in the amount of American steel made by the basic oxygen process.

The United States is remarkable for the richness and variety of its mineral wealth. Across the border in Canada also there are vast resources of some of the minerals in which the U.S.A. is not singularly favoured: for instance, nickel, in which she is only 12 per cent self-sufficient. Deficiencies in bauxite (only a quarter self-sufficient) and asbestos are matched by surpluses in Canada. Apart from these shortcomings, the Americans are well endowed with iron and copper as well as, of course, with coal and oil. The United States is also the leading producer — and exporter — of the alloy minerals vanadium and molybdenum. But despite such assets, Americans are still concerned at their working deficiencies. Even in iron, there have been growing imports since the end of the Second World War, although massive supplies are now being exploited in Canadian Labrador; and in lead and zinc, the deficiency has grown with time. Defence-minded America was worried by shortages exhibited during the Second World War and in many cases still more during the period of the Korean War. From a strategic point of view, shortages have been particularly significant in the minerals — antimony and chrome are outstanding examples — found in great quantities in the Communist States.

U.S. Minerals — 1960 Production and Degree of Self-sufficiency[4]

Mineral	Unit	U.S. production	Production as a percentage of consumption
1. Vanadium	thous. sh. tons	5	226
2. Molybdenum	thous. sh. tons	34	195
3. Copper	thous. sh. tons	1,140	96
4. Iron ore	thous. long tons	88,777	82
5. Titanium	thou. sh. tons	795	71
6. Mercury	thous. flasks	32	65
7. Tungsten	thous. sh. tons	3·3	57
8. Zinc	thous. long tons	432	45
9. Lead	thous. sh. tons	244	42
10. Bauxite	thous. long tons	2,096	26
11. Cobalt	thous. sh. tons	1	20
12. Nickel	thous. sh. tons	13	12
13. Chromite	thous. sh. tons	107	9
14. Asbestos	thous. sh. tons	45	6
15. Mica (sheet)	thous. sh. tons	120	6
16. Antimony	thous. sh. tons	0·6	5
17. Manganese	thous. sh. tons	80	4
18. Platinum	thous. oz. (troy)	10	3
19. Industrial diamonds	million carats	0	0
20. Tin	thous. long tons	0	0

United States policy has been sensitive to any reliance upon Soviet, or even neutralist, sources. In this respect South-East Asian tin may be considered, to some extent, vulnerable to Communist pressure. The underdeveloped countries may, in their own interest, have reservations about the operation on their domestic territory of foreign, including American, companies, or of combinations of industrial concerns with American and other members. Dean Frasché has said: 'We must recognize that emerging nations are no longer willing to exist as mere suppliers to other nations that enjoy the advantages of advanced industrial economies'.[5] It is always possible for revolution to bring about a change in the strategic pattern of mineral availability: 'the change in Cuba's political alignment denied the Free World about 15 per cent of its annual nickel production'.[6]

In addition to American shortages and to political and economic difficulties in the West, there has to be set the story of steady advance in the Communist East. Notable progress in the Soviet Union has occurred in the petroleum and natural-gas industries. Despite the fears of some that Soviet oil could demolish the price structure of the West, there have been other voices raised to suggest that rapidly expanding economies in the East will absorb most production there.[7] With chromite, American industrial consumers have shown themselves ready to take Soviet ore, to the discomfiture of other chromite producers. With uranium, on the other hand, Thoman has said that there are 'sizable exploitable quantities' in both the Communist and non-Communist world. He reports, perhaps just as significantly, that over 70 per cent of the uranium production of the Western world comes from the United States and Canada.[8]

The Steel Industry

The familiar concept of the concentration of American industry within the north-eastern quadrilateral is still valid today, but not to the same extent as in the first quarter of the twentieth century. At that time the localizing factors of raw materials, power, and communications all tended to nucleate production around coal, and near inland water transport. Now, as previously, the waterways of the Ohio and its contributory streams — especially the Mononga-hela — and the New York State Barge Canal carry an enormously important traffic, as does the Mississippi itself. Added to these routes and to the Illinois waterway, and competing with them to some extent, is the St. Lawrence Seaway. This still developing artery of trade tends, in part, to diminish the stature of the older routes, but also adds to their through trade. On the Seaway, the ore traffic from Minnesota eastwards is pre-eminently important, the main routes still being from Mesabi, Cuyuna, and Gogebic to the Erie lakeside sites and to Chicago. The traffic through the Soo canals at Sault Ste. Marie is such as to dwarf the tonnages passing through either Suez or Panama. Since the 1920s and the partial collapse of America's economy in the Great Depression, new and vital factors have made themselves felt with regard to the location of industry. Some of these elements were discernible before, if only in embryo.

The Location of Industry

The United
States — The
Organization
of Abundance

FIG. 15.1   Aerospace industries of the U.S.: the South
Aerospace has helped to transform the Deep South.

Changes in
Location
In all the countries of the world, electric power has become a factor in industrial location. At times it has seemed to provide a negative effect, in removing the strict control that coal availability exerted as an element in any energy situation. Changed patterns of supply have also worked to alter the location of major industries. Bethlehem Steel was responsible, in 1922, for the venturesome establishment of plants in new locations: at Sparrows Point, in Maryland — convenient for imported ore — and at Lackawanna, near Buffalo. The Second World War led to the development of steel production on the Pacific coast: over 3 million tons is now made annually in California.

The textile-manufacturing industry, once overwhelmingly concentrated in New England, is now largely based upon the Piedmont region of North Carolina, South Carolina, Georgia, and Alabama. The Second World War also encouraged the growth of the shipyards of the San Francisco area and San Diego, although more ships are in fact built on the coast of the Gulf of Mexico, and more still in the central Atlantic Coast region.

New York, Connecticut, Michigan, and Ohio are still significant centres of the aircraft-manufacturing industry, as are Dallas and other Texas cities and Seattle, but the most important aircraft-manufacturing region now is Southern California, where the largest plants are located in the outer suburbs of the Los Angeles complex. There is fierce competition for contracts between giant corporations

208

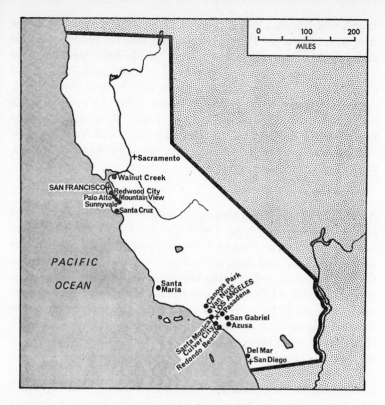

FIG. 15.2   Aerospace industries of the U.S.: California

California is the world's largest centre of these industries, which
are concentrated especially around Los Angeles and to the south
of San Francisco.

(Douglas, Boeing, Martin, Lockheed, General Dynamics, North
American Aviation), on whose operations whole communities
depend for their livelihood.

Important missile and associated industries are to be found in
New England, particularly in Massachusetts. In this state occurs
10 per cent of American 'space spending'. Here are to be found the
units of the electronics industry, centred upon the Massachusetts
Institute of Technology, and deployed along U.S. Route 128. Such
plants are also being built in old cities like Atlanta and Charlotte
and, still more, in the fastest growth areas of the south, in the states
of Florida and Texas (Fig. 15.1). Installations are found at Fort

H   H.G.P.

209

The United States — The Organization of Abundance	Worth and Daytona Beach. There are similar developments, in the American interior, at Tulsa, Phoenix, and Denver; and more atomic and missile centres in the states of Mississippi, Alabama, and Tennessee. Cape Kennedy is at the hub of high-speed building and development in eastern Florida. But as with aircraft construction, the foremost area for the missile and space industries is on the South California coast (Fig. 15.2), at Long Beach, Pasadena, Redondo Beach, Santa Monica, Sunnyvale, Palo Alta, and Van Nuys. In California also are the important naval laboratories of Point Mugu, China Lake, and San Diego.

Comparisons with the Soviet Union

American experience suggests comparison with the more deliberate and calculated redeployment of Soviet industrial strength, carried out a generation ago under fear of attack from the West. War accelerated what had been started some years previously: namely, the partial eastward shift of the industries of European Russia. The overriding motive behind this movement had been strategic: it was more than deployment, it was evacuation. In the era of Panzer divisions and wars of movement, it was essential to convey as much of the fabric of industry as was possible across the Volga, even to the Urals or beyond. America had no such compelling urge at that time. American mainland shores were not invaded during two world wars. In the Polaris age there are no safety zones left, but it is still logical for an American government to pursue policies of dispersal, and to welcome industrial growth in the interior. The headquarters of the Strategic Air Command, for instance, is at Omaha, Nebraska.

The North-East Region

Most United States industrial workers are still to be found north of the Mason-Dixon line (the limit of the old slave-owning states) and east of the Mississippi. The figures for 'productive workers' (the classification is that of the U.S. Census of Production) show 66 per cent in the North-East Region in 1962. But this numerical advantage has been eroded more and more — the region had 69 per cent of productive workers in 1939. It was during the period after 1951 that the great migration of skilled workers occurred. During the years 1931–51 the increase in the percentage of total productive workers to be found in the three Pacific Coast states had grown by only 2 per cent.[9] But during the years 1950–62 the population of

FIG. 15.3   Chicago, city of the Middle West

Chicago remains the chief focus of an economically and strategic-
ally vital region (see Fig. 20.6, for Chicago city).

California alone grew phenomenally, by 60 per cent. By 1964 there
were 18 million people in the state.

In the North-East are to be found the largest consumers of steel, **Consump-**
pre-eminent among which is the automobile industry. The **tion of Steel**
Southern Lakeland region (Fig. 15.3), in which Detroit remains
supreme, has kept 80 per cent of the national output of automobiles:
Michigan is by far the most important state. Ohio, followed by
Michigan, leads in machine-tools and accessories; the order is
reversed for cutting tools and jigs. Ohio leads again in the manufacture of metal-working machines. It is not surprising that, in the
food products, machinery, and farm-machinery industries, Illinois
should lead, since Chicago is the largest food market in the world.
In all of these branches of engineering there is an overwhelming
regional concentration upon the area east of the Mississippi, north
of the Ohio, and south of a line from St. Paul to Port Huron. Here
are to be found almost all of the foundry and machine-shop products
and the manufacture of electrical machinery. In the two last
activities, southern New England, eastern Pennsylvania, and New
York State are important. The pull of the markets — west of
Chicago and east to New York City and the other Atlantic Coast

Aluminium

conurbations — is discernible in the trades with consumer-industry outlets.

An interesting example of the interworking of various localizing factors is provided by the aluminium industry, in which the United States is easily the world's largest producer. The main locational difficulty in the manufacture of aluminium concerns the stage after mining and reduction, and involves the smelting of alumina at temperatures of around $1,775°$ C. $(3,225°$ F.$)$. To produce such conditions, hydro-electric power has often been used, for instance at Kitimat in British Columbia. In the United States a similar control operated to establish the plants at Massena, in New York State, within reach of Niagara, and at Alcoa (named after the Aluminium Company of America) in the Tennessee Valley. The latest projects using hydro-electric power are to be found in the Columbia Valley. The reduction plants that make alumina do not require such great amounts of power; this accounts for the fact that in Arkansas, where native bauxite is reduced, natural gas is used for fuel. Similarly, the East St. Louis plants, in Illinois, use local coal.

**Techno-
logical
Progress**

America, in company with other leading industrial nations, is concerned to keep in the forefront of technological development and the commercial application of scientific knowledge. The defence departments are allied with the programme directed by the National Aeronautics and Space Administration (N.A.S.A.). Spending on space programmes has reached extremely high levels: N.A.S.A.'s approved budget for 1964 was $5,300 million; but this will be dwarfed by 1970, when total American spending is likely to reach $20,000 million per annum.[10]

Much of the most significant scientific work in industry, in this generation, has been done by chemists. From the laboratory have come breakthroughs in the utilization of petroleum by-products, and their transformation into chemicals, plastics, and fibres. Great advances have been made in non-ferrous metals and the manufacture and utilization of alloy steels. Electrical engineering progressed very quickly after the Second World War, and out of the skill of engineers, using the products of metallurgy and chemistry, came a new and rapidly expanding sphere, in electronics. The electronics industry multiplied the value of its products ten times between 1940

and 1950, and during the next decade the value nearly trebled
again, most of this second increase being due to defence requirements in the fields of 'supersonic aircraft, guided missiles and space
technology'.[11] Meanwhile, in the United States, as in Western
Europe and Japan, and to a lesser extent in the Soviet Union, the
television boom continues, accompanied by an impressive expansion
in the entertainment industries using electronic devices.

At the back of all American achievement is the production of power.
Resources plus capital provide the conditions for the creation of
positive wealth, and in the field of power supplies the Americans
have been in the forefront by developing coal, oil, gas, water, and
atomic power for industry.

America claims almost a third of usable coal reserves in the world.

American and Other Coal Reserves[12]

	Producible coal ($\times 10^9$ *metric tons*)	*Percentage of world total*
U.S.A. . .	753	32·5
U.S.S.R. .	600	25·8
China . .	506	21·8
West Germany	143	6·2
U.K. . .	85	3·7

It is well known that much of America's coal is easy to mine, the
comparative thickness, evenness of seams, and absence of faulting
lending themselves to large-scale mechanization. Production is high,
and productivity higher than in most countries of the world. During
periods of national crisis there has been an inducement for all-out
effort: in the bituminous coal industry, during the war period 1939–
44, productivity rose by 59 per cent,[13] and this in spite of the fact
that productivity in an 'old' industry, such as coal, could be expected
to rise at a slower rate than that of 'new' industries, such as oil and
gas.[14] The overall economic prospects for coal-mining must eventually deteriorate, as seams become worked out, and even industries
possessing 'captive' mines of their own will have to look elsewhere.

Nevertheless, for some years to come, America is likely to be one
of the two leading coal-producers in the world. The Soviet Union
has now overtaken her as leader. With the continuance of present

trends, the gap between Russia and America will widen, to America's detriment. China is still, apparently, a long way behind, American estimates giving the Chinese production as 241 million tons for 1963. (American production in that year was 459 million short tons.)

The industrialized countries of the world have, in recent years, shared experiences in power development; there has been a transformation in the sources of energy. In Britain this has been a continuing process, the end of which is not yet in sight. Her domestic supplies of petroleum are negligible, her water-power resources small compared with the still immense coal reserves; but nuclear generation is already a practical proposition. Both oil and nuclear fuel will contribute significantly to the production of electricity in Britain by the end of this decade. In many other industrial fields, and on the railways, oil is already playing a vital role as fuel. For town gas production, oil and natural gas are becoming increasingly important. In the United States this trend became established earlier than in any other country. During the 1950s oil overtook coal as a source of energy in the U.S.A. By the end of that decade, gas also had overtaken coal. In 1964 the respective percentage proportions of total sources of energy in the U.S.A. were: oil and gas, 68·5; coal, 27·2; water power, 4·2 per cent. It was estimated in 1962 that the United States, while possessing nearly one-third of the proved petroleum reserves of the world, would provide, after 'ultimate recovery',[15] only 14 per cent of total world supplies. The Soviet Union, by the same reckoning, with 7·4 per cent of the world total of proved reserves, would provide 16 per cent after ultimate recovery.[16]

The rate of increase of proved reserves has fallen significantly in the U.S.A. since the Second World War. During the same period, American imports have risen, quantitatively, and relative to domestic production. It is clear that the United States must become more and more dependent upon foreign sources. American output is very carefully regulated, as was demonstrated during the Suez crisis, when foreign consumers had to wait upon a temporary decision to step up American production.

Russian oil production has expanded rapidly — from only 37·9 million tons in 1950 to 239 millions in 1965 — and the Soviet Union seems far from having reached her peak. The Soviet target for 1970 is 390 million tons. Eventually, the Russians will reach the same critical point as the Americans, but a generation or more later. During the intervening time, the Soviet world may well be in a strong position *vis-à-vis* the West, regarding the power situation in the light of the high cost of nuclear processes. This situation could change, however, owing to the decreasing cost per unit of energy produced by large-scale nuclear stations.

In the United States, methane has been used on a large scale since pre-Depression days, although the landslide in favour of conversion to gas came about only as a result of the construction of pipelines for long-distance transmission in the late 1940s. As with oil, many attempts have been made to assess American wealth in terms of ultimate reserves. The estimate made by Weeks in 1958 was more than doubled by Zapp in 1961.[17] The wealth of conflicting estimates, of which these are only two, makes it hazardous to evaluate the true ratio of gas reserves to consumption, or to form an opinion of future relative prospects. However, Hume estimated in 1962 that 'at the 1961 rate of production, the reserves in the U.S. were equal to 19·9 years' supply'.[18] This seemed to err on the side of pessimism, although the situation had been rendered acute by the greatly increased use of gas. Hubbert considered that there were only ten years' more supply of gas than of oil: 'in the United States, the culmination in the production of crude oil is expected to occur before 1980'.[19] Schurr has commented[20] on the discrepancy between the estimates, both for oil and gas, on the part of Hubbert and Zapp, there being a difference of 1 : 3 between the two men's estimates of the ultimate reserves of natural gas; but Hubbert's lower figure was issued in 1956; Zapp's in 1961. It is fortunate for the Americans that they can draw on large Canadian supplies, including those in Alberta. The flow of gas is now south-westwards into Washington, Oregon, and California, and southwards also across the St. Lawrence at Buffalo. (Soviet gas deposits are huge, and there has been a spectacular increase in production during the past decade.) It so happens that there are very large oil elements to be found in the American states of Colorado, Wyoming, and Utah, and that across the border there are huge, and largely untapped, deposits in the tar sands of Alberta, in the McMurray district of the Athabasca River Valley. It has even been said that the oil content of these sands is equal to the total exploitable oil reserves of the world.[21]

Opinions differ on the advisability of a greater use of hydro-electric power, but are agreed that water-power potential is several times greater than the total consumption of energy today. Some regard water as the ultimate source. 'Unlimited'[22] it certainly is, in the sense that the source is renewed by nature, but there are clearly

limits, quite apart from expense, to the utilization of hydro-power.
The chief practical difficulty is the nature of the water supply, which
unlike the fossil fuels — coal, oil, and gas — can only really compete
in those industries that positively demand the use of electric current
in large quantities.

Hydro-electric power production has been linked with irrigation
on the Western Plains. In the Tennessee Valley, the achievement of
the multi-purpose Federal Authority has been especially remarkable
for the extent to which it has combated the serious erosion of the
soil wealth of the whole region between the middle Appalachians
and the Mississippi. But it is also important because it offers a
source of cheap power. There has indeed been an impressive growth
in per-capita income in the territory covered by the T.V.A. One
interesting feature of power development in the U.S.A. is the
competition between Federal and private producers, there being no
nation-wide nationalized concern such as we have in Britain.

Nuclear Power

Nuclear power developments are in hand in many of the wealthier
countries: uranium is plentiful in the world, though expensive to
process, and the Americans, predictably, have made tremendous
efforts to develop this industry, with its strategic as well as industrial
implications. The major uranium deposits of the U.S.A. are to be
found on the Colorado Plateau, which continues from the state of
Colorado into the neighbouring states of Utah, Arizona, and New
Mexico. More uranium is to be found in the sandstone and lignite
ores of Wyoming and the Black Hills of Dakota. A surplus of
uranium concentrate has accumulated, at least in the U.S.A.,
because of over-optimism about the speed with which industry
would change from conventional to nuclear fuel. It has been stated
in Britain that American nuclear power is now 'on or near the
threshold of competitiveness with conventional power'.[23] But even
in the regions of New England and California, where industrial
activity is intense and transport costs of coal are comparatively high,
the Government's Commissioner has said that nuclear power is
unlikely to be competitive before 1968.[24] Schurr[25] refers to a later
report of the United States A.E.C., to the effect that atomic power
would become competitive 'throughout most of the U.S. in the
1970s', but comments, with some reason, that the Commission has
an axe to grind in this matter. The future of the atomic power
industry is somewhat uncertain. A good deal may depend upon the

provision of cheaper fuel, and upon the development of more sophisticated processes, involving the use of breeder reactors, which allow low-grade fuel to be used.[26]

Nuclear
Power

The United States is the most affluent nation. It possesses far more motor-cars than any other country, and produces more automobiles than the rest of the world combined. The U.S.A. has the largest motion-picture industry, centred around California's Hollywood, even though some of the giant sets are now closed down and major effort confined to 'epics' supplemented by work for television. Production of television receivers has been remarkably resilient. After a falling-off in the later 1950s, production quickly recovered to over 7 million sets in 1963.

Radio and
Television

Output of Television Receivers in the United States[27]
('000)

1950	.	.	7,464
1955	.	.	7,757
1960	.	.	5,708
1961	.	.	6,177
1962	.	.	6,471
1963	.	.	7,130
1964	.	.	8,120

Radio, as a large-scale manufacturing industry, antedated television by about a quarter of a century. In these and allied fields, some of the key discoveries and advances were made by Americans:

1844   Morse sends a telegram from Baltimore to Washington.
1876–81 The telephone is patented by Alexander Graham Bell.
1878   Thomas A. Edison patents his phonograph.
1879   Edison invents the first practicable incandescent bulb.
1880   Eastman patents the first successful roll film.
1888   Eastman's portable roll-film camera.
1889   Edison's Kinetoscope movie camera, using a continuous roll of film.
1915   The first transcontinental telegraph line: New York–San Francisco.
1923   The first transatlantic radio-telephone.
1927   A.T. & T. carried out the first transmission of television signals from New York to Washington.
1956   First transatlantic telephone cable laid.
1964   Syncom 3 satellite relays television pictures.

The United States — The Organization of Abundance

The radio and telecommunications industries are dominated by a few giant corporations, the biggest of which are:

Manufacture and Communications

1. The Radio Corporation of America (R.C.A.).
2. The American Telephone and Telegraph Company (A.T. & T.).

Broadcasting

3. The National Broadcasting Company (a subsidiary of A.T. & T.).
4. The Columbia Broadcasting System.

The private-enterprise basis of broadcasting in the U.S.A. is in strong contrast to the State control operated in Britain and many other countries.

Television is commercially a product of the years since the Second World War. On 1 January 1948, television sets in use by the American public numbered only 190,000. By 1951 there were 10,550,000; by 1960, 52 million.[28] The United States has about three times the number of receivers to be found in Britain, West Germany, and France combined.

America and the New Revolution

Technological advances, if they occur too fast, can create considerable social distress, the chief factor being unemployment. Critical local situations have developed from the introduction of new processes, using new materials that bring different relationships between the raw-material content and power contribution as twin elements in the final cost. The changes have been especially severe in communities based upon a single industry or a single plant.

In the United States, automation has made a significant and growing impact upon patterns of employment and unemployment incidence. The new age has brought a new vocabulary, with such terms as 'technological unemployment'. Assembly-line techniques, such as those of the car industry, would seem to be well suited to the introduction of automation, but Dunning and Thomas have said that, even with cars, no more than 30 per cent of production potential is 'capable of being automated'.[29] As against this, telephonic communications do lend themselves to automotive techniques; these, the same authors suggest, could displace 100,000 workers in the decade 1963–73.[30]

Government and administration cannot be indifferent to the impact of these new techniques. The rapidity of change and growth has been demonstrated in the electronics industry since 1950, and the impact of new forms of production is making itself felt in Washington as well as Whitehall.

A number of commentators have pointed to differences in American official opinion on these matters. There has been a long-standing insistence that governments must interfere in industry as little as possible. As in Britain, there has been concern that 'the U.S. nation's resources of scientific expertise are being too heavily pre-empted by the defence and aerospace industries'.[31] Some authorities in the U.S.A. have sought to combat the prevalent idea that technological advance is 'possibly the major cause of recent unemployment',[32] and have pressed for positive growth. There have been indications of an advance in relations between management and labour about automotive processes; notable moves have been made in meat-packing, in steel, and in shipping.[33] In Britain, important related studies have been undertaken by the T.U.C.'s General Council.

The New Frontier of progress, however, has not touched districts such as east Kentucky, where the desperate poverty of eighteen mountain counties brought new promise of Federal intervention. The causes were long-standing: 'by 1930 primitive hillside farming methods and ruthless over-cutting of the region's timber have left the mountains raw and subject to erosion, causing silting of streams and increases in flooding . . . the collapse of mining in the 1950s, through automation in the mines and a national shift to other fuels, left an unnaturally large population in a worn-out land'.[34] In the Deep South, vast problems of colour exist to aggravate the difficulties of economic readjustment, but in places spectacular new industries of the space age have transformed whole regions.

America and the New Revolution

NOTES

1. G. Schroeder, *The Growth of Major Steel Companies, 1900–1950* (Johns Hopkins Press, Baltimore, 1953), p. 36.

2. Ibid., p. 216.

3. Ibid., p. 48.

4. Dean F. Frasché, *Mineral Resources: A Report to the Committee on Natural Resources* (U.S. National Academy of Sciences and Research Council, Washington, D.C., 1962), p. 8.

5. Ibid., p. 13.

6. Ibid., p. 22.

7. Robert E. Wilson, 'Petroleum', in *American Enterprise: The Next Ten Years*, ed. M. R. Gainsbrugh (Macmillan, New York, 1961), p. 212.

8. Thoman, *The Geography of Economic Activity*, p. 265.

9. Carlson (ed.), 'Populations and Their Resources', in *The Economic Geography of Industrial Materials*, p. 20.

10. *Financial Times*, 20 July 1962, quoting *Investors Chronicle*.

11. Donald C. Powers, 'Electronics', in *American Enterprise: The Next Ten Years*, ed. Gainsbrugh, p. 234.

12. Hubbert, *Energy Resources*, p. 37.

13. N. H. Leonard, 'The Bituminous Coal Industry', in *The Structure of American Industry: Some Case Studies*, ed. W. Adams (Macmillan, New York, 1950), p. 49.

14. Marvin Frankel, 'Distributing Productivity Gains: The Historical Record', in *American Enterprise: The Next Ten Years*, ed. Gainsbrugh, p. 318.

15. Ultimate recovery = total amount recoverable from wells.

16. Hubbert, *Energy Resources*, p. 74.

17. Ibid., p. 77.

18. George S. Hume, in *Financial Times* supplement on 'World Energy', 24 Sept. 1962.

19. Hubbert, *Energy Resources*, p. 90.

20. S. H. Schurr, 'Energy', *Scientific American*, vol. 209, no. 3 (Sept. 1963), p. 118.

21. Trevor M. Thomas, 'Exploitation of the Athabasca Tar Sands, Alberta', *Geography*, vol. xlviii, pt. 3, no. 220 (July 1963), p. 332.

22. J. G. Warnock, in *Financial Times* supplement on 'World Energy', 24 Sept. 1962.

23. *Financial Times*, 27 Nov. 1962.

24. Wilson, 'Petroleum', in *American Enterprise: The Next Ten Years*, ed. Gainsbrugh, p. 216.

25. S. H. Schurr, 'Energy', *Scientific American*, vol. 209, no. 3 (Sept. 1963), p. 124.

26. Hubbert, *Energy Resources*, p. 110.

27. *Statistical Abstract of the United States*, 1965, p. 815.

28. J. G. Glover and R. L. Lagai, *The Development of American Industries: Their Economic Significance* (Simmons-Broadman, New York, 1959), p. 800.

29. Dunning and Thomas, *British Industry: Change and Development in the Twentieth Century*, p. 178. They refer to examples from the Ford Motor Company.

30. Ibid., p. 180.

31. Michael Shanks, 'The Automation Problem: Too Much or Too Little', *Financial Times*, 6 Nov. 1963.

32. T. L. Johnston, 'American Faces the Challenge of Automation', *The Times Review of Industry and Technology* (July 1963), p. 78.

33. Ibid.

34. 'East Kentucky's Cycle of Despair', *The Times*, 21 Jan. 1964.

The Soviet Union – from Poverty to Wealth

The Soviet economy provides a very large field of investigation to the economist, to the statistician, to the sociologist, and to the geographer. Sources of information are not lacking now, although there still persists some lingering doubt about the reliability of agricultural production figures. Since the earliest days of what was once regarded as a hazardous economic experiment — it is now accepted as an accomplished fact — there has been an organizational schism between industry and the land. Perhaps nowhere do farmers take kindly to regimentation; perhaps it is because of their nearness to, and special relationship with, the soil; but there have been numerous instances, not least in Communist China, as well as in the Communist States of Eastern Europe, to show the perils of large-scale collective farming.

Growth

In industry the picture has been very different. There, the record is one of remarkable and progressive development. Soviet policy is based upon growth and founded upon an industrial achievement that has been all the greater for the difficulties it has encountered: 'After the First World War and the Civil War, it took the U.S.S.R. about six years to bring industrial production back to the pre-war, 1913 level',[1] although Soviet Russia has not been alone in enduring the catastrophes of war, devastation, defeat, and famine.

The Second World War, like the First, involved a tremendous disturbance to the Russian economy. In Britain, the dislocation of war was considerable, but it by no means approached the scale it did in the East. It was not until 1948 that the Soviet Union caught up with the level of industrial production in 1940. In Soviet Russia's own assessment of its industrial achievement, two features predominate: one is the backward glance to 1913 and pre-revolutionary conditions; the other, the forward, planner's look, welcoming comparisons with Russia's rival, the United States.

The Soviet Five-Year Plans 'for the economic development of the U.S.S.R.' have run as follows:

1st Five-Year Plan: October 1928–1932.
2nd   "   "   "   1933–37.
3rd   "   "   "   1938–42. Only partially fulfilled because of war-time conditions.
4th   "   "   "   1946–50.
5th   "   "   "   1951–55.
6th   "   "   "   1956–60.

In 1957, after work had begun to implement the Sixth Plan, decisions were taken to commence a longer-term plan, to run from 1959 to 1965.

It goes without saying that the planner is a most important part of the Soviet bureaucracy. The machinery of planning has been used to alter materially the distribution of the manifold resources of the U.S.S.R. and their apportionment among the different sectors of society, to alter and control the location of industry, to channel labour to new enterprises and new regions, and to provide materials and manpower for a rapidly expanding economy.

The machinery of administration grew up around the State Planning Commission, later to become the State Planning Committee (Gosplan). Behind the administrators, and advising them, are bodies of experts, and the task of all is to anticipate rather than to direct. The function of direction belongs rather to departmental managers.

The Soviet Plans have helped to shape developments in West European countries with political systems very far removed from the single-party Soviet State. The planning philosophy of the Soviet has been inseparably tied to this one-party control: the Communist Party Central Committee is a sort of Soviet 'Cabinet' in executive charge of the whole national scheme: the 'Inner Cabinet' is the Politburo of the Central Committee. In 1962, 'two new bureaux of the party's Central Committee — one for the guidance of industrial production, and one for the guidance of agricultural output'[2] — were created. It was intended that these supervisory bodies should operate efficiently inside the republics of the Union; the 'economic areas' of the separate republics have been consolidated. In the largest administrative division of the Soviet Union — the Russian Soviet Federal Socialist Republic (R.S.F.S.R.) — the number of such areas was reduced, in 1963, from sixty-two to not more than twenty-four, and in the Ukraine from fourteen to seven. The function formerly exercised by the State Planning Committee, to review annually performance in Five- or Seven-Year Plans, was transferred to a new body, the National Economic Council.[3] Since the earliest days of Soviet planning, the system had depended upon the allocation of targets of production to industries and individual enterprises. Performance was measured in terms of annual achievement of the target set. In 1965 there was a major change. The former production plan was to be 'replaced by a sales plan. A factory will still have an overall target, but it will only count as fulfilled when goods have actually been sold'.[14]

Planning

In an undertaking as vast as the direction of one of the two most powerful nations on earth, there is a clear danger of the machinery of administration becoming excessive and unwieldy. Centralism may produce not clarity, but confusion. One way out of this is to subdivide functions at the centre: central direction will remain, but there will be an increased delegation of responsibility for planning and anticipation to sub-committees. Delegation was to increase within the Union structure of the U.S.S.R. The Soviet Union, it is well known, is organically a federation, but it has always been assumed that the Russian part of it should remain supreme. In 1957, it was deemed administratively opportune to recognize the shift in emphasis from almost total dependence on European Russia to interdependence between the old and new centres of economic growth. In particular, it was thought desirable to set up an industrial agency for Central Asia.

After the fall of Khrushchev, who had been responsible for the measures of decentralization undertaken in 1957, there was considerable re-thinking of the problems of regional responsibility in the U.S.S.R. One of the difficulties had been the tendency for some of the regional councils (*sovnarkhozy*) 'to give priority to their own needs over those of their neighbours'.[5] The map of the major economic regions of the U.S.S.R. (Fig. 16.1) illustrates the administrative changes that ensued, especially in regard to the crucial Urals region and its eastern borderland. The Urals–Tyumen area, shown by Alampiev,[6] embraced a huge expanse of forest land and tundra in the West Siberian Plain, as well as the metallurgical centres of the South Urals. Mellor has seen, in the large economic region, a concept based largely on 'an analysis of present needs and capabilities'[7] that is strikingly different from the type of region commonly found in the West.

Regional Development

223

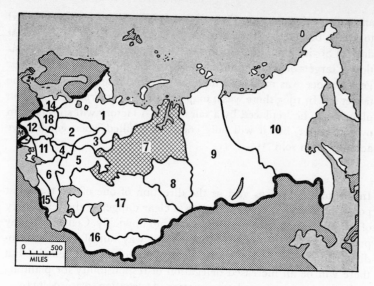

FIG. 16.1   Major economic regions of the U.S.S.R., 1964
The Soviet Union, like other countries, has difficulties with the
creation of convincing regional economic divisions. The heavily
industrialized Urals Region includes a stretch of the barren Arctic
coast.
Regions: 1. North-western; 2. Central; 3. Volga–Vyatka; 4.
Central Black Earth; 5. Volga; 6. North Caucasian; 7. Urals;
8. West Siberian; 9. East Siberian; 10. Far Eastern; 11. Donets–
Dnieper; 12. South-western; 13. Southern; 14. Baltic; 15. Trans-
caucasian; 16. Central Asian; 17. Kazakhstan; 18. Byelorussian;
M. Moldavian Republic.

Energy

Soviet strength has been founded on the progress of heavy industry,
mining, and power production. A generation ago, the Soviet Union
was fifth or sixth in the world in coal output. Now she is first,
surpassing the United States. After a rapid rise from 261 million
metric tons in 1950 to 391 million tons in 1955 and 513 million tons
in 1960 (for bituminous coal and lignite combined), production
began to level off: it was 578 million tons in 1965. But coal is still by
far the biggest element in energy supplies in the Soviet Union. In
this respect the U.S.S.R. contrasts with North America (Fig. 16.2).

One striking feature of Soviet heavy industry has been the eastward movement of the focus of production. (In the U.S.A., the
movement has been in the opposite direction.) Mining, by its
physical nature, is restricted to a location; but here, too, there have

224

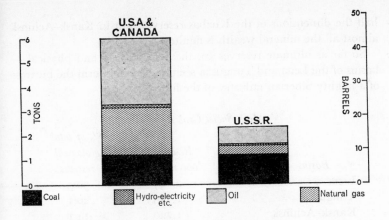

FIG. 16.2   Soviet Union and North America — energy-consumption patterns

Anglo-America still has a big lead, although the Soviet Union is making considerable progress in the production of oil and gas.

been considerable changes in the Russian economic scene. Mik-hailov related how production from the Donbas field had fallen from 87 per cent in 1913 to 61·9 per cent of total Union output in 1935. Actual production was: 1913, 25·3 million tons; 1935, 67·4 million tons.[8] There had been some production, even in 1913, from the Kuznetsk Basin and also from the East Siberian coal region, but in each case output was minute in comparison with the vast reserves available. At that time neither field produced much more than our own East Kent mines do today. In 1960, production in the Donbas had risen to the huge figure of 188 million tons, but by this time the basin yielded only 37 per cent of total Union production. This one field now produces more than any single country in the world, except the United States and Britain.

Significant coal deposits are more widely distributed in the U.S.S.R. than in the U.S.A. In America, output in Pennsylvania–West Virginia is about equal to that in the Soviet Donbas. In the U.S.A., however, there is no second area of concentration as important as is the Kuzbas in Russia. The proved reserves of the Kuzbas are about equal to those of European Russia, but production from the Kuzbas (Fig. 16.3) is still much lower than that from the Donbas. Further east, there are big proved reserves in the Kansk–Achinsk field, alongside the Trans-Siberian railway, amounting to

half the dimensions of the Kuzbas reserves; but in Kansk–Achinsk
almost all the mineral wealth is lignite.[9]

So far as ultimate reserves go, the geological — and physical —
basins of the Lena and Tunguska seem destined to form the buttress
of a mighty Siberian industry of the future.

Main Soviet Coal Reserves[10]

Basins	Reserves in '000 mill. tons	% of total geological reserves
Lena	2,647	30·5
Tunguska . . .	1,745	20·1
Kansk–Achinsk . .	1,220	14·1
Kuznetsk (Kuzbas) .	905	10·5
Taimyr . . .	583	6·7
Pechora . . .	344	4·0
Donetz (Donbas) .	240	2·8

In the early years of the Revolution, Lenin is credited with having
foreseen the basic role of electrification in the transformation of an
economy. The growth in output of electrical installations is impressive. By 1950 the amount of electricity generated was almost double
the 1940 figure. Since 1955 it has been doubling itself every six
years; although some authorities have doubted whether even this
rate will suffice to keep pace with the planned growth of industrial
production. Soviet Russia has a very large power potential, measured
by her resources of coal, lignite, petroleum, gas, and hydro-power
potential. The plentiful oil supplies, greater than those of the United
States, more than offset her smaller coal reserves, as calculated by
Averitt.[11] Petroleum production topped 200 million tons for the first
time in 1963. Soviet gas resources have been quoted as being much
smaller than those of the U.S.A.[12] American production of methane
in 1958 was greater than the planned Soviet output for 1972.
Nevertheless, Soviet gas production is increasing at a far faster rate.
During the period 1945–57 the growth was sixfold as compared with
threefold in the U.S.A.; during the period 1953–57, gas output in
the U.S.S.R. increased, annually, by 29·2 per cent, in the U.S.A.
by only 6·1 per cent[13]; and in the single year 1962–63, Soviet output
grew by a quarter.

It is an important fact that a very big percentage (87 per cent,
according to Hodgkins)[14] of all proved Soviet gas reserves is to be

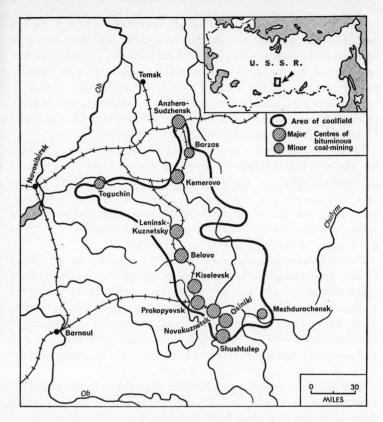

FIG. 16.3   The Kuzbas coalfield
This field, centrally placed in the Soviet Union, still has only half
the output of the Donbas.

found in European Russia, west of the Urals. This gives the same
sort of geographical imbalance as obtains in the American coal
industry.

The significance to the Soviet economy of natural gas lies particularly in its being a cheap source of power. This is because,
measured in units of production against numbers employed, labour
productivity in the methane fields is more than twice that achieved
in oil production, and twelve times that of coal.[15] But gas must be
piped or carried to the consumer. Hence the importance of the long-
range pipelines, including the one from Bokhara–Khiva, the producing region in Central Asia, to the centres of metallurgy in the Urals.

The time-lag between the original conception of power stations and their completion is such that long-term planning is a prerequisite of the successful operation of the industry. The water-power resources of the Soviet Union have been tapped to a far smaller degree than those of the United States. Whereas the curve representing the increase in installed capacity of hydro-electric power is likely to level off in the U.S.A. after the end of this century,[16] in the Soviet Union it is likely to continue to climb more steeply.

In working out Soviet energy plans, I. Novikov, Soviet Minister for Power Plant Construction, stated the cost 'per kilowatt of installed capacity . . . has gone as high as 4,000 roubles'[17] in the case of hydro-electric stations. On the other hand, 'new large thermal power plants will make possible a reduction in relative outlay per kilowatt of installed capacity to 800 roubles . . . and to 670 roubles on plants operating on natural gas'.[18]

Unused water-power potential there is, in plenty, in the Soviet Union. One feature of her physical geography is the tremendous spate of water — the largest volume being carried by the River Yenisei — running to waste northwards across the Siberian tundra. There have been a number of mammoth schemes to divert some of this vast resource of potential irrigation southwards, into the arid and semi-arid zones of Kazakhstan. The partial harnessing of these rivers to produce power is already a fact.

The biggest of power stations, either planned or in the process of construction, is Krasnoyarsk on the Yenisei. This was originally designed to produce 3,200 MW, but further plans increased it to at least 5,000 MW. Subsequent sources have quoted its capacity as 6,000 MW.[19] The Irkutsk station on the upper Angara is in operation, producing 4,500 MW; the Bratsk station, lower down the Angara, was designed for 3,200 MW but has been increased also to 4,500-MW capacity. The station at Volgograd (the former Stalingrad) was intended for 2,300-MW capacity, later increased to 2,500 MW; the Kuibyshev station, also on the Volga, has been changed from 2,100 to 2,300 MW; and on the same river stands a 1,000-MW plant, at Saratov. Despite the availability of water power, numerous pronouncements have been made,[20] indicating that the proportion of power produced from hydro-sources will not increase during the next two decades, although in the period 1960–80 Soviet energy demands are expected to multiply ten times. During the period 1960–64, Soviet hydro-electric production increased by 52 per cent; thermal production by nearly 60 per cent.

One source has suggested that the pace of development has been such that the power industry, in places such as Siberia, has run out of consumers, while in European Russia a power shortage has appeared.[21]

The Soviet Union is ahead of Britain in the development of high-voltage transmission lines. In Russia there are now nearly 4,000 miles of 500-kV lines in operation, notably between Votkinsk and Sverdlovsk; but transmission capacity is far from having reached its limit, and in 1962 a 800-kV cable was opened between Volgograd and the Donbas.

In their attitude to nuclear power, the Soviet leaders and planners have, in general, been motivated by considerations similar to those influencing their contemporaries in the West. However, the Chairman of the Soviet State Atomic Energy Committee was quoted as saying that 'areas do exist in the U.S.S.R. where, even now, nuclear power is competitive'.[22] The result of this thinking has been to give at least qualified approval to the large-scale use of nuclear power in industry, even if only on a selected number of sites. The same source quotes Professor Emelyanov as having disclosed 'a plan to build several 1,000-MW breeder reactor stations'.[23] The largest atomic plant in the first generation of nuclear power stations went into service in 1958 with a capacity of 100 MW. This was later to be raised to 600 MW. The second generation of stations included Belvyarsk and a new Voronezh plant. There is no reason to anticipate a decline in the progress of the generation and transmission of power in the Soviet Union. The U.S.S.R. passed the figure for the combined output of the E.E.C. countries in 1959, and in 1966 had established a comfortable lead over them.

The record of the Soviet iron and steel industry is impressive. Only 4·2 million tons of pig-iron was produced in 1913, pig-iron that Mikhailov called 'the metal base of old Russia'. In 1927–28 output was actually less than this: 3·2 million tons. In both years, production in Britain was about two and a half times as great. By 1937 Soviet production was twice that of Britain. Now it is three times the British output. Only United States production tops that of the U.S.S.R., though there is still a considerable margin between them.

Output of steel has risen with the progress of the Five-Year Plans and the massive programmes of capital building, reconstruction, and farm mechanization. Perhaps the most remarkable advances in steel production were made during the periods 1928–40 (4·2 to 18·0 million tons) and 1940–55 (18·0 to 44·5 million tons). The first of these periods put the Soviet Union among the world-class industrial Powers; the second increase was achieved in the teeth of war and its aftermath. Since 1955, production rose steeply year by year, to reach nearly 90 million tons in 1965. The Soviet Union is well favoured by the magnitude of her ore resources, concentrated in the Ukraine — particularly around Krivoi Rog — and in the Urals.

In the U.S.S.R., as in other major industrial nations, iron and coal are not found together. Occasionally, locational compromises are reached, as on the northern shores of the Sea of Azov where the Zhdanov works are able to draw on the lean iron ore of Kerch in the eastern Crimea as well as on the coal of the Donbas. Cole and German report that there are more than 2,000 million tons of medium-grade ore at Kerch. There is also about the same amount of high-grade ore at Krivoi Rog, west of the Dnieper, where there are big pig-iron works. But the main centre of the Ukrainian iron and steel industry is the Donetz coalfield. The chief producing towns are Donetzsk, Makeyevka, and Yenakiyevo. The steel mills on the Dnieper, near the hydro-electric stations at Dnieprodzerzhinsk and Zaporozhe, are rather closer to iron than coal. In the Union as a whole, it is noteworthy that the steel industry is more widely distributed than is the pig-iron. The Ukraine produces over 55 per cent of the Union's iron ore, half of its pig iron, but only 40 per cent of its steel. The second great region for iron and steel is the central and southern Urals, particularly at the centres of Nizhny Tagil and Magnitogorsk, both near to iron ore, at Pervouralsk, near Sverdlovsk, and at Chelyabinsk respectively. Coal is short in the Urals, but is plentiful far to the east in the Kuzbas, so the 'pendulum' scheme[24] was begun to transport iron eastwards from the Magnitogorsk deposits, and coal from the Kuzbas west to the Urals. Pounds and others have referred to the economic strains produced by the physical distance between the Urals and the Kuzbas, especially since 'the better Magnitogorsk ores, like those of Minnesota, are nearing exhaustion'.[25] But many countries are now having to rely more heavily than hitherto upon the leaner ores.

The Second World War was instrumental in developing the eastern areas' steel industries at a time when most of Russia west of the Volga was occupied and much of it devastated. Since pre-war days the output of Urals steel has increased much faster than that of the Ukraine.[26] The Kuzbas region has a number of typical growth points: for instance, Stalinsk (renamed Novokuznetsk), Kemerovo, and Prokopievsk. West of the Kuzbas, on the River Ob, are Barnaul and Novosibirsk — one of the big cities of the Soviet Union. A similar growth-point is to be found at Karaganda in Kazakhstan, where coal and tungsten are mined. In Kazakhstan are to be found nearly half the copper, lead, and zinc reserves of the whole Union; but oil production is small.

Growth of West Siberian Cities
('ooos)

City		*1939*	*1959*	*1964*
Novosibirsk	. .	404	887	1013
Novokuznetsk				
(Stalinsk)	. .	166	377	410
Barnaul	. .	148	320	373
Kemerovo	. .	133	277	343
Prokopievsk	. .	107	282	292

The efficiency of transport is an important consideration in countries as large as the U.S.A., the Soviet Union, and China. All of these are countries with very large populations, with established centres of heavy industry, but with new growth industries, in some instances many miles removed from the older nuclei.

In America there has been fierce competition, under conditions of free enterprise but not without governmental interference, between the different forms of transport. As long ago as the mid-nineteenth century, the older methods of transport competed for the commercial exchanges of America's industrial revolution and for the traffic that moved ever further westwards. As in Britain, the struggle was between inland water communication, railway, and road. Unlike Britain, the contest was not in many areas weighted heavily against water operators. Canal and river traffic was, and still is, of vital importance, especially in the industrialized north-east. And recently, the position of the shipping lines has been fortified by the construction of the St. Lawrence Seaway. (In 1962 nearly 27 million tons of cargo were carried through its locks and canals.) U.S. Government support for the Seaway was given only after fierce opposition by competing interests, represented especially by the

railway and the East Coast ports. But the tonnage carried on the
Seaway is increasing. In 1962, for the first time, Chicago dealt with
over 1 million tons of cargo.[27] In America, as in Britain, the railways
are fighting for traffic. As in Britain, the railways' share of total
freight has dropped — from 60 to 40 per cent over the past fifteen
years.[28] The traffic has been lost, very largely, to the roads. One
suggested solution, even less popular in the United States than in
Britain, has been a government subsidy for the railways; another
has been rationalization, involving wholesale pruning and closure.
In commercial terms, rationalization would entail amalgamation,
the most spectacular such merger being proposed for two north-
eastern giants: the Pennsylvania Railroad and the New York
Central. The history of these two lines covers the industrialization
of the most important manufacturing region in the world. Their
union has been approved by the Federal Transport Commission,
but the same body has not agreed to a parallel merger between the
Baltimore–Ohio and Chesapeake–Ohio systems.

One advantage in railway operation shared by Russia and the
U.S.A. is the long run. The railway managers in Britain think they
have proved from the example of France that the elimination of
many short runs would bring back the solvency that has eluded
them. In France there has been a striking increase in the freight
traffic carried — measured in ton-miles — over the period 1952–62;
it has grown faster than passenger traffic. In Britain, on the other
hand, freight tonnage since 1955 has shown a serious decline.

The big cities, which the railways helped to create, have continued to grow and to provide increased freight for the trunk lines.
Transport forms react to the general climate of industry. Changes
occur because they are demanded by the transport-users, or because
they emerge from the situation created by an inadequate supply of
transport facilities. In Russia, industrialization came late. The
Trans-Siberian link was completed more than a generation after
the meeting of the tracks in the U.S.A. The railways still represent
a growth industry in Asia. This is well shown by Cole and German.
The relative role of railway transport has declined only very slightly,
as compared with 1937, while the actual tonnage of freight carried
by rail, as represented in ton-kilometres, has quadrupled.

The statistics combine to give a picture of the still overwhelming
importance of the railway to freight carriage. But there has been a
movement — slow, it is true, though definite — showing a comparative advance in the competing transport forms. To this extent,

232

Soviet Freight Traffic — Percentage carried by Different Transport Forms[29] *(ton-kilometre basis)*			
	1955	*1958*	*1960*
Rail	83·4	81·2	79·5
Water (coastal and mainland)[30]	11·7	11·9	12·4
Road	3·6	4·8	5·6
Pipeline	1·3	2·1	2·5

Williams's uncompromising assertion — 'the Soviet economy is and always has been a railway economy'[31] — requires partial qualification. Williams has provided illuminating material on transport fares in the U.S.S.R., where water-carrier rates are commonly fixed at 30 per cent below those obtaining for rail.[32] This gives an interesting comparison with the position in the United States, where railways have complained bitterly for many years of the existence of discriminatory regulations, taxation provisions, and public facilities favouring their competitors. American railways once held a virtual monopoly of long-distance traffic, affording a source of valuable local revenue. Williams has discerned a peak in the dominance of the railway in the Soviet Union, occurring just before the Second World War affected the U.S.S.R. He compared the 87 per cent of freight traffic handled by railways in 1940 with the 61 per cent carried in 1913.[33]

Railways are especially important for the moving of mineral ores, metals, and cereals. The main axes of transport for the traffic of heavy industry are north–south in the zone Moscow–Donbas and east–west from the Urals to the Kuzbas. At right-angles to these main flow-lines are the movements from the Donbas to the Dnieper and from Magnitogorsk in the southern Urals to Chelyabinsk and Sverdlovsk. The Turksib trunk line was one of the first major transport achievements of Communist Russia. Since the inter-war period, Karaganda and Central Asia generally have become even more important as sources of non-ferrous minerals, and these have increased as elements in Soviet rail-freight cargo.

Some impact has been made by the completion of the Volga–Don Canal, opened in 1952, connecting Moscow via the Moskva and Oka rivers to the Volga and thence with the Sea of Azov and the Black Sea, but the Soviet Union, even in its European portion, has no Mississippi or Ohio. The Dnieper and the Don 'do not effectively tap the Donbas',[34] while, in contrast, the less exotic northern

233

streams — the Dvina and Pechora — 'are vital to the development
of the area in the absence of railways'.[35] There is another most
important factor: Soviet trade is very largely inward-directed: this
is Soviet traffic, orientated to Soviet needs. The Russian economy
is not nearly so dependent as the American upon foreign trade, and
by far the largest element in Soviet trade — 71 per cent in 1961 —
is provided by the commercial exchanges with her own Communist
partners in Eastern Europe and, to a smaller extent, with China.
The Chinese traffic has dropped spectacularly since the ideological
schism between Moscow and Peking.

Since the Second World War, the Russians have carried through
a very large programme of electrification on their railways. The
Five-Year Plan of 1946–50 included electrification of over 5,000
kilometres of track, almost doubling previous achievements. The
1965 Plan provided for the Moscow–Kursk–Belgorod–Donbas electrification to be continued via Rostov-on-Don into the Kuban and,
later, to the resort of Mineral'neye Vody in the foothills of the
Caucasus (see Fig. 16.4). Actual freight traffic by rail increased
strikingly, from 970,500 million ton-kilometres in 1955 to 1,850,000
million in 1964.[36]

In passenger transport by air, the Soviet Union has witnessed
spectacular quantitative and qualitative growth, as shown in the
speed of aircraft used and in the numbers of passengers carried.
Performance standards (speed and range) of Soviet aircraft have
been comparable with the best in Britain and the United States.
The Soviet Union is able to conduct internal proving flights over
distances greater than any available to other countries. The number
of passengers carried by air inside the Soviet Union more than quadrupled during the period 1957–63. Aeroflot has not lagged behind
other airlines in design, and there have been indications that the Soviet
planners are working on the basis of attaining Mach 2 speeds by
1970. This would be within striking distance of the Anglo-French
Concord's Mach 2·2 (Mach 1 = the speed of sound, 760 m.p.h.).

It seems to be generally agreed that for freight transport, air is
much less important than other transport media in both the U.S.A.
and U.S.S.R., although there is some difficulty in arriving at a
common basis of comparison. Cole and German[37] have referred to
the situation in 1958, when United States airlines and railways each
accounted for less than 4 per cent of total passenger movements,
including those by private motor-car, since which time, the airlines
in America have progressed and railways have continued to decline.

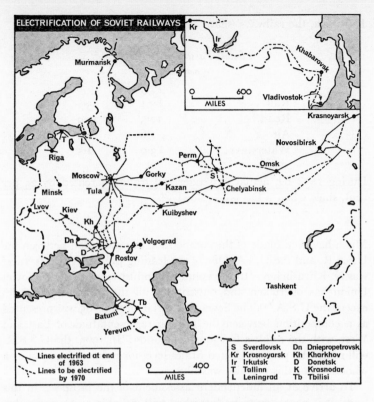

FIG. 16.4   Electrification of Soviet Railways — a trans-
continental service

The Trans-Siberian railway is still the main artery for east–west
freight traffic.

Statistics of public transport tend to over-emphasize the significance
of the airlines. Nevertheless, air transport has made spectacular
advances since 1951. *Jane's Worlds Railways* provides the following
data for inter-city traffic in the United States:

United States Passenger Traffic (Revenue-Earning)[38]
(per cent)

	1962	*1963*	*1964*
Rail . .	24·70	21·65	19·7
Road .	26·05	25·46	24·3
Air . .	45·90	49·68	53·0
Waterways .	3·35	3·21	3·0

235

In Russia, the railways' share of traffic has also fallen.

Soviet Passenger Traffic[39]
(per cent)

	1955	*1958*
Rail . . .	83·1	75·1
Road . .	12·3	20·2
Air . . .	1·6	2·2
Waterways . .	3·0	2·5

During 1958–62, actual passenger rail traffic increased by 25 per cent, since when it has fallen slowly.[40]

U.S.A. and
U.S.S.R. —
Competition
in
Production

Much has been made of the competition in production between the U.S.S.R. and the U.S.A. One of the leading publicists of this 'race' was N. Khrushchev: 'In the volume of industrial output, the Soviet Union has overtaken and outstripped all the capitalist countries except the U.S.A.'[41] The Seven-Year Plan of 1959–65 was presented as a competition between the leading representatives of East and West, with the result a foregone conclusion: 'In 1965, the U.S.S.R. will reach the present United States level for industrial output as a whole'[42]; but this promise was illusory.

To arrive at an independent assessment of the prospects in this 'race' it is necessary to be furnished with reliable and comparable data. Not everyone is satisfied with Soviet statistics, with their reliability or consistency; yields are often more revealing than are mere output achievements. It is necessary to know both input and output in order to determine efficiency. Nove has pointed out some of the dangers in comparisons made by the Soviets themselves. (In this case he is thinking of a superficial resemblance that might be seen between conditions in the Soviet Union and reality in some of the Afro-Asian States): 'part of the "magic" of the Soviet example also lies in the acceptance of official Soviet growth-rate statistics which, were they really correct, would indeed be evidence of magic. . . . Of course, rapid industrialization of the U.S.S.R. is a fact. But, properly deflated, the figures compare reasonably with Japan'.[43]

There is no doubt that growth-rates, when insecurely based, are bad foundations on which to judge situations. Soviet officials are fond of comparing prevailing conditions with those that obtained before the Revolution. The base figure is normally that for 1913,

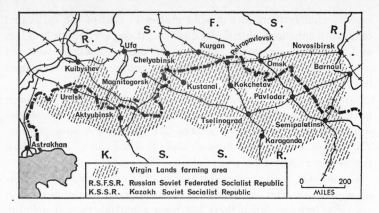

FIG. 16.5   The Virgin Lands

The Virgin Lands scheme has proved extremely costly in low-rainfall years.

although occasionally 1917 is taken. To use the latter[44] is rather like accepting the production of the disaster year 1945 as a basis from which to judge post-war achievement of German industry. The arbitrary 'benchmarks' chosen for purposes of comparison are often those of 1928, the year when the succession of Five-Year Plans was inaugurated, 1940 (the last year of 'normality'), and the years that mark the beginning and end of Plans. It is, perhaps, comforting to read from an authoritative American source — and after stating the uncertainties of assessment and prediction — 'When all is said, Soviet data, with their many faults, do provide a basis for assessing Soviet industrial performance and growth, if carefully used and interpreted'.[45] A cautionary note having been introduced, we can accept that striking, even sensational, advances have been made in some sectors of the Soviet economy.

Soviet agriculture remains something of a liability. In 1954–56, 88 million acres of virgin and long-fallow lands in the climatically marginal regions of Kazakhstan, West Siberia, and the Lower Volga (Fig. 16.5) were brought under the plough; but there has not been a commensurate increase in production. One hazard in such environments has been described by Uvarov: 'The first ploughing of virgin grassland results in immediate reconstruction of its fauna; many species, including beneficial ones, are eliminated, but a few

Set-backs in Agriculture

237

rapidly change their diet of wild grasses to that of the cultivated
ones, with enhanced nutritional qualities; their populations build up
and a plague develops'. The Soviet programmes encountered
'severe set-backs through devastations caused by hitherto innocuous
insect species'.[46]

Grain output in the U.S.S.R. was less, in 1961, than it had been
in 1958. 1963 was a year of major disaster and 1965 also (Fig. 16.6a)
was marked by more crop failures but 1966 was a bumper year.
The Soviet Union, in a normal year, produces more wheat than
Anglo-America and less coarse grains (Fig. 16.6b).

Communist States generally have had scant success with gran-
diose plans for land development. China suffered continual crisis in
1960–62, but since then there has been a partial, though definite,
recovery. Climate is a hazard in China, as it is in the Soviet Union,
against which there can be no national insurance except the maintenance of a stock of hard currency to finance emergency imports
of grain. The net result of ploughing the marginal dry-farming
areas of Kazakhstan has been to increase national output, but to
decrease overall yields.

Agricultural Progress in the U.S.S.R. and the U.S.A.

Compared with pre-war conditions, there has been a very big
decrease in rye acreage in Russia. In 1960–61 there was only 63 per
cent of the 1934–38 acreage under rye. Wheat showed a huge
increase with the ploughing of the virgin lands, but there has lately
been a comparative decline. Oats has decreased but barley and
maize have been encouraged.

In the U.S.A. we find that the area under the five prime cereals
— wheat, rye, barley, oats, and maize — in 1934–38 was 197
million acres; in 1960–61 this had shrunk to 174 million. Total
American production of these cereals, in 1934–38, was 92,000
thousand metric tons; in 1960–61, 173,000.

In the U.S.S.R., taking the same five cereals, the area sown in
1934–38 was 251 million acres; in 1960–61, 278 million. Soviet
production in 1934–38 was 98,500 thousand metric tons; in 1960–61
it had grown to 126,900 thousand.

Overall yields in the U.S.A. increased dramatically during this
period, chiefly because of the great success of maize, output of which
had more than doubled by 1961, and that from a decreased acreage.
This was a phenomenal achievement, the more so because it came
from a farm population a quarter less than the peak post-war year

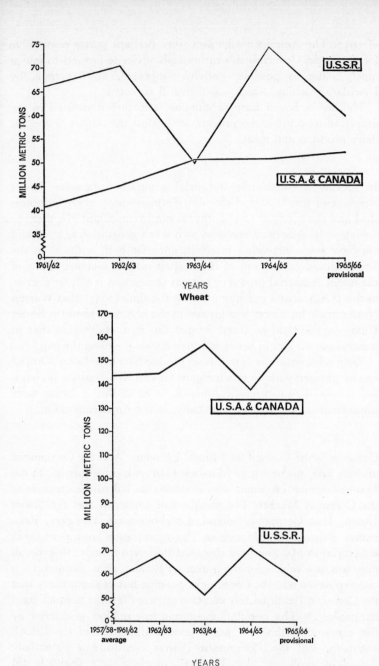

Agricultural
Progress in
the U.S.S.R.
and the U.S.A.

Wheat

MILLION METRIC TONS

U.S.S.R.

U.S.A. & CANADA

YEARS

1961/62 1962/63 1963/64 1964/65 1965/66 provisional

Coarse Grains

MILLION METRIC TONS

U.S.A. & CANADA

U.S.S.R.

YEARS

1957/58-1961/62 average 1962/63 1963/64 1964/65 1965/66 provisional

FIG. 16.6 Food grains — Soviet and U.S./Canadian
shares of world production

Wheat production is normally higher in the Soviet Union than in
Anglo-America. Maize output has languished and Siberian gold
has had to be sold to pay for Canadian supplies.

of 1947. The American advances were perhaps partly responsible
for the Soviet Government's rather rash advice to farmers to sow as
much maize as possible — advice supported, at that time, by
Lysenko's teaching, which was then still accepted.

The lag in Soviet farm production is further illustrated in the
graphs of total industrial growth, set against the output figures for
dairy products and meat.

Industrial Comparisons with the West

In seeking a worthwhile industrial comparison between Soviet
Russia and the U.S.A., Cole and German chose as their indices
steel and electricity.[47] Coal output is not so important in either the
Soviet or the American economy as it was a generation ago: oil and
gas have been increasing in significance for both nations. In the
Soviet Union gas has one of the steepest rates of increase of any of
the major industrial products, but gas production is still far greater
in the U.S.A. Total energy output at the time (1955) that Warren
Nutter made his survey was greater in the U.S.A. than in the Soviet
Union in the ratio of about 8 : 3.[48] But it is undeniable that in
mineral output and in heavy industry Russia is closing the gap.

Yield is important in agriculture; productivity in industry. Output
can be pursued without much regard for cost. It is feasible, perhaps,
for Russia to out-produce America, even if this is being done
unprofessionally and uneconomically, as the Americans claim.

The Soviet Union and Comecon

Comecon is the Council for Mutual Economic Aid: the Communist
answer, first, to America's Marshall Plan and, subsequently, to the
Franco-German economic *rapprochement* that led to the creation of
the Common Market. The members of Comecon are: the Soviet
Union, East Germany, Poland, Czechoslovakia, Hungary, Roumania, Bulgaria, and Mongolia. The organization has a permanent
secretariat in Moscow. It is supposed that such a body, in general,
must act as a vehicle for the pursuit of Russian aims. Comecon is a
concern devoted to the Communist policies, but 'it seems likely that
the Comecon Headquarters and Council are the scene of much hard
bargaining'.[49] The population — some 325 million — covered by
this economic alliance is much greater than that of the E.E.C.
countries, and the Communist Powers constitute a potentially
formidable economic bloc. However, much of their wealth is still
very little realized. Comecon seeks to further joint development by

means of a division of labour among the member States, especially in all branches of engineering, in the growth industries that are familiar to the West, such as plastics and artificial and synthetic fibres, and in certain branches of the chemical industry, including synthetic rubber.[50] A sensitive point of the Eastern economies was stressed by the emergency imports of grain from North America in the autumn of 1963. At the same time great amounts of wealth have been expended — perhaps squandered — in the search for increased production and productivity. By itself, the expenditure of capital through increased purchases of fertilizer and machines may prove to be disappointing: inputs may rise 'without corresponding rises in outputs'.[51]

Industrial production has advanced in Eastern Europe. The combined steel output of the buffer States is about equal to that of the United Kingdom. All of them have made substantial development plans on the Soviet model. Poland produced 9 million tons of steel in 1965 — about the same amount as Belgium; Czechoslovakia, almost as much. Poland is one of the leading world coal producers, her output being about one quarter that of the United States.

Recent political developments in the Soviet Union have been paralleled by changes in the relationship between Soviet Russia and the other East European Communist countries. It has been claimed that Roumania, in particular, has frustrated the original Comecon objectives: her 'refusal to play the role of primary producer undermined Comecon's first attempts to integrate and rationalize the Eastern European economies'. And again: 'Roumania is determined to develop her own resources, regardless of costs'.[52] But the positive, and developing, links between the Communist countries remain, although the ideological conflict between Soviet Russia and Communist China is still unresolved.

There has been a steady increase in trade between the Comecon countries and the West, and in the traffic between Britain and the Communist Powers, including China (the Americans are still opposed to a significant increase in trade with the Communist Chinese). Soviet exports to the U.K. in 1964 stood at £90 million. British exports to the Soviet Union in the same year were worth £40 million. However, foreign trade is still relatively unimportant to the Soviet Union, representing only about 3 per cent of the

I H.G.P.

country's gross national product. This is about the same percentage as Britain's trade with Communist Europe represents, expressed as a percentage of her total foreign trade.[53]

There has been some indication that Washington has reconsidered its attitude towards trade with at least a major part of the Communist East. Since the beginning of the Cold War, there has been a ban upon the export of strategic commodities to the Soviet Union, to the smaller Communist Powers, and to China. The suggestion now is that consumer goods might be offered on a big scale to the large markets in Eastern Europe. Even with strategic goods, there might be some room for manœuvre: as has been pointed out, the term 'strategic' is open to wide interpretation.[54] One big new factor introduced into the situation since 1963 has been the massive shipments of wheat permitted by the U.S.A. Policy changes regarding the disposal of American food surpluses have to be passed by relevant committees of the U.S. Senate, as well as by the Administration. There are political as well as economic reactions to be considered. In any such move, the interests of the farming states of the Middle West have to be borne in mind.

In any sort of relationship between Western Europe and the Communists, political considerations are also important. Opposition by Federal Germany, as well as by the U.S.A., combined to frustrate plans to sell British-made steel pipes to the Soviet oil industry. Italy, on the other hand, partly through the State-controlled Ente Nazionale Idrocarburi (E.N.I.) Corporation, has greatly extended her trade with the U.S.S.R., of which a big element has been the import of Russian oil. A trade agreement with Russia was signed in 1963 by which Italy was to purchase around 45 million tons of crude oil, over a period of six years. This was to be the national figure of imports by Italy. E.N.I.'s separate agreement with the Soviet Union, reached as part of the general contract, included the purchase of 25 million tons of oil by the Corporation.

The Soviet rulers may find that, in order to meet the same crisis demand for certain imports — for instance, food grains — they will again, as in 1963–64, have to export a sizeable part of their gold production. It has been suggested that the reason why Soviet gold is not more readily available to finance normal trade abroad, is that the Siberian gold industry is uneconomic by comparison with the West. Figures have been suggested that give the Soviet worker a productivity only one-fifth that of his American counterpart; and this is coupled with a cost of production at least five times greater

242

than the Western average. Nevertheless, Soviet gold sales to the West increased sharply after 1955, and reached a total of over $1,500 million during the five years, 1960–64.[55]

The pattern of Soviet foreign trade has not been fixed for all time. Its comparative unimportance at present may be a clue to the dimensions of the changes that can occur. Very large increases in Soviet trade, carried by a rapidly expanding Soviet mercantile marine, are promised with the underdeveloped countries.

NOTES

1. N. A. Voznesensky [Chairman of the State Planning Commission of the U.S.S.R.], *Five-Year Plan for the Rehabilitation and Development of the National Economy of the U.S.S.R., 1946–50* (Soviet News, 1946), p. 37.

2. 'Soviet Economic Re-organisation', *Financial Times*, 20 Nov. 1962.

3. *Keesing's Contemporary Archives*, 19223A, 2–9 Feb. 1963.

4. Michael Connock, *Financial Times*, 4 Oct. 1965.

5. *The Times*, 20 Nov. 1964.

6. P. Alampiev, *Economic Areas in the U.S.S.R.*, trans. L. Lempert (Progress Publ., Moscow, 1964), pp. 38–44.

7. Roy E. H. Mellor, *A Geography of the U.S.S.R.* (Macmillan, 1964), p. xiv.

8. N. Mikhailov, *Soviet Geography*, 2nd ed. (Methuen, 1937), p. 61.

9. Hodgkins, *Soviet Power: Energy, Resources, Production and Potentials*, p. 165.

10. Ibid., p. 9.

11. Given in Hubbert, *Energy Resources*, pp. 37, 46.

12. G. S. Hume, in *Financial Times* supplement on 'World Energy', 24 Sept. 1962.

13. Y. Maksaryov (ed.), *Technical Progress in the U.S.S.R.* (For. Lang. Publ. House, Moscow, 1960), p. 96.

14. Hodgkins op. cit., p. 138.

15. Ibid., p. 145.

16. Hubbert, *Energy Resources*, p. 98.

17. *Pravda*, 3 Feb. 1959, given in *Current Digest of the Soviet Press*, vol. xi, no. 11 (Joint Committee on Slavonic Studies, Washington, D.C., weekly).

18. *Pravda*, 26 Nov. 1959, given in *Current Digest of the Soviet Press*, vol. xi, no. 47.

19. *Guardian*, 27 June 1962.

20. See especially *Financial Times*, 25 Oct. 1962, referring to a contribution by Mr. Lavrenenko to the World Power Conference.

21. 'Soviet Power Shortage a Threat to Development', *The Times*, 17 Aug. 1965.

22. *Financial Times*, 8 Nov. 1962.

23. Ibid.

24. N. N. Baransky, *Economic Geography of the U.S.S.R.* (For. Lang. Publ. House, Moscow, 1956), p. 40.

25. Pounds, *The Geography of Iron and Steel*, p. 152.

26. R. S. Theman, *The Geography of Economic Activity*, p. 475.

27. *Financial Times*, 17 Jan. 1963.

28. *Financial Times*, 19 Oct. 1962.

29. *The World's Railways, 1965–66* (Sampson Low, 1967), p. 249.

30. J. P. Cole and F. C. German, *A Geography of the U.S.S.R.* (Butterworth, 1961), p. 1, provide a separate figure for freight carried by river: 1955–56, 8 per cent; 1958–59, 3 per cent.

31. Ernest W. Williams, Jr., *Freight Transportation in the Soviet Union* (Princeton U.P., 1962), p. 1.

32. Ibid., pp. 70–71.

33. Ibid., pp. 84–85.

34. Ibid., p. 5.

35. Ibid.

36. *Jane's World Railways, 1965–66*.

37. Cole and German, *A Geography of the U.S.S.R.*, p. 66.

38. *Jane's World Railways, 1965–66*.

39. Ibid.

40. Ibid.

41. N. S. Khrushchev, *The Way to Further Economic Progress* (For. Lang. Publ. House, Moscow, 1959), p. 46.

42. *Soviet Handbook, 1959–65: Statistics and Data Relating to the Soviet Seven-Year Plan* (Soviet Booklet, no. 57, London, 1959).

43. A. Nove, *The Soviet Economy: An Introduction* (Allen & Unwin, 1961), p. 305.

44. As in *Soviet Handbook, 1959–65*, Table 3.

45. G. Warren Nutter, *Growth of Industrial Production in the Soviet Union* (Princeton U.P., 1962), p. 13.

46. Sir B. Uvarov, 'The Insect Threat to Developing Countries', *New Scientist*, no. 403 (6 Aug. 1964).

47. Cole and German, *A Geography of the U.S.S.R.*, p. 263.

48. Nutter, *Growth of Industrial Production in the Soviet Union*, pp. 373–5.

49. *Financial Times*, 10 Aug. 1962.

50. *Financial Times*, 23 Aug. 1962.

51. *The Times*, 7 Nov. 1963.

52. *The Times*, 20 July 1965.

53. M. H. Fisher, 'Trade through the Iron Curtain', *Steel Review*, no. 18 (B.I.S.F., April 1960).

54. *The Guardian*, 23 Sept. 1963.

55. *The Times*, 31 Aug. 1965, quoted International Monetary Fund estimates.

India – Problems of Food Supply Chapter 17

Food is only one of a number of indices to living standards, but in underdeveloped economies it is the most important. The food situation must be considered precarious in a country like India, where the mass of the people have never been adequately fed. Income is desperately low for millions who are always hungry and often near starvation. Industry is important, especially as a token of what might be, but it has so far made little impression on living standards.

Food Production

The greatest concentration of population in the world is to be found in Asia, east of 67° E. longitude and south of 40° N. latitude. In China alone there live more than a fifth of the human race. The main food of all these people is rice; what happens to the acreage under rice and its productivity is therefore of vast importance to all mankind, because, should famine strike Asia, the results cannot now be expected to be confined to that continent.

Considerable stocks have to be held against the danger of shortages due to climatic difficulties. Periods of drought may be succeeded by flood, and governments hold reserves sufficient, it is hoped, to cope with the worst crisis. Such supplies are likely to be heavily taxed during drought.

The greater part of production in the poorer countries is not marketed at all, but consumed by the farmer and his family; it is production for subsistence. The estimated percentages kept by Indian farmers for their own use are: wheat, 63; rice, 69; maize, 76; and millets and sorghums, 74–81 per cent.[1] Contrast this with the position in Britain, where no more than 1 per cent of total agricultural output comes under the heading of subsistence production.[2]

Recurring crisis is inevitable in a situation where population is increasing at an accelerating rate. In 1965 it was claimed that Indian food production had overtaken the rise in population,[3] but this was not borne out by British[4] and other sources and was belied by the crisis of 1966. It is not contested that food imports have risen steeply in recent years.

The area under rice has continued to increase, so that now, as in the past, there is more land under this crop in India than in any other country in the world. But it is estimated that the Chinese had an approximately equal acreage in the 'good years' of 1957–58 and 1958–59.

Area under Rice — India and China[5]
('ooo acres)

	Average 1951–52 to 1955–56	1959–60	1960–61	1961–62	1962–63	1963–64
India	75,800	83,573	84,333	85,731	86,325	88,026
China (estimated)	69,400	73,000	77,000	75,000	76,000	77,000

Indian production has also moved ahead, but because of the paltry yields output is smaller than in China. The Japanese produce over a third as much rice as the Indians from less than a tenth of the acreage.

Production of Rice — India and China[6]
('ooo tons; milled rice equivalent)

	Average 1951–52 to 1955–56	1959–60	1960–61	1961–62	1962–63	1963–64
India	25,972	31,187	34,028	35,100	31,410	36,306
China[7]	45,400	52,000	50,000	52,000	53,000	51,000

Inside India, there is a very wide difference in the accomplishments of the growers in the various states, the yields of the leading rice states varying between 400 and 1,000 lb. to the acre. The biggest producers are[8] in the Ganges Valley (Fig. 17.1).

The Soviet Russian and Chinese Communist organizers of production set targets for achievement; the Indians, also, have their National Plan. Individual peasants in the Indian subcontinent have,

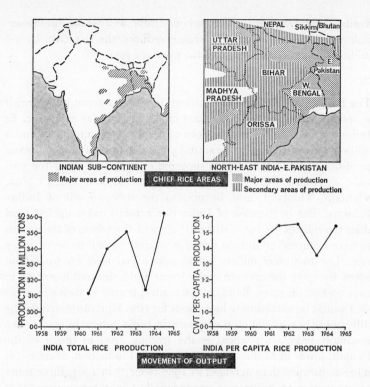

FIG. 17.1 Rice production in India
Total production has increased but has failed to improve the
food situation for a rapidly rising population. Failure of the
monsoon can soon produce famine conditions.

presumably, a simpler target — survival from one year to the next.
In the famine tracts of southern India, lying in the lee of the Western
Ghats, 'average rainfall' figures hold an academic interest for the
geographer. The farmer is more concerned with reliability, in a
zone where precipitation variability can be as high as 32 per cent:
this for a station — Bellary — where the annual average fall is no
more than 19·46 inches.[9]

In Uttar Pradesh State, a break in the rainfall early in the month
of August, when the rice crop is due to be transplanted, means that
precious days of growth are lost — for good. If the rains stop in
September, as may happen to the monsoon in a capricious year,
'the crop is almost wholly lost, for the available supply of water in
ponds is used up for irrigation in September and no supply is

available for October.'[10] Throughout India, as a whole, 'unfavourable weather' in the 1962–63 season reduced the rice crop by 2·8
million tons, as compared with the previous year.

Other Food Crops

The South-East Asian food problem does not concern only rice; it
is necessary to consider other food crops, in India as elsewhere. In
Indonesia in 1960, 11 million tons of cassava were produced and 2
million tons of maize, as against 13 million tons of rice. Climatic
conditions ensure that rice is supreme over the whole of the vast
zone extending from Japan, through central and south China,
Vietnam, Thailand, and Burma, to the subcontinent of India–
Pakistan. But in the case of India rice actually takes up less land
than the millets. In 1950, Russell[11] showed the whole of the millets
to have occupied 78 million acres, as against 75 million acres under
rice. The two chief millets, jowar and bajra, took up 59 million
acres. By 1963, the acreage under jowar and bajra had increased to
over 70 million acres. Bajra, in particular, is able to thrive in areas
that would be exceedingly hazardous for rice. Kuriyan[12] stresses the
differences in regional crop emphasis in India, where in places 'rice
is almost unknown': wheat is the leading crop in much of the
Punjab; jowar in Maharashtra (Fig. 17.2). Production, of course, is
more significant than acreage; in 1950 twice,[13] in 1964, three times
as much rice as millet was produced; but in the two years that
followed, failure of the monsoon brought general disaster to parts
of northern India.

Where people are living near to, and often below, the subsistence
level, the price of food is all-important. In most of India millet is
the cheapest cereal, and it is from cereals that the choice has to be
made, representing, as they do, 'for a very large part of the population . . . the sole intake of food'.[14] Marketable rice may be sold in
order to buy larger quantities of other foods for consumption.
China, in 1964, sold abroad an estimated 720,000 tons of rice, in
order to import cheaper wheat.[15]

Soil Improvement

Measures to raise productivity may involve large-scale irrigation
and, perhaps still more urgently, drainage projects. The results of
the application of modern aids to farming are seen in the rice-
growing regions of Japan, where the intensity of input of the major
fertilizers is a hundred or more times greater than in India and

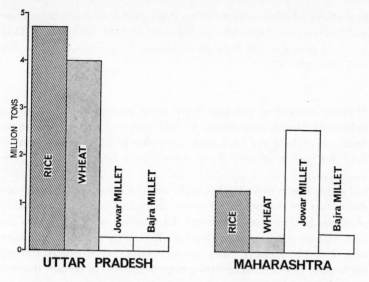

FIG. 17.2   India — regional bias in food production

Rice is the chief food grain of most of south-east Asia, but millet is more important in much of India, especially to the poorest people.

yields are the highest in Asia. In many of the arid regions and much of India, even animal manure is not always available to stimulate plant growth. Thus dung may well be used for fuel, where wood is scarce and expensive and other heating materials are beyond reach. In China, on the other hand, there has been a long tradition of the ruthless application of all manures, including human night-soil, to the land. Yields in China are noticeably better than in India–Pakistan; but it is not always feasible to apply fertilizers heavily, since, in the interests of efficiency and safety, they should be conveyed to plants in solution.

Soil conditions are of enormous local significance in the fight for greater productivity. Arakeri[16] points to the problems arising from the widespread laterite soils of Bombay and West Bengal, where fertility is high for the first three or four years, but exhaustion is likely to follow. If fertilizers are then available, they can make a decisive difference to performance. There is a comprehensive survey of soil conditions in Dobby's *Southeast Asia*.[17] Fertilizers and soil surveys require more capital than the peasant proprietor possesses. He lacks the machinery applicable to terrace conditions and the pesticides and selective weedkillers that could do so much to increase yields. However, herbicides and sprays, like the American STAM F-34, do exist that are capable of ridding the paddies of jungle rice and other weeds.[18]

Farming Methods

Shifting cultivation practices have been blamed for some of the failures of Asiatic agriculture. Arakeri writes of primitive tribes, in India, scratching the land with a wooden plough, 'which may or may not have a wooden share', who till the land for two or three years, content with a wretched yield, and then move on to another hill slope, where more land is exploited and exhausted.[19] Such conditions are, of course, by no means as typical of India as of other countries further east — Sarawak, for instance, where Polomka has said that six times as much land is affected by shifting cultivation as is settled by farmers.[20] But one must note that, to others, shifting cultivation has been acceptable, even desirable, in certain tropical conditions.[21]

Land Tenure

Feudal or semi-feudal systems of land tenure, rather than mere physical disabilities, may often lie at the root of agricultural stagnation and distress. Antiquated farm organization may, of course, be accompanied by appalling failure to apply mechanized solutions. This certainly applies where, according to the National Sample Survey taken during the period 1955–57, 'in about 97 per cent of the villages, tilling was done with the help of animals. Only 0·4 to 0·9 per cent of the villages had [a] power-driven system'.[22]

The main obstacle, apart from poverty, that prevents the use of new machines, is the fragmentation of holdings. Vera Anstey has stated the problem that consolidation poses in a free society: 'if this entails an increase in the size of many holdings, many cultivators will lose their holdings'.[23] In eastern Uttar Pradesh, Shafi[24] reports, there is less than half an acre of land cropped, per head of population, in either the summer or the winter growing-season. A fifth of an acre of land, per head of population, is *double cropped* — it produces in both seasons. Russell[25] speaks of East Pakistan, where more than half of the farms are of less than three acres; Khusro, of the state of affairs at independence, in 1947, when one-third of Indian farms were of less than $2\frac{1}{2}$ acres, and even these were commonly divided into three fragments in Uttar Pradesh and Bengal.[26] The

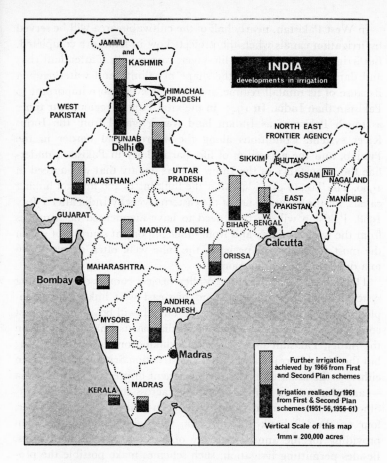

FIG. 17.3   India — developments in irrigation

Irrigation is of critical importance in maintaining production,
especially in the Ganges valley and in eastern India.

land reform that was to create viable farms out of such small plots
had ended 'in fiasco'.[27]

The biggest factor in food production in southern Asia, as in any
rice environment, is the availability of copious supplies of water.
India's target for her Third Plan (1961–66) was to put 90 million
acres under irrigation and so 'to cover about 50 per cent of the land
which is believed to be irrigable'[28] (Fig. 17.3).

Irrigation

India —
Problems of
Food Supply

In West Pakistan, nearly half of the cultivable area will be served by irrigation canals when the projects now in hand are completed. But irrigation, the potential life-saver, carries with it attendant risks and dangers, especially in the shape of salinity and waterlogging. Because of its rainfall regime, irrigation is even more important to Pakistan than India. In 1947, in the vital Punjab region, four times as much Pakistani as Indian land was irrigated from the Indus River system. Conditions along the international border in the Punjab, and the necessities of life, particularly in Pakistan, underline the importance of the Indus Waters Treaty that was agreed in 1960. The Treaty provides, after the building of 460 miles of linking canals, for the exclusive use of the eastern rivers by India after 1 July 1968. Pakistan will by then need to have augmented her supplies from the western rivers and from other important sources, of which the most significant is, perhaps, the tube well, often driven down to a depth of 250 feet or more.

The link canals of the Indus Valley project comprise an imposing system with five north–south and two east–west links. After completion, the irrigation network of the Punjab will be among the best co-ordinated schemes in existence. India has its Bhakra scheme on the Sutlej, Pakistan its Warsak undertaking on the Kabul River; but the Lloyd Barrage and Canal Construction Scheme is older than either — the main dam is an achievement of pre-war British India — and depends on a mighty barrage across the Indus at Sukkur. Since then, seven main canals have been built out from the river, four on the left bank and three on the right, the complete plan providing for the annual delivery of water to 5·45 million acres. Besides permitting irrigation, such schemes make possible the provision of desperately needed power.

Foreign Aid

Non-Communist and Communist countries alike have not been slow to come to the aid of the underdeveloped regions. Pakistan, for instance, is said to have received £1,500 million worth of help from the United States up to the end of 1965. The Colombo Plan — in full, the 'Colombo Plan for Co-operative Economic Development in South and South-East Asia' — came into force in 1951, being intended 'to provide the framework for the development programmes of the Asian member countries' until 1957. Later extensions carried this date forward to 1966. Members of the Colombo Plan Consultative Committee include the present British Dominions and former colonies of the South-East Asia region, as well as the U.K., Canada, Australia, and New Zealand, Indonesia, Vietnam, Cambodia, Laos, Japan, the Philippines, and Thailand. The United States attends meetings as a full member.

The body within the U.S. Department of State responsible for the administration of the economic assistance programmes of the American Government is the Agency for International Development (A.I.D.).

There has been a steady increase in the volume of British overseas aid; the most spectacular product of this aid is the steelworks erected at Durgapur, in West Bengal, built by a consortium of thirteen British steel and engineering companies. Loans have been made by the British Government and by British banks and the Indians have also drawn on our general-purpose aid. Besides this monetary aid, there has been indirect financial assistance: Indian engineers have been trained here, and British engineers have gone out to help with construction and operation.[29]

The industrial achievements of India are real and impressive, but their contribution to living standards has been small in relation to total needs. The nature of the industrial problem can be stated in terms of energy, by the per capita consumption per annum of fuel and power, expressed in coal equivalent: India had by 1960 attained a figure of a mere 0·15 tons. Contrast this with the position of Japan, which had achieved 1·40 tons by that date. India's Third Plan (1961–66) provided for a 70 per cent increase in overall industrial production, but the Indian Government's Planning Commission has itself cautioned: 'It must be recognized that Indian industry, considerable as it is, is still too small to make a real impact on the living standards and employment of the mass of the people, or radically alter the structure of the economy'.[30] Only a tenth of India's national income comes from industry; the figure for Japan is one-third. Even spectacular projects, such as the nuclear power station being built at Tarapur, can make little difference to the overall picture.

The position of Pakistan is of a country even less developed than India. Countries such as these may be tempted by the attractions of over-ambitious industrial programmes; but the Chinese, having decided to divert decisive amounts of capital to heavy industry, especially to metallurgy, have had to re-think their national economic policy in the face of agricultural crisis. Pakistani development projects include steel mills, but they are small by world standards. The Rawalpindi Government has recognized that overall economic solutions must depend upon the successful development of agricultural resources. This is emphasized in Pakistan's Second Five-Year Plan: agricultural development 'in the past years was overshadowed by an almost exclusive attention paid to the improvement of the industrial sector of the economy'.[31]

There is now a general recognition that the essential economic problem is how to improve native food supplies, in circumstances where production has deteriorated, rather than improved, since the pre-war years. The magnitude of India's crisis can be appreciated from the size of the aid that has had to be furnished to avert starvation.

NOTES

1. K. C. Abercrombie, 'Subsistence Production and Economic Development', F.A.O., *Monthly Bulletin of Agricultural Economics and Statistics*, vol. 14, no. 5 (May 1965), p. 3.

2. Ibid.

3. A. M. Khusro, 'Success and Failure in a Grand Design', *The Times* supplement on 'India', 14 Aug. 1965.

4. Barclays Bank Economic Intelligence Dept. report on 'India', 5 Aug. 1965: 'the production of cereals has failed to keep pace with the expanding population'.

5. Commonwealth Economic Committee, *Grain Crops*, p. 134.

6. Ibid., pp. 136–7.

7. Estimated.

8. H. R. Arakeri *et al.*, *Soil Management in India* (Asia Publ. House, 1958), p. 264.

9. K. Sita, 'Dry Farming in Peninsular India', *Indian Geographical Journal*, vol. xxxv, nos. 1–2 (Jan.–March and April–June, 1960), p. 23.

10. M. Shafi, *Land Utilization in Eastern Uttar Pradesh* (Muslim Univ. Press, Aligarh, 1961), p. 63.

11. Sir J. Russell, *World Population and World Food Supplies* (Allen & Unwin, 1954), p. 324.

12. G. Kuriyan, 'Rice in India', *Indian Geographical Journal*, vol. xx, no. 4 (Oct.–Dec. 1945), p. 158.

13. Russell, op. cit., p. 324.

14. Ibid.

15. 'F.A.O. Meeting on Rice Problems', *Monthly Bulletin of Agricultural Economics and Statistics*, vol. 14, no. 5 (May, 1965), pp. 14–17.

16. Arakeri, *Soil Management in India*, pp. 269, 275.

17. E. H. G. Dobby, *Southeast Asia*, 7th ed. (Univ. of London Press, 1960), pp. 74–84.

18. E. W. French and W. B. Gay, 'Weed Control in Rice Fields', *World Crops*, vol. 15, no. 5 (May 1963), p. 199.

19. Arakeri, *Soil Management in India*, p. 280.

20. Peter Polomka, 'A Nation Based on the Land', *The Times* supplement on 'Malaysia', 16 Sept. 1963.

21. D. R. Stoddart, 'Geography and the Ecological Approach', vol. l, pt. 3, no. 228 (July 1965), p. 248, referring to C. Geertz. See also L. D. Stamp, *Africa: A Study in Tropical Development* (Wiley, 1964), p. 144, quoting Lord Hailey.

22. *India, 1962* (Govt. of India, New Delhi, 1963), p. 172.

23. V. Anstey, 'Land Reform in India', *Journal of Local Administration Overseas*, vol. i, no. 2 (H.M.S.O., April 1962), p. 92.

24. Shafi, *Land Utilization in Eastern Uttar Pradesh*, p. 70.

25. Russell, *World Population and World Food Supplies*, p. 338.

26. A. M. Khusro, *The Times* supplement on 'India', 14 Aug. 1965.

27. Ibid.

28. Indian State Planning Commission, *Towards a Self-Reliant Economy: India's Third Plan, 1961–66* (New Delhi, 1961), p. 197.

29. See White Paper, *Aid to Developing Countries*, Cmnd. 2147 (H.M.S.O., 1963).

30. Indian State Planning Commission, *Towards a Self-Reliant Economy*, p. 215.

31. *Pakistan, 1961–62* (Dept. of Information, Karachi, 1963).

Chapter 18 East and West Africa – Problems and Opportunities

Food Production
Most agriculture in tropical Africa, where so many countries have recently achieved independence (Fig. 18.1), is in the form of native farming, directed, in the main, to food production for local use, despite the fact that by far the greater part of certain world crops — cocoa, palm oil, and sisal — comes from West and East Africa. (From West Africa, also, comes one-fifth of the world's groundnuts.) But even in the case of the vegetable oils, much production is for local food consumption. There is more variety in food production in tropical Africa than in many of the rice lands of South-East Asia. Rice can be grown with success in this part of Africa, as it can in Egypt, but more important, especially in savanna country, are the alternative cereals, particularly the millets and maize. In all Africa, about twice as much maize as wheat is grown, and three times as much maize as rice. Locally more important than maize over wide areas of central and western Africa are the root crops such as cassava, yams, and sweet potatoes. Cassava is the leading food over much of the Congo basin, as are yams over a huge swathe of territory inland from the Guinea coast, extending from the Ivory Coast to Eastern Nigeria[1] (Fig. 18.2). In Sierra Leone, the chief food crop is rice.

Organization
African farming carries with it a stigma of inefficiency that is largely deserved; but Russell has shown that in one vital respect — the care of the soil — traditional native methods have been remarkably successful in reducing erosion below the levels obtaining elsewhere. Under the old-established African system, crops are grown together on the same land; they are not separated into specialized plots. Since the various harvests occur at different times, some plant growth is always taking place, which serves to protect the soil.

The gap in achievement between richer and poorer countries is due, above all, to the difference in input of capital directed to technological experiment and development. The African lacked the

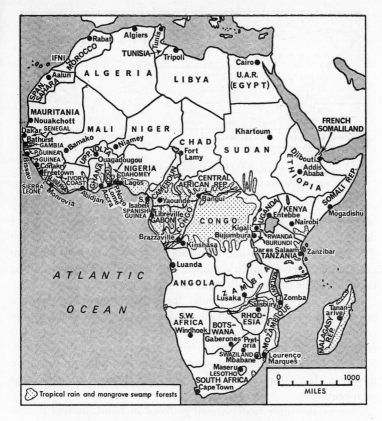

FIG. 18.1 The new Africa

Africa has a large number of states newly independent from colonial rule. In Central Africa the rain forest of the equatorial zone provides conditions often congenial to plantation crops and to economic activities in which European interests may still be important: based on original map by George Philip and Son.

wheel that the Eurasian possessed for longer than written records tell; nor did he have the plough.

Obstacles to Production

There are obstacles to production, lying beyond the realm of physical environment: one of these is the significance of cattle in African, as in Hindu, society; but in Africa the most significant element in animal husbandry is social rather than religious. Russell expresses graphically the role of cattle as a bride-price, where

257

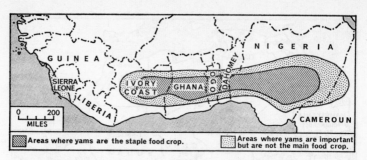

FIG. 18.2   West Africa — yam cultivation

The yam is a mainstay of food production in a large part of
West Africa. (After Coursey.)

'numbers only count, the quality of the animals having no more
significance than the condition of a £1 note, so long as it is intact'.[2]
The position of women in African society is an important factor in
production: they often do as much heavy work as the men, tilling
the fields while the menfolk look after the cattle.

Poverty can prevent, or render ineffective, measures to reduce
crippling disease in plants. One of the most notorious enemies of
production is swollen shoot, carried by the mealy-bug, that affects
cacao; the only complete answer is the destruction of infected trees.
There have been frequent reports of native resistance to dramatic
measures, but strong and determined government can overcome
such obstacles.

Poverty and undernourishment go hand in hand: hunger itself is
the enemy of progress. Vitamin and protein deficiencies are responsible for a fearful mortality, especially among children, for
premature death among adults, and for a drastic reduction of
efficiency. One of the most grievous ailments is kwashiorkor, a
protein deficiency that has decimated the child population of areas
such as the eastern Congo. Hunger and its accompanying weakness
reduce resistance to disease, which is not confined to the illiterate
or the uncivilized elements of the population. Insect carriers — the
tsetse fly and the mosquito — are no respecters of persons. But the
poorer, the more ignorant or superstitious a people, the more likely
are they to lack the wherewithal to combat disaster. The insect
pests can be kept down by spraying: British and German chemists
have been to the fore in the provision of the necessary chemical
weapons, but unfortunately the sprays are too expensive to be
bought by the individual farmer.

In tropical Africa, as in many other poor areas, progress in land use and in the application of soil science is hampered by existing systems of land tenure, the most serious handicap being the fragmentation of holdings; of course, the solution would be consolidation, but to this policy 'in general, the natives strenuously object'.[3]

There are radical answers — in particular, Socialism and Communism — available in other parts of the world. In Ghana, under State Socialism, a large-scale experiment was commenced between 1961 and 1963, with the establishment of nearly one hundred State farms.[4] Administrative solutions can be more simple, perhaps involving merely the recognition of existing holdings where, as in Kenya, 'it became evident that individual Africans, in many areas, had evolved something like full ownership'.[5] Government ownership of much of the land in Uganda was taken to imply that Crown land was 'held in trust for the use and benefit of the African population'.[6] Independence in these African countries has sometimes brought great changes in land ownership: the Kenyan White Highlands Settlement Scheme involved the transference into African hands of about a million acres that were formerly European-run. But, as Elspeth Huxley has pointed out, many of these plots were not the best land, being 'of low potential with a rainfall of 30 inches or less'.[7]

Since the inter-war years, there has been a notable increase in the proportion of land under cash crops, which have become more important both to individual farmers and to governments seeking revenue for development purposes. A choice does not always have to be made between cash and subsistence farming: cotton and groundnuts, for instance, being annuals, can be taken into a systematic farm rotation.[8] The congenial climatic régime in much of tropical Africa has encouraged experiment and interchange. Fibre and beverage plants, as well as foodstuffs, have been introduced from similar climatic environments elsewhere. Sisal is a native of Yucatán, in Central America, but was taken to Florida and from there to East Africa. The tea of Malawi (formerly Nyasaland) originated in China; Ghana's cacao, in Brazil; but both *robusta* coffee and the oil palm are native to West Africa. The drain on foreign exchange has promoted the development of Urena Lobata, a plant native to West Africa, but formerly unimportant there (see above, p. 29): huge quantities of sacking material are needed to move

Cash Crops

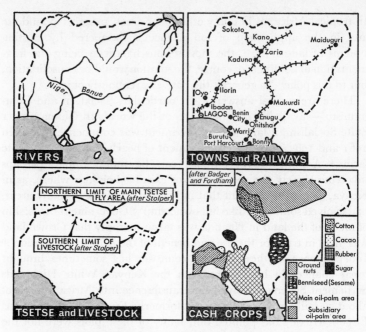

FIG. 18.3   Nigeria — the background to production

Nigeria is a country of very wide regional differences — climatic,
economic and social.

the cocoa crop, and experiment has resulted in the commercial
production of Urena as a substitute for jute.

There have been powerful advocates of novelty in land use:
success, it has been said, 'has been most apparent when related to
the sound establishment of new introductions — coffee, tea, irrigated
rice — and least apparent in efforts to improve subsistence on old-
established practices without reform of land tenure'.[9]

The countries of West Africa vary as to their cash-crop specialization: cacao is supreme in Ghana, whose cocoa exports, which had
been a mere 40 tons in 1896, had risen to 420,000 tons by 1962.
(The previous peak had been in 1936. 311,000 tons had been sold
abroad in that year, after which swollen shoot decimated the crop.)
Nigeria is more versatile, principally because of its greater area
(Fig. 18.3). The rain forest inland from the Niger delta furnishes
very valuable timbers, including mahogany and satinwood. The
climate that encourages this equatorial forest also favours the growth
of the oil palm, cacao, and rubber, just as it is suited to the food

crops rice and cassava. North of the forest, sesame, which the Nigerians call benniseed, is important around Makurdi. In the corresponding region of Western Nigeria, a 15,000-acre sugar estate has been established at Bacita, on the Niger. The north, beyond Kaduna, is the region for cotton; and beyond Zaria, for groundnuts, with an overlap between the Zaria and Kano regions. Many of these plants are not exclusive in their requirements. Some products, notably the oil palm, can furnish both cash and subsistence; and the quality of crops varies greatly from site to site. Nigeria's cocoa tonnage is less than that of Ghana, but quality is appreciably higher: 99 per cent of it is Grade I, 'a higher percentage than that of any other country'.[10] The dangerous condition of *monoculture*, where one crop is overwhelmingly important, is illustrated by the example of Gambia, which is almost entirely dependent for foreign earnings upon groundnut exports. A similar imbalance prevails in the former French territories of Mali, Senegal, and Niger, in the same latitudes.

Tanzania is the world's chief source of sisal, to which about 250,000 acres are devoted. In 1963, 214,000 tons of sisal was exported, nearly four times as much as came from Kenya, production being centred in the area between the coast and the Central Plateau; and Tanzania is the second East African producer of cotton. From Zanzibar and Pemba come most of the world's cloves, to which over 60,000 acres are devoted. In much of East Africa, in contrast to the West, large segments of commercial life are controlled by immigrant, often non-African, people; immigrants have also supplied the capital and management for farms and estates. Many of the sisal plantations are owned by Britons, Indians, or Greeks; most of the large clove properties by Arabs or Indians. In Zanzibar, the coconut industry is also important. The large cotton crop of Uganda, worth nearly £15 million in 1960, is cultivated by Africans working smallholdings, some as little as three acres. But the cotton ginneries are Indian-owned, as are the two largest sugar estates in Uganda. Coffee balances the cash-crop picture in Uganda, and it produces about an equal amount of revenue. *Robusta* coffee is grown in Buganda Province, and *arabica* in Bugisu. By far the most important cash crop in Kenya is coffee, which is worth more than the next two most valuable products — tea and sisal — combined. Most Kenya coffee comes from European-owned plantations. These are chiefly to be found to the north and east of Nairobi and in the Rift Valley. African production is becoming more significant, as for instance in the Meru district, to the north-east of Mt. Kenya. The African crop, processed and marketed largely through co-operatives, now accounts for almost one-third of the total national output; but the contrast in productivity is shown by the figures for the 1962–63 season: European estates provided 22,000 tons from 70,000 acres; African growers 10,000 tons from 63,000 acres, mainly in the form of smallholdings. In 1960, only a tenth of Kenya's tea acreage belonged to Africans; this rose to 23 per cent by 1964. Sisal is important in the drier areas. As much land is under sisal in Kenya as in Tanzania, but the yield is far less. Kenya's pyrethrum, used for insecticides, is grown by some 1,100 Europeans and over 26,000 Africans (most of them in co-operatives). Pyrethrum sales abroad realize over £2 million; wattlebark and bark extract about £1 million. By 1965 the measures of reorganization begun at independence had resulted in the division of 900,000 acres of large-scale former European farms, which became African subsistence holdings. The break-up was partly responsible — though drought was a major factor — for the serious fall in cash-crop production, particularly of maize.

Animal Husbandry

Among the African tribes of the savanna, animals are a vital part of economic life. It is in these areas of fluctuating rainfall that there exist special local factors, often dependent upon tradition and tribal custom, often resistant to change, that affect critically the agricultural prospects of the new nations.

In Nigeria, with its population of about 55 million people, animals are confined mainly to the north and the numbers are uncertain, but the national totals are thought to be about 6 million cattle, 3 million sheep, and 11 million goats. Some sources say there are as many as 20 million sheep and goats. The natural control over animal husbandry in the centre and south is provided by the tsetse fly, which induces sleeping sickness in cattle, and is kept at bay even in the north only by a massive programme of injections.

Russell estimated that one-quarter of the available land in Africa was so heavily infested with tsetse that 'all domestic animals, except poultry, are completely excluded'.[11] In Guinea, a breed of cattle, the Ndama, has been found that resists the tsetse.[12] But on the other side of Africa the pest completely precludes the rearing of cattle 'from the wetter regions of dense bush and forest'.[13] In Uganda, the areas of most serious infestation are located in a belt about fifty miles wide

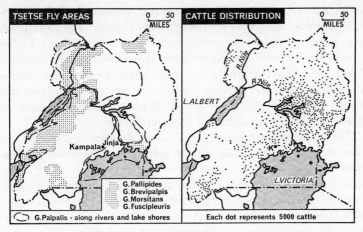

FIG. 18.4 Uganda — cattle distribution and tsetse-fly areas

Uganda shows the connection between cattle rearing and freedom from tsetse. (After K. C. Edwards and *Atlas of Uganda*.)

(Fig. 18.4), extending down the western side of the country. Here there are almost no cattle to be found, while in the whole of the country there are about $3\frac{1}{4}$ million head. Edwards has described the measures taken in Uganda to assist the native farmer in the clearance of tsetse-infested land, and the limited success achieved.[14]

Many of Kenya's cattle exist in climatically marginal semi-arid country. In 1961 a year-long drought was broken by excessive rainfall in the autumn, when the months of September, October, and November brought a normal year's rainfall in many places, and flooding caused disastrous losses of animals and crops. Disease is known and predictable. What often seems worse is the damage caused by ignorance and short-sighted greed. There is a striking passage in the Report of Kenya's Director of Agriculture for 1961, referring to the Southern Province: 'Grazing schemes completely broke down during the year due to gross over-stocking and the non-payment of fees. The last vestige of grazing control broke down in February . . . since when hordes of cattle have been grazing illegally'.[15]

Industrially, East and West Africa are regions of potential, rather than actual, achievement. Production of electricity, for instance, is very small compared with that of the European or other **Industry** industrialized countries. Ghana's electricity output in 1963 was 470 million kWh: this was 1/330 the figure for Britain. (The corresponding populations in that year were: Ghana, 7 million; United Kingdom, 53·8 million.) There is mineral wealth in both East and West Africa, particularly in the West; but in the East one-third of the value of mineral exports is accounted for by the product of a single great installation — the Williamson diamond mine at Mwadui, the biggest diamond 'pipe' in the world.

There is some petroleum production in the west: 3·8 million tons of crude, in 1963, from Nigeria; 0·9 million from the newly independent Gabon. Nigeria is a major producer of tin: fifth in the world, in 1963, with 8,868 tons. (Tanzania produced a mere 252 tons in that year.) Ghana is important for manganese, but her output is only about one-third of South Africa's, and one-twelfth of the Soviet Union's. Nevertheless, manganese, gold, and diamonds together bring in a quarter of Ghana's revenue from exports. Two-thirds of the value of Sierra Leone's exports come from diamonds and iron ore.

Diamonds accounted for 57 per cent of Sierra Leone's total exports during the period 1960–62, production having increased remarkably since 1955. Though much of the output is highly mechanized, some is still hand-dug by individual Africans who treat mining as an ancillary occupation to cash-crop or subsistence farming.[16] Total figures of diamond production in West Africa can be only conjectural, because of the vast scale of illicit digging and smuggling.

The relatively small achievements of East and West Africa in mineral production may be dwarfed in the near future. There are considerable riches of iron and copper on the edge of the Sahara, and impressive prospects for the development of hydro-electric power nearer to the coast. Ghana has its own 'Aswan Dam' — the Volta River project, opened in 1966, which will produce 768 MW of electricity, making possible the utilization of Ghana's considerable bauxite reserves (estimated at over 200 million tons). Nigeria has a Six-Year National Development Plan for 1962–68[17]; its total cost is £676 million, £420 million being marked down for the private sector.[18] A group of Federal enterprises in the electrical engineering field is centred around the construction of dams on the Niger, at Kainji, Jebba, and Shirono Gorge. Kainji will be among the world's major undertakings: the output planned for 1980 is 980 MW.[19] In East Africa, the Nile has been dammed at the Owen

Falls to produce power for Uganda. Total electricity output in that country, in 1963, was only 497 million kWh, but this represented an advance of more than 230 per cent since 1957. Power production will grow, and also power needs. On the Guinea coast, new oil refineries are under construction or are planned. Those at Tema (Ghana), Port Harcourt (Nigeria), Abidjan (Ivory Coast), Dakar (Senegal), and Monrovia (Liberia) will have combined initial capacity of 4·6 million tons.[20] Petroleum consumption in East is much smaller than in West Africa.

Industry

NOTES

1. D. G. Coursey, 'The Role of Yams in West African Food Economics', *World Crops*, vol. 17, no. 2 (June 1965), pp. 75–76.
2. Russell, *World Population and World Food Supplies*, p. 237.
3. Ibid., p. 236.
4. J. Gordon, 'State Farms in Ghana', *World Crops*, vol. 15 (Dec. 1963), p. 466.
5. *East Africa Information Digest, 1962* (East Africa Information Office, London, 1962), p. 27.
6. Ibid., p. 28.
7. Elspeth Huxley, 'A Look at Settlement Schemes', *Kenya Today* (June–July 1963), p. 10.
8. Russell, *World Population and World Food Supplies*, p. 236.
9. R. J. M. Swynnerton, 'Kenya's National Crops Policy', *Kenya Today* (June–July 1963), p. 26.
10. W. F. Stolper, 'The Development of Nigeria', *Scientific American*, vol. 209, no. 3 (Sept. 1963), p. 171.
11. Russell, *World Population and World Food Supplies*, p. 237.
12. Ibid., p. 293.
13. Ibid., p. 256.
14. K. C. Edwards, 'The Importance of Biogeography', *Geography*, vol. xlix, pt. 2, no. 223 (April 1964), pp. 91–92.
15. Kenya Dept. of Agriculture, *Annual Report for 1961*, vol. i (Nairobi, 1962), p. 58.
16. Commonwealth Economic Committee, *Non-Metallic Minerals* (H.M.S.O., 1964), p. 186.
17. Barclays Intelligence Dept., *The Federation of Nigeria*, August 1963.
18. Ibid.
19. 'Harnessing the Power of the Niger', *Financial Times*, 30 Oct. 1962.
20. B. S. Hoyle, 'New Refinery Construction in Africa', *Geography*, vol. xlviii, pt. 2, no. 219 (April 1963), p. 191.

Chapter 19 Brazil and the Latin-American Scene

Brazil and the World Market

The dimensions of Brazil are impressive. She occupies over 47 per cent of the area (Fig. 19.1) and contains almost half of the total population of South America.

The world-renowned symbol of the Brazilian economy is coffee, but this has not always been Brazil's first crop. She has, in fact, been remarkable for having had a succession of products, each of which has dominated her export trade. At different times, Brazil depended very largely for foreign exchange upon the sale of dyewood, sugar, gold, diamonds, cotton, and rubber.

The dyewood was red timber — '*pau brasil*' — from which the country got its name. Camacho[1] identifies this as the first item in a cyclic series that confirmed Brazil as a one-crop economy.

Few of the foods and fibres were, in fact, indigenous in the tropical and subtropical sites with which they are now so closely identified. Sugar was brought to Brazil from the Cape Verde Islands, and retained its dominance as an export for a much longer period than did any of the later primary products. Brazilian sugar, as Celso Furtado has said, was the first plantation crop to make an impact upon the European economy. Sugar brought prosperity to Portuguese — and later Dutch — planters who produced it, along the north-east coast at different times between the start of the sixteenth and the end of the seventeenth centuries. The Dutch left Brazil after 1654, introducing sugar planting to the Caribbean and so ending the monopoly held by the Brazilian coastlands.[2]

Brazilian rubber went to satisfy the requirements of the automobile industries of Europe and North America in the first decade of this century. It supplied the wealth to sustain the building of Manaus, capital of the Amazonian rubber empire. In 1905 rubber provided 36 per cent of Brazil's exports; in 1906, 31 per cent; but production declined, because of the greater efficiency of the East Indian plantations, assisted by a natural calamity — blight — which ruined the Brazilian holdings.

The organization of commodities and of commodity trade in the

Brazilian Provinces
1 Rio Grande do Norte   6 Federal Territory
2 Paraíba   7 Espírito Santo
3 Pernambuco   8 Rio de Janeiro
4 Alagoas   9 Guanabara
5 Sergipe   (see inset)

Colonies
A Dutch Guiana   B French Guiana
(Surinam)

0   400
MILES

FIG. 19.1   Provinces of Brazil

The federal capital, Brasília, is far removed from the economic
capitals, São Paulo and Rio de Janeiro.

tropical world was for long in the hands primarily of the Dutch and
the Portuguese. The Dutch were responsible for the introduction
of the Arabian coffee shrub into the East Indies. Later, they took
it from Java to Guiana. From Cayenne, in French Guiana, the
Portuguese, in some secrecy, took the seedlings and seeds of coffee,
and transplanted them near Belém, at the Amazon mouth.[3] The
'coffee cycle' in Brazilian economic history, which lasted from 1830
until 1940, was virtually brought to an end by Vargas, 'a political

leader from a non-coffee state' (Rio Grande do Sul), as Ganzert called him. Vargas, when President before the Second World War, decreed that no new coffee trees should be planted.[4] There has been a tremendous attempt on the part of Brazilian governments to diversify production and exports, but coffee still accounts for 50–60 per cent of foreign earnings. Brazil, it is true, is less dependent than Colombia upon coffee; but the two countries have been drawn into various international attempts to reach an understanding about crop disposal. Despite the increase in African coffee acreage, Brazil still produces 43–44 per cent of the world's supply. In the post-war years, agreements among the leading coffee-producers have been rather more successful than hitherto, and much more effective than in the case of cocoa. In order to avert commercial catastrophe, Brazil has withheld from the market as much as 40 per cent of her crop[5]; but it has now been recognized that still more drastic and permanent measures are necessary. It was proposed to the International Coffee Organization in 1965 that producing nations should begin to curtail, not only sales, but also output, by placing a ceiling on acreage planted with coffee.[6]

Commercial Dangers

While the prices of most world products have risen, a number of commodities, including coffee, have become cheaper: between 1955 and 1963 its price fell from 85 U.S. cents to 40 cents per pound. But the cost of essential capital equipment has risen considerably. This has been serious enough for Brazil, but disastrous for countries like Colombia and El Salvador, dependent on coffee to the extent of 70–75 per cent for their export earnings. Coffee accounted for 54 per cent of Haiti's exports in 1960. Similarly, 63 per cent of Bolivia's export revenue came from tin; 64 per cent of Chile's from copper; and in northern Latin America — especially in Honduras, Panama, Costa Rica, and Guatemala, the banana is a key export commodity. The world's most important banana exporter is Ecuador. The natural calamities of sigatoka and Panama diseases, along with soil exhaustion and hurricane havoc, have reduced the share of production held by the Central American countries; but the most dangerous aspect, for the monocultural banana economies, has been the very large increase in world output. New plantations were developed, after the 1950s, in many parts of the West Indies, including the British Windward Islands. Increased output was absorbed up to 1964 by greatly increased demand, especially in

West Germany and other Western and Central European countries; but at the end of 1964 banana prices suddenly collapsed.

American investment has long played a vital part in South and Central America and in much of the Caribbean. Goodyear and Goodrich, and the Italian Pirelli Company, have Brazilian subsidiaries with plantations in the state of Pará, and Firestone have big plantations in southern Bahia. (The Ford plantations on the River Tapajós were sold to the Brazilian Government.⁷)

Until recently, the third most important field for U.S. investment in all Latin America was Cuba, much of the capital being in public utilities, especially railways, tramways, telephones, and telegraph. Most of the other American investment in Cuba was in sugar and tobacco. In 1960 factories, railways, and other services were nationalized by the Castro régime.

Latin Americans are increasingly conscious of the undeveloped resources within their borders and of the extent to which already-developed wealth is flowing abroad. Between 1957 and 1960 two-thirds of new foreign capital entering Brazil was American. Brazil is second in Latin America as a field for United States investment, first place being taken by Venezuela, where nearly 40 per cent of American investment is in petroleum. More than half the American stake in Brazil is in manufacturing: in São Paulo there are plants run by Goodyear, Firestone, General Electric, General Motors, Ford, Armour, and Wilson. Foreign companies altogether control more than two-thirds of the automobile and well over half of the pharmaceutical industry of Brazil.

In Central America, cash-crop and plantation production is largely controlled by American companies or their subsidiaries. In the 'banana republics', the chief economic power is the American United Fruit Company.

Nationalization has long been a frightening possibility for foreign companies in Latin America. The Mexicans created a sensation as long ago as 1938 by expropriating the property of the oil companies; but almost all other mineral output in Mexico is still foreign-owned. Less than 10 per cent of production from mines and metal plants is Mexican-owned. Perhaps more important than the earlier events in Mexico was the, albeit temporary, Asian example of the Iranian Government's nationalization of the Anglo-Iranian Oil Company in 1951. In South America there was pressure against the oil companies

269

in Brazil and Peru. It was even more significant in Argentina, where oil investments, worth about £150 million, belong to such foreign concerns as Shell and Standard Oil of New Jersey.[8] Venezuelan oil production is important to all the large international companies except British Petroleum. The biggest oil-producer in the world, Standard Oil of New Jersey, derives half of its oil from Venezuela; Royal Dutch-Shell, nearly half. In Venezuela, also, half of the proved iron-ore reserves are in areas leased to two very large American corporations.

One view is that economically South America must always occupy a place subordinate to the positions held by North America and industrialized Western Europe: 'economic independence for Latin America is only a relative possibility. As an absolute, it would be neither attainable nor desirable. . . . Some must always be hewers of wood and carriers of water'.[9]

The chief Latin-American economic grouping is the Latin-American Free Trade Association (L.A.F.T.A.), concluded at Montevideo in 1961 by Brazil, Argentina, Chile, Mexico, Paraguay, Peru, and Uruguay, who were later joined by Colombia and Ecuador.

**Resources
and
Develop-
ment**

The contrast between potential and development is shown by the fact that, while hevea is a native of Brazil, nearly one-third of her rubber consumption is imported from South-East Asia. Her forests are vast and varied, but 20 per cent of her woodpulp requirements are imported, along with 70 per cent of her newsprint consumption.[10] It is symptomatic of economic change that Petrobras of Brazil has started large-scale production of synthetic rubber: of total rubber production, in 1962, 45 per cent was synthetic.

Latin America has a remarkable variety of mineral resources, most notable being the precious minerals — gold and silver, petroleum, copper, lead, zinc, tin, and bauxite. Brazil is not one of the leaders in developed minerals, although her iron-ore reserves are vast. One assessment[11] places about a quarter of the world's iron reserves in the south-eastern parts of the Sierra do Espinhaço, mainly around the headwaters of the Rio Doce. This seems to accord with the Brazilian Government's own figures. Production from the Itabira field in 1962 was 10 million tons, of which 7·8 million was exported; and the ore was rich, having a 70 per cent ferrous content. In manganese, Brazil is the third world producer. The most important area is in Amapá, in the Amazon delta.

In Venezuela there is almost a Brazilian-type contrast between the affluence of Caracas and the oil trade and the poverty of the interior. Offshore are the thriving, bustling refineries on the Dutch islands of Aruba and Curaçao. The chief basis for long-term economic optimism in Venezuela lies in the potentialities of the industrial complex built around the town of Santo Tomé de Guayana, where the Caroni River provides plentiful hydro resources. The intention is to introduce cheap hydro-electric power for the manufacture of products — aluminium, pulp, paper, manganese, and chemicals — that would then be exported to North America and Europe.[12] Mexico possesses an impressive range of mineral wealth apart from petroleum. She is a world-class producer of silver, lead, and zinc. Most of her mineral production goes to the U.S.A. which owns nearly all the mines. Chile is second in the world in copper production, most of her output being in the hands of the American giants, Anaconda and Kennecott Copper.

Resources and Development

Brazil in 1965 had 84 million cattle and 56 million pigs — twice as many cattle, and fifteen times as many pigs, as Argentina. Brazil has only 40 per cent as many sheep as Argentina but twice as many goats.

Stock-Rearing

There are a number of zones of concentrated cattle rearing in Brazil:

1. *The South,* especially in the province of Rio Grande do Sul. This province is bordered by cattle-conscious Uruguay on the south. Here is pampa country ideal for beef cattle.
2. *The São Paulo Plains and Uplands,* bordered on the west by the River Paraná. Their biggest market is in São Paulo itself.
3. *Southern Mato Grosso and Goias provinces,* containing the upper Paraguay and the right-bank tributaries of the Paraná. Schurz has likened the Brazilian trails, the *boradas,* necessary to take the cattle to market, to the old drives eastwards to Kansas City in the U.S.A. The Noreste railroad, he says, 'is completely inadequate for the task of moving the vast supplies of cattle to market'.[13] The opening of the interior to cattle by the farmer-adventurers of São Paulo is well described by Camacho.[14]
4. *The 'Mineral Triangle'* of the state of Minas Gerais centred upon Barretos in neighbouring São Paulo state. Here are the fattening stations for the cattle overlanded from Mato Grosso and Goiás.

5. *The Sertão* — 'far interior' (Hunnicutt)[15] — of the north-east, the country of drought-resisting vegetation, where there is a catastrophic uncertainty of rainfall, with great floods succeeding long, dry years. This is a land of tragedy, of hope eternally deferred.

6. *Marajó Island*, at the mouth of the Amazon.

7. *The Campos Geraes*, the northern grasslands bordering on Venezuela.

The climatic uncertainties of the Sertão are repeated in the tropical grasslands (llanos) of Venezuela, where cattle deaths and heavy weight losses have been common during the dry season. Just as serious is the frequent excess of rain in June–August, with cattle losses due to drowning or attack by alligators. Schurz describes the ordeal of cattle on Marajó Island, where their natural enemies are jaguars and snakes.[16] One may contrast the uncertainties of stock-rearing in the Brazilian interior with the highly organized efficiency of the Argentinian industry.

Land Tenure in Latin America

Conditions of land tenure in South America invite comparison with countries like India where there is also payment of rent in the form of service, and where the peasant has a holding that may often be minute, although big farms occupy a completely disproportionate share of the total farm area (Fig. 19.2). The most extreme case occurs in Mexico, where 74 per cent of holdings — being those under 5 hectares — occupy 1·3 per cent of the total available area. In Ecuador, the average size of these farms of under 5 hectares is only 1·7 hectares (Crossley). On the *haciendas* (estates) of the plateau country of Andean America there are large-scale survivals of serf-dom, alongside quite inadequate peasant holdings. In Brazil, grave social implications attach to the pattern of land distribution. Saco, using statistics collected by the Inter-American Committee for Economic Development (I.C.A.D.), allots only 10 per cent of farming land to the smallest holdings, the *minifundia*. But these tiny properties represent 32 per cent of all Brazilian farms.[17] Crossley attributes to the under-5-hectare holdings (22 per cent of the total), a mere 0·5 per cent of the farmland. According to Saco, the biggest farms and plantations, the *latifundia*, though only 3 per cent of all holdings, take up 59 per cent of the farm area. Crossley puts 1·6 per cent only of all Brazilian holdings in the over-1,000-hectare category; but they take up 51 per cent of the farm area. In Argentina,

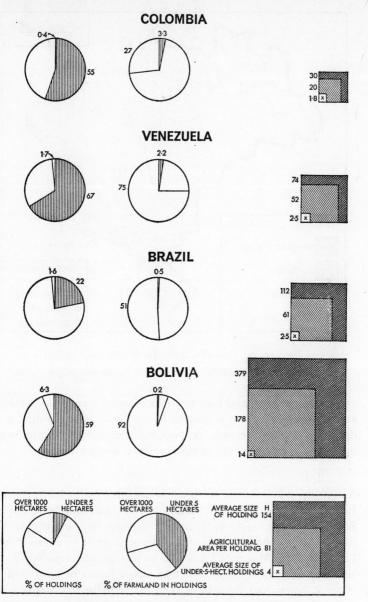

FIG. 19.2   Size of farm holdings in Latin America

A comparison of land tenure in Brazil and in the other South
American countries show the extremely small proportion of their
area occupied by smallholdings.

K   H.G.P.

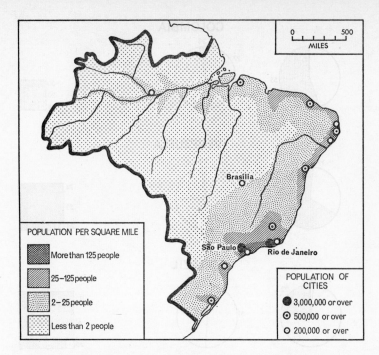

POPULATION PER SQUARE MILE

More than 125 people

25–125 people

2–25 people

Less than 2 people

POPULATION OF CITIES

● 3,000,000 or over

◉ 500,000 or over

○ 200,000 or over

FIG. 19.3   Brazil — distribution of population

Brazil's crowded coastlands contrast with her largely empty north.

75 per cent of farmland is in holdings of more than 1,000 hectares: agriculture there is not a struggle for existence on a minimal plot, dependent upon an erratic, perhaps even temporarily non-existent, market; it consists mainly of industrialized beef production.

Aid   American aid to Latin America is organized principally by the Institute of Inter-American Affairs, the Organization of American States (O.A.S.), and by powerful private bodies such as the Rockefeller Foundation. The Foundation is active in Brazil, Chile, Colombia, and Mexico; O.A.S. and its services are important in all countries except Argentina. Aid from abroad must be buttressed by effort at home, and there have been major redistributions of land, especially in Mexico and Bolivia; but in some cases progressive measures have foundered upon the lack of a scientifically-based national plan. Elsewhere, they have generated more violent social and political pressures.

The very striking concentration of population in Brazil (Fig. 19.3) is in the south-east, within the triangle Rio de Janeiro–São Paulo–Belo Horizonte, with secondary concentrations on the north-east coast and around Curitiba and Porto Alegre in the south. The concentration of manpower and skill around Rio and São Paulo has been emphasized, rather than diminished, by the fitful development of the new capital, Brasília. This creation of President Kubitschek, a place where 'order, logic and planning reign supreme',[18] seems to conflict with the geographical *raison d'être* of the dynamic centres of industry and commerce. São Paulo has grown, since 1940, from 1 to 4½ millions. During the period 1950–60 the total population of the major towns and cities of Latin America (those holding over 100,000 people) increased by half.

Regional
Imbalance

Regional Imbalance

In 1962 the whole of South America had an installed electrical capacity of only some 10 million kW.

Energy

Electricity — Installed General Capacity, 1962[19]

	Electricity capacity (mill. kW)	% of world capacity	Population in millions	% of world total
U.S.A.	174·0	37·85	177·7	6·35
U.S.S.R.	59·3	12·9	210·5	7·5
U.K.	35·0	7·6	52·2	1·87
Japan	21·2	4·6	92·7	3·32
South America	10·1	2·2	134·6	4·82
Africa	8·1	1·76	260·3	9·3

The figures cover the whole range of wealth and destitution in South America. It is notable that, deficient though the South Americans are in electric power, they are ahead, absolutely, of Africa, which possesses a population nearly twice as large. On the other hand power reserves in South America are high, Brazil being credited with the fourth-greatest potential in the world. She has very little coal but, it is thought, considerable oil reserves in the state of Bahia. The South-Central region produces 90 per cent and consumes 88 per cent of all Brazil's electric power. Electrification is progressing at speed, but national output is retarded by the poverty of the Northern and North-East regions. The result is that Chile, Argentina, and Uruguay have larger per-capita consumption of electricity.

The power situations of Brazil and Peru have some points of similarity: on the negative side, in their lack of coal; positively, in their hydro-power potential. Their selva backgrounds are similar; but southern Peru's desert area, watered by short, swift streams from the mountains, is almost unique. The need there for irrigation is acute; the most notable river running into the Pacific, and tapped for power, is the Santa, around which a multi-purpose scheme has been started, modelled on the American T.V.A.

Transport

Transport in the underdeveloped lands goes hand in hand with general economic progress. But contrasts between progress and torpor, between Brazilian coastlands and the Sertão, existed from the earliest days of settlement. The South-East did not become the principal region for economic growth until coffee became dominant in the nineteenth century. Before that, the North-East coast region had been economically supreme, its lead being based on tobacco, cacao and, later, cotton.

In Brazil, the contrast of cultures is strikingly presented in its transport forms. The South-East has had railroads since 1853, while the traffic of Amazonas is still largely river-borne. On the other hand, the railway network of the region between Belo Horizonte and Curitiba is comparable with that of the United States Middle West at the start of this century, while the network of Rio Grande do Sul is almost equal to that of the Argentine pampas. In 1958 there was completed the Trans-Andean line from Santos to Arica in northern Chile, crossing the Andes at over 4,000 metres (13,000 feet), via Corumbá and Santa Cruz in Bolivia.

Spectacular roads exist. President Dutra was credited with the dictum: 'To govern means to build roads.' There is a good road— the Via Dutra — between Rio de Janeiro and São Paulo. What has been lacking is a north-south link between the prosperous provinces and Amazonia, linking with the Pan American Highway system of the south (Fig. 19.4). Much effort is now being devoted to constructing such a throughway from the new capital, Brasília, via Imperatriz, to Belém. The result, during the period 1959–64, has been to increase the population of Imperatriz from 6,000 to 20,000, and the marketable rice crop from 8,000 to 500,000 sacks. The road barely exists at the moment, and is liable to be interrupted by wet-season rains. However, it is now possible, during the dry season, to expect delivery of goods from São Paulo to Belém by lorry in under a fortnight.

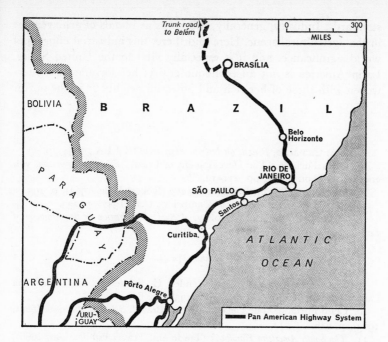

FIG. 19.4 Pan-American highway system of south-east Brazil

Southern Brazil is well-served, interior Brazil, ill-served, by roads.

Airlines could transform the economic situation in Brazil. Panair do Brasil has expanded both passenger and freight traffic in spectacular fashion. Comparison here may be made with mainland China, which with its limitless physical and economic potential now possesses a chain of modern airfields, fully adequate to take the largest commercial airliners and important international flights. Both countries have vast areas, ill served by the older forms of transport, but which will eventually be adequately linked by air.

Brazil and the other Latin American countries present a fascinating mosaic of growth and change. Natural conditions often favour settlement, but population pressure is severe in some regions. There are great areas of excessive plant growth, deserts, and zones of water shortage, where irrigation is needed but little applied. Production has grown, but a faster population expansion has reduced living

The Future for Latin America

standards. Industry, generally, still exists as islands of achievement in the agricultural scene. Here and there, this industrial effort is of world significance, and it is especially vital to the United States. Latin America is not an economic entity: her fortunes are interwoven with those of her rich and powerful neighbour in the north.

NOTES

1. J. A. Camacho, *Brazil, an Interim Assessment* (R.I.I.A., 1954), p. 29.
2. Celso Furtado, 'The Development of Brazil', *Scientific American*, vol. 209, no. 3 (Sept. 1963), pp. 211–12.
3. W. Schurz, *Brazil, the Infinite Country* (Robert Hale, 1962), p. 193.
4. F. W. Ganzert *et al.*, *Brazil* (Cambridge U.P., 1947), p. 233.
5. F. Benham and H. A. Holley, *A Short Introduction to the Economy of Latin America* (Oxford U.P., 1960), p. 103.
6. *The Times*, 9 Aug. 1965.
7. Schurz, *Brazil, the Infinite Country*, p. 49.
8. *The Times*, 12 Nov. 1963.
9. Donald E. Worcester and Wendell G. Schaeffer, *The Growth and Culture of Latin America* (Oxford U.P., 1956), p. 811.
10. Celso Furtado, 'The Development of Brazil', *Scientific American* (Sept. 1963), p. 216.
11. *The South American Handbook* (Trade and Travel Publications, 1966), p. 611.
12. *The Times*, 20 April 1964.
13. Schurz, *Brazil, the Infinite Country*, p. 205.
14. Camacho, *Brazil, an Interim Assessment*, p. 32.
15. B. H. Hunnicutt, *Brazil, World Frontier* (Van Nostrand, 1949), p. 47.
16. Schurz, *Brazil, the Infinite Country*, p. 206.
17. Alfredo M. Saco, 'Land Reform as an Instrument of Change — with Special Reference to Latin America', F.A.O., *Monthly Bulletin of Agricultural and Economic and Statistics*, vol. 13, no. 12 (Dec. 1964), p. 3.
18. 'Brazilian Tale of Three Cities', *The Times*, 18 Jan. 1964.
19. *Financial Times* supplement on 'World Energy', 24 Sept. 1962.

A prosperous world is a medium for rapid development of transport, but there may be a considerable gap between potential and achievement. The railways, if modernized, could possibly do much to ease the pressures of life and work in Britain's industrial centres, but such measures depend upon the necessary government expenditure. There is no general agreement upon the solutions to our transport problems, only a consensus of opinion that, with time, the difficulties are sure to multiply.

Potential and Achievement

The possibilities of ocean transport are still immense. It is now practicable to construct ships bigger than ever before. The newest passenger vessels are no larger than 45,000–50,000 tons, but cargo-ship tonnage increases every year, with 200,000-ton tankers being built here and abroad, and still larger vessels are planned. The potential of the railway has, in the past, been limited by safety considerations, by signalling problems, and by the nature of the track; but in the 1965 Beeching Report, provision was made for a very considerable improvement in freight speeds, over certain railway trunk lines by 1984. This expectation was quoted as justifying considerable expenditure on such routes. On the sea, there is much less physical control, although limits on size operate when it comes to port handling, estuarine working, and canal transport. Movement through the super-canals — Panama, Kiel, and Suez — is circumscribed by the draught of channels or the size of locks, nevertheless Suez traffic increases year by year. The reason is that Suez provides the chief arterial route for the movement of petroleum. The figures of Suez Canal traffic show more and bigger ships, carrying more cargo but fewer passengers. Cities such as Amsterdam depend upon canals for their economic life, and the North Sea Canal locks are vaster even than those of Panama. Aircraft are not constricted by the physical limits that inhibit road, canal, and railway operators, and the faster planes now being built will attract still more passengers from slower transport forms.

Suez Canal Traffic[1]

Year	Number of vessels	Net tons ('000)	Number of passengers ('000)	Receipts (£E'000)
1961	. 18,148	187,059	323	51,887
1962	. 18,518	197,837	270	53,957
1963	. 19,146	210,498	298	71,294
1964	. 19,943	227,911	270	77,697
1965	. 20,289	246,817	291	85,792

In France, physical conditions favour water communication between the eastern tributaries of the Seine (Fig. 20.1). In the United States, the trans-continental routes of the late nineteenth century were those of the railway. Now the railways are fighting new competitors and have replied with various measures of rationalization, comparable to those proposed in Britain. America's roads have brought people and goods, carried by the world's largest fleet of motor vehicles, to choke her skyscraper cities. Railways are still being built in important areas of the world: for instance in Central Asia and in the North-West Territories of Canada; but in Western Europe railway lines are being taken up, and the new tunnels through the Alps are for road traffic. Nevertheless, the very success and popularity of motor-cars have created vast problems that a streamlined rail organization may in part be required to solve.

Canal Operation

The canal is an excellent transport medium in the congenial physical conditions of the plains of northern Europe or of the New World. On the North European Plain, single barges may be of 1,350 tons: such are the 'European' barges of the Rhine–Moselle waterway that links Koblenz and Thionville by a channel with a minimum depth of 10, and width of 120 feet. The West German section of the Mittelland Canal is to be similarly deepened. The picture of the French waterways is of vast freight movements — and perhaps of still greater potential — in the east and north-east, and in the intermediate zone between these regions and Paris.

The position is far different on Britain's waterways, where the standard barge remains at 60 tons capacity. On British canals, coal is still by far the most important load representing about 4 million

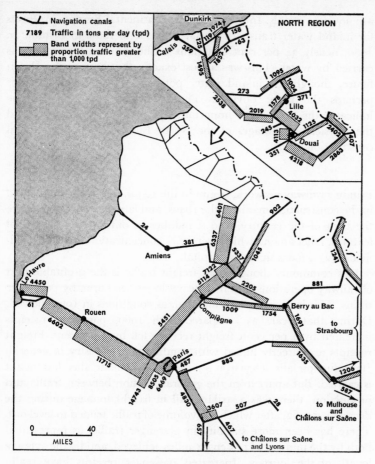

FIG. 20.1 Inland waterways of Northern France and
Paris region

There is a great concentration of water traffic: (a) on the Seine;
(b) in the north-east; (c) on the canals following the right-bank
tributaries of the Seine.

tons of cargo per year — and some of the largest and latest power
stations, such as those at Skelton Grange and Ferrybridge, are sited
on canals.[2] Oil is second to coal as a canal cargo in Britain, accounting for over 2 million tons per year: the most important routes for
oil are the waterways of Yorkshire, the Trent–Humber basin, and
the valley of the Severn. Mineral ore is admirably suited to canal
transport, though the main iron deposits in the Jurassic scarplands

are not near canals. In many parts of continental Europe, prospects for inland water transport are far superior to those in Britain. In 1960, nearly 34 per cent of freight traffic in West Germany was carried by water. This was almost exactly the same as the Dutch figure, though the inland water potential of the Netherlands is perhaps the more obvious. The waterways map of Europe indicates the very great importance of her navigable rivers and the physical advantages of the North European Plain for canal construction.

Railway Operation

Britain's railway network, begun in the 1830s, massively augmented in the construction mania of the 1840s, and largely completed before the turn of the century, had a number of outstanding locational features, chief among which were: (1) concentration upon the coal-fields; (2) a focus upon the capital.

It is commonly thought that freight traffic is the profitable part of railway operations, whereas heavy losses are borne by passenger trains. This is an over-simplification, as conditions in 1961 showed. During that year, as compared with 1960, passenger receipts increased by 4 per cent; freight receipts fell by 3 per cent. Freight receipts are directly linked with conditions in industry in general. If production falls, if less iron is mined or steel made, then less freight is carried. But apart from the general relation between traffic and production, there was a striking fall in freight tonnage during the decade 1952–62, after which the volume of traffic tended to level out. There has been more stability in passenger traffic, as represented both by the number of passenger-miles achieved, and by the average length of the journey. Increased passenger receipts have really come from fare increases; and in 1964 reached £167 million per annum.

British Railways — Estimated Passenger-Miles[3]
(million)

1951–55 average	.		20,523
1956–60 average	.		21,938
1961	.	.	21,061
1962	.	.	19,772
1963	.	.	19,300
1964	.	.	19,874
1965	.	.	18,713

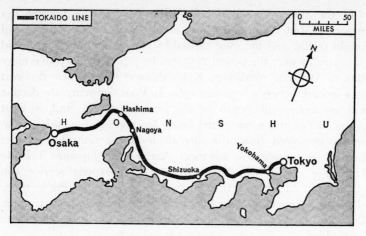

FIG. 20.2   Japan's Tokaido Line

The electrified Tokaido Line is a purpose-built route connecting
Japan's two biggest cities.

The pattern of fares has to be seen, however, against a background
of steeply rising costs. One must also notice the scale of the 'central
charges', principally representing interest payments on compensation stock.

Munby comments on the importance of itemizing figures of profit
and loss.[4] Coal traffic and petroleum movements (now 10 million
tons per annum) are profitable. Other mineral, general merchandise
and passenger traffic, habitually lose money.

It may be a slight consolation to our railway managers to know
that other countries have similar difficulties in resisting competitors.
The United States railways have already felt the growing strength
of the hauliers (and of the teamster associations that man them).
But it was only in 1960 that American roads, for the first time,
carried half as much as rail, and air freight is still extremely small
in comparison with the other forms. Pipeline distribution of oil and
gas continues to grow, both absolutely and comparatively.

U.S. — *Volume of Domestic Inter-City Freight Traffic*[5]
(*per cent*)

Year	Rail	Motor vehicles	Inland water[6]	Oil pipeline	Air
1962	43·66	22·44	16·60	17·24	0·06
1963	43·02	23·78	16·00	17·11	0·09
1964	42·91	23·82	15·95	17·22	0·10

In the Soviet Union, rail freight traffic has also become less important, but it still commands almost 80 per cent of all inland freight traffic, and the total carried by rail, in ton-miles, increased considerably over the period 1955–60. In Japan, the picture is more akin to 'Western' conditions. Rail's share of freight there declined by a seventh between 1958 and 1960. In West Germany, the decline was less steep — one-tenth for the period 1956–60. Rail, in most places, is fighting a rearguard battle for business but, using techniques borrowed from the aircraft industry, railway engineers have made considerable advances. Abroad, the Japanese Tokaido Line (Fig. 20.2) has shown what a real express service can accomplish. At home, British Railways are now planning in terms of 75 m.p.h. speeds for their liner trains; and this is only a beginning. Comparable speeds have been reached by the new services to Lancashire.

The Railway as a Service

The concept of railway operations as a community service is common today, but such an attitude has been resisted by railway managers. Margetts compared the railways with the different treatment habitually accorded to industry in general, stressing the 'insistence on treating a railway concern differently from other means of production and transport, and demanding that it should continue to do things which any commercially-minded concern would stop doing'.[7]

On Britain's railways, it was said, 'revenue does not pay for the maintenance of the track and the maintenance and operation of the signalling system, quite apart from the cost of running trains, depots, yards, and stations. Also, it is found that the cost of more than half of the stations is greater than the receipts from traffic which they originate'.[8]

The 1963 'First Beeching Report' proposed to discontinue many stopping trains on passenger services, both on branch and main lines. The Report proposed greatly to modernize freight services: (i) by the progressive closing of small stations to uneconomic freight traffic; (ii) through 'the attraction of more siding-to-siding traffics suitable for through-train movement'.[9] There were envisaged 'livery trains' serving major company requirements, and rail–road liner trains carrying fast flows of traffic made up of important small consignments.

'Freight sundries' traffic was to be concentrated on about one

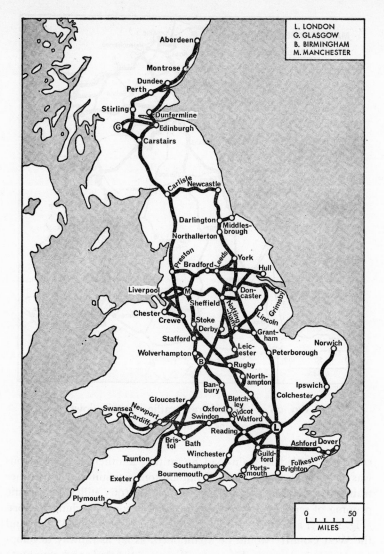

FIG. 20.3   British Rail — routes selected for development
The plans for Britain's railways show a pruning and concentration
of main-line services, and capital development.

hundred depots. One result of the change of government in 1964
was to slow down the implementation of the Report. Its findings
had included an estimate that 8 million tons of additional traffic

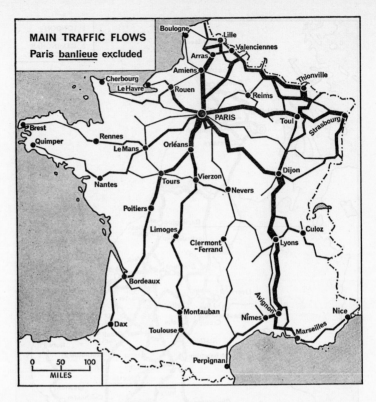

MAIN TRAFFIC FLOWS
Paris banlieue excluded

Boulogne
Lille
Valenciennes
Arras
Amiens
Cherbourg
Le Havre
Rouen
Reims
Thionville
Brest
Quimper
Rennes
Le Mans
Orléans
PARIS
Toul
Strasbourg
Nantes
Tours
Vierzon
Dijon
Poitiers
Nevers
Limoges
Clermont-Ferrand
Lyons
Culoz
Bordeaux
Avignon
Dax
Montauban
Nîmes
Nice
Toulouse
Marseilles
Perpignan

0 50 100
MILES

FIG. 20.4   French rail traffic — main flows
Paris remains the all-important focus.

could be carried in train-load quantities; another 30 million tons
was 'favourable to rail'; and 16 million tons was suitable to the liner
trains of a combined road–rail service. In 1965 still more drastic
pruning of services was proposed in the 'Second Beeching Report'
(Fig. 20.3): according to this, a large part of Scotland, Wales, and
the West Country would be abandoned, as far as railway development was concerned. The 1965 Report estimated, and sought to
provide for, a huge increase in the carriage of oil by rail during the
period 1964–84, a decrease in the traffic in coal, and a very large
rise in the movement of iron and steel. One may compare the
situation that prompted the British proposals with the situation in
France (Fig. 20.4), where there is very pronounced regional concentration of rail traffic.

The Transport Act of 1947 nationalized much road traffic. It was followed by de-nationalization in 1953, although not all public holdings in long-distance haulage were discarded and sold. There resulted a dual pattern, with private hauliers, on the one hand, and British Road Services (B.R.S.), the largest single road hauliers, on the other.

It has been suggested that the problems of roads and railways may demand the services of an arbiter, perhaps centrally placed: 'transportation problems will have to start being considered as a whole by some special executive planning body which will not be for or against a motor car, or for or against the railways, etc. — a body, in fact, which will take all existing means of transportation, develop them and apply them together on the basis of thorough studies of the situation in the country as a whole.'[10]

Many authorities, national, local, and professional, have been perturbed at the crisis in road movement produced by the pressure of fast-increasing traffic. One of the results of the general concern was the Buchanan Report of November 1963. The statistical foundation for the Report's recommendations — assessed 'by projecting past trends' (Fig. 20.5) — was the 'prospect in Great Britain of 18 million vehicles (including 12 million cars) by 1970' and 'of 27 million (including 19 million cars) by 1980'.[11] The social foundation for the assessment was the assumption that, of a population that would increase at a rate undreamt of in the 1930s, the vast majority would wish to travel by car. The Report relied upon a forecast of population growth to a figure of 74 million in 2010, and upon the possession of 1·3 cars a family by that time. It was calculated that by 1990, by which time the number of car-less families would have declined drastically, the growth rate of car purchase would also be decreased severely. By 2010, 'saturation point was likely to have been reached — most of the people wanting cars would, by that time, have secured them'.[12] The number of cars on the road would continue to rise if the population increased. Apart from that, domestic car production would be devoted to the replacement of existing vehicles — a state of affairs that is already being reached in some areas of the United States. The Report saw a major issue in the public attitude to the re-planning of towns in the rapidly approaching crisis period of the Motor Age. There had been wholesale opposition to the idea of demolition and reconstruction of

Government
Intervention

Government
Intervention

Road Traffic

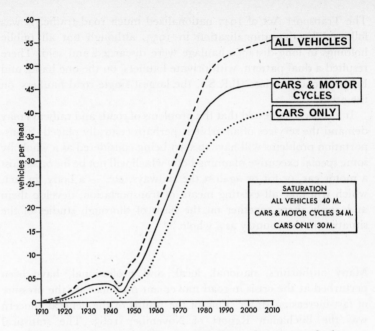

FIG. 20.5   Road traffic in Britain — forecasts of the
Buchanan Report

Predictions are that the increase in vehicles will start to level off
well before the end of this century, but that saturation will be
reached only in about the year A.D. 2010: 'most of the people
wanting cars would by that time have secured them'.

historically attractive, but economically impracticable and inadequate, route-ways in our town centres; and the conclusion was
drawn that 'if major physical changes are out of the question in
historical towns, there must be a reduction of accessibility'.[13]

The concept of reduced access, along with restriction on road-
users, is at the heart of most proposals for accommodating the
expected vast increase of vehicles — primarily private cars — to the
continuance of town life. In London, difficulties arise particularly
from the degree of cross-traffic induced by the increasing importance
of routes to the coast, and from 'the desires of through traffic'. The
Americans have seen critical road situations as primarily urban
problems, so that recourse has been had to Freeways and Expressways that are often elevated and cut across their cities in a fashion
that Britain has so far seen on only a very limited scale. The interchange for the Dwight D. Eisenhower and John F. Kennedy

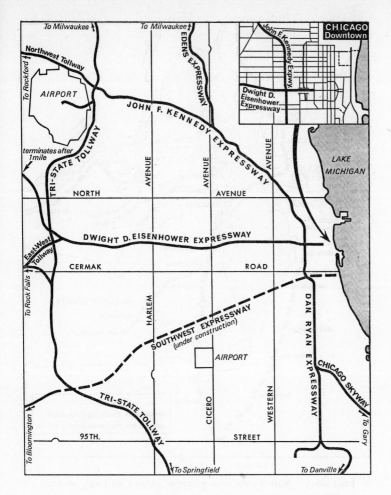

FIG. 20.6 Urban motorways of the New World —
Chicago

Events in American urban transport help to show us the British
pattern to come.

Expressways in Chicago takes up valuable land to the west of the
business section (Fig. 20.6).

Highly significant from the vehicle-use point of view has been the
suggestion for a mass reversion to public transport. In the United
States there have been a number of examples of this awareness. In
California, a city railway seventy-five miles long (Fig. 20.7), with

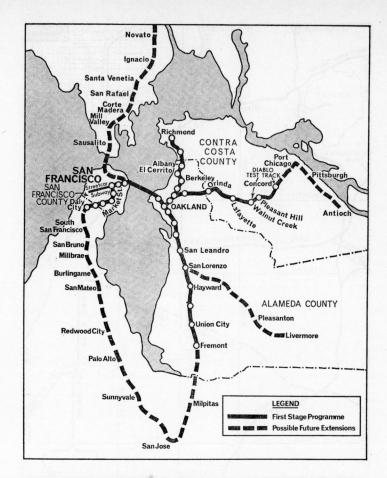

FIG. 20.7 San Francisco express urban railway system
Conditions of road chaos and expense have helped to produce in
central California a reversion to public transport.

an underground link below San Francisco Bay, has been initiated
as a matter of urgency. It is jointly financed by the local authority,
backed by a public bond issue, and, for the Bay Section, by the
California Toll Bridge Authority.[14]

The Buchanan Report objected, in an important passage, 'to the
slavish adoption of a ring road as a standardized pattern'. But the
London Motorway provisional plan shows a box of 'cross routes'
surrounding the Central Area (Fig. 20.8).

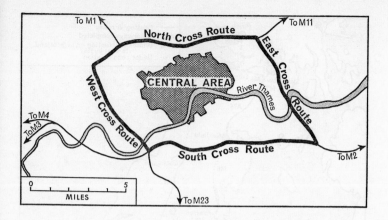

FIG. 20.8   London urban motorway plan
London's plans for urban motorways will still leave the central
area untouched.

Liverpool has approved a scheme for $3\frac{1}{2}$ miles of six-lane motor-way, much of it elevated.[15] Paris is building an east–west motorway, about eight miles long, on the lower quays of the Seine. This imaginative concept is to link the quay-roads, where necessary (and entirely on the right bank of the river) by tunnels, passing under the approaches to the Pont des Invalides and the Pont de la Concorde.[16] For Paris, as for other cities, the most intractable problem concerns 'peaks.' Special difficulties must occur in capitals that are also industrial centres or, like Paris, have an island centre. In New York, the rivers present transport problems on a far greater scale; tunnels have been used, more than bridges, to cross the Hudson. The Japanese have also used a tunnel to connect the Honshu road system to Shikoku. Coastal highways such as U.S. Route No. 6, which crosses Chesapeake Bay in magnificent fashion, can make use of both bridge and tunnel. The problems arising from the international link projected for the English Channel are of a different dimension; but the British and French — with the help of American engineering — have, in principle, decided on a tunnel in preference to a bridge to link Britain to Europe. Britain's motor-ways will soon afford direct links between London and Carlisle and London and South Wales (Fig. 20.9).

FIG. 20.9   U.K. motorways

Britain began slowly with motorway construction. The story of
the M4, for instance, is one of frustrating and protracted delays.

**Air
Transport** For many years planes have been getting bigger and faster, and this
has helped to push airports further out from the city centres. As
against these well-established tendencies, we now see significant
innovations, first military, and ultimately civilian, to introduce
craft using vertical and short take-off and landing techniques. It is
fortunate that this development has come to the aid of urban
planners, since many city airfields cannot now handle the largest

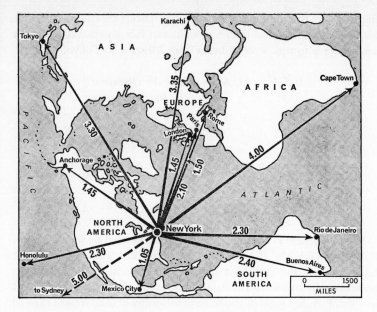

FIG. 20.10   A smaller world — 2,000 m.p.h. travel times
from New York (in hours and minutes) by S.S.T.

and fastest planes; and much faster craft will shortly be coming into
service. The bigger airlines are likely to be at very considerable
advantage in the re-equipping of their fleets with these supersonic
giants. The Anglo-French Concord is being built to fly at Mach 2·2;
and it is thought that the first Soviet supersonic craft are likely to
be slightly faster than this; the first of the new range of American
machines is intended to be faster still, perhaps reaching Mach 3.
One feature all the models will share: they will be extremely
expensive; but they will make the world a still smaller place (Fig.
20.10).

Many think that the achievement of safer — and quieter — flying
would be preferable to the attainment of extraordinary speeds; also,
that more attention should be paid to freight. But the pressure of
competition will undoubtedly compel even the most reluctant
operators to buy the new machines.

The greatest density of air traffic is to be found over the United
States, where three operators each exceed the carrying capacity of
either of Britain's State-owned corporations. The biggest passenger-
carrier in the world is Aeroflot, the Soviet airline, which now has

flights direct to London as well as to New Delhi; the quickest regular air route from London to New Delhi is in fact now via Moscow. A new route is to run across Siberia from Moscow to Tokyo.

U.S.A. and U.K. — Major Air Operators[17]

Airline	Number of planes	
	Passenger fleet	Cargo fleet
American . .	174	14
T.W.A. . .	153	13
P.A.A. . . .	100	23
B.E.A. . . .	95	6
B.O.A.C. . .	70	2

Most passengers crossing the Atlantic are carried by the American P.A.A. or T.W.A. P.A.A. does not have any routes within the United States, but in 1963 it carried 24·9 per cent of the 2·5 million passengers flying the North Atlantic, as compared with 22·8 per cent in 1962. P.A.A.'s total of 160 million ton-miles of total freight carried in 1961 had increased by 1963 to 206 million.

To meet competition from the Americans, European airlines have made a number of mergers and associations: B.O.A.C. with Cunard Eagle on the North Atlantic route, and with Air India and Qantas on routes to the Far East. In Europe, an outsize combine — Air Union — has been formed by the association of the near-monopoly national airlines of France, Italy, Belgium, and West Germany.

In America, there is a strong east-west pattern, focusing particularly on Chicago. On the West Coast there are two outstanding terminals in San Francisco and Los Angeles, between which cities and New York non-stop flights are now a commonplace. In the East, there is dense traffic between Boston, New York, Philadelphia, Baltimore, and Washington. However, New York is supreme as a link with the Old World.

The United States is a sufficiently large country for there to be highly important provincial air centres: besides Chicago, these include Kansas City, St. Louis, and Salt Lake City. There are Great Circle routes across the U.S.A. itself and from both West and East Coasts to Europe. In America there has been a constant increase in both freight and passenger traffic. During 1962 there were 73 weekly all-freight services between Los Angeles and New York, as compared with about 500 passenger flights; across the North Atlantic, there were 46 all-freight services.[18] During the period 1957–63, international air traffic commencing in the United States more than doubled. During the same period, internal American air traffic increased by 51 per cent. In Britain, there is a large and growing movement by air between the London region and Yorkshire, Lancashire, and Central Scotland; and from South Coast airports, such as Lydd, to the Continent.

In the United States, more and more people are using planes instead of trains and buses. It is interesting to compare the American figures with those for Japan, which may be westernized in many respects, but is far behind the United States in the volume of revenue-earning air traffic. The proportion of such American traffic

Passenger Traffic, 1960 (Revenue-earning)
(per cent)

	U.S.A.[19]	Japan[20]
Rail . . .	27·6	76·3
Road . .	25·5	23·0
Air . . .	43·5	0·3
Waterways. .	3·4	0·4
	100·0	100·0

carried by air trebled between 1950 and 1960; by 1962, it had increased further, to 45·9 per cent. One sees, meanwhile, that the private car is still devouring an overwhelming proportion of total traffic between towns, although since 1961 (a watershed year), the car has lost a little ground to the airlines.

U.S. — Volume of Domestic Inter-City Passenger Traffic[21]
(per cent)

Year	Rail	Commercial motor carriers	Private automobiles	Inland waterway	Air
1950 .	6·87	5·59	85·16	0·25	2·13
1955 .	4·32	3·84	88·16	0·26	3·42
1960 .	2·84	2·62	89·73	0·35	4·46
1962 .	2·51	2·66	89·80	0·34	4·69
1963 .	2·23	2·63	89·69	0·33	5·12

Transport	The advantage of the sea for the carriage of bulk cargo has been bluntly stated by Keenlyside: 'it is much the cheapest per ton-mile, for all forms of transport'. In the passenger trade some sea transport has held its own, but there has been a comparative decline: move- ment by sea has barely held its own; air travel 'has expanded sharply'.[22] The importance of the sea in Britain's history needs no stressing. Ocean communications are still vital to her economic existence. However, there has been a great increase in passenger traffic by air to America and to the Dominions during the past generation, and this has been achieved at the expense of the shipping companies, some of which have partially covered themselves by investing in air transport.	
Ocean Passenger Transport		

A large majority of the people travelling from Europe to the United States or Canada now go by air. The result of intense com- petition between the different transport forms, and between competing airline operators, has been to keep fares generally low. Tourist fares by sea, for instance to New York, are considerably cheaper than the lowest 'group' fares available by air. Shipping companies have thus been able, with difficulty, to maintain their absolute figures of passengers carried to North America, over the period 1961–63. Some ocean passenger traffic is made up largely of migrants. This applies to Australia, where the number of immigrants from Britain has fluctuated around an average of 57,000 per annum.

Emigration to Australia and Ocean Passenger Traffic[23]

Year	Passengers carried by sea from Britain to Australia	Period 1 July to 30 June	Emigrants to Australia from Britain (total)
1960	56,400	1960–61	34,700
1961	59,600	1961–62	27,000
1962	55,300	1962–63	41,700
1963	62,400	1963–64	54,630
1964	66,700	1964–65	.....

The Australian traffic, of course, is notable also for the sizeable number of people travelling back to Britain, the figure for this having fluctuated, since 1960, between 30,000 and 34,000 per annum. The figures for movements by sea to Australia may be compared with those for air transport, in which there was an 82 per cent increase in 1963 as compared with 1962; but the statistics for total air travel to Australia showed a consistent upward trend during the period 1961–63, whereas those for sea were erratic.

Passenger Movement by Air between Australia–New Zealand and the U.K. [24]

Year	To U.K.	From U.K.
	('ooo passengers)	
1961 . .	5·1	7·7
1962 . .	6·3	10·0
1963 . .	7·1	19·6
1964 . .	8·9	37·3

A contrasting pattern in the two competing transport forms is also shown in the figures for Atlantic traffic where the trend is much more strongly in favour of air. Many more people are

Passenger Movement by Air and Sea between the U.K. and North America
(U.S.A. and Canada) [25]
('ooo passengers)

Year	To U.K.		From U.K.	
	Air	*Sea*	*Air*	*Sea*
1961 . .	392·5	129·8	398·2	121·2
1962 . .	446·1	130·8	458·7	128·4
1963 . .	507·1	125·5	527·7	127·1
1964 . .	639·0	114·8	670·3	115·4

travelling between Britain and North America; but nearly all of the new traffic is going to the air operators.

Sea transport can offer much greater comfort and amenities: the reasons why people choose to forgo them lie in the advantages of saving time. Year by year planes are travelling at greater speeds, and the disparity in the performances between ship and plane will increase as supersonic aircraft come into service.

In the cargo trade, things are very different: the freight-carrying airline still operates at a very considerable disadvantage compared with the shipowner. This is so, despite the increasingly frequent reductions in air-freight rates. A number of attempts have been made to average out costs for different forms of transport. Thus Bengtson and Van Royen have produced comparative figures, although the terms in which these are presented make it plain that only some of them are averages: a direct comparison is made between the average costs per ton-mile of freight by rail ($0.02), road ($0.05), and air transport ($0.15). But ocean-going freight can go 'as low as' $0.001; river barges 'can move bulky freight' for $0.004, while Great Lakes freighter rates have had 'a rock bottom' of $0.0008 per ton-mile.[26] Thoman has offered an alternative range of comparison, which he presents as 'generalized averages': these give Great Lakes freights 'as low as' $0.001; and ocean freights as $0.002 per ton-mile.

Most freight traffic across the oceans is likely to be carried by ship for a very long time to come; but the airlines are still struggling to reduce their freight rates to an economic level. Improvements, however, continue to accumulate in ship operation: the Japanese, for instance, have made remarkable progress with automative processes; and there has been a very large advance in the efficient handling of specialized bulk cargoes, such as oil, coal, ores, and grain, especially at such Continental ports as Antwerp, Amsterdam, and Rotterdam, which have benefited from the expansion of trade among the Common Market countries. Rotterdam has grown more quickly than her rivals, but is more dependent upon petroleum, which, in its crude form alone, accounts for almost two-thirds of Rotterdam's imports and, refined, makes up a quarter of her exports. The main ports of the Low Countries — Amsterdam, Rotterdam, Antwerp, and Ghent — between them, have more traffic than New York and London combined.

Of the Port of London's total traffic of 59 million tons handled in 1965–66, 26 million tons was petroleum and 12 million tons coal, these two items taking up nearly two-thirds of all traffic.[27] New York has an even larger proportion — 70 per cent — of bulk cargo in its total foreign traffic, much of which is carried in specialist vessels. Efficiency of handling may be promoted by the concentration of traffic in a few ports (nearly a third, by value, of all United Kingdom trade passes through London); but great problems of inland transport are likely to ensue in a country such as Britain, which is not endowed with a comprehensive system of waterways to move the goods from the docks.

Handling techniques, generally, are in a process of transformation. For some time containers have been used on a larger and larger scale on ship, lorry, and train. They can be refrigerated for food movement, which is a most important matter to a country so dependent on imports as Britain. Now, roll-on-roll-off vessels are coming into service that are capable of handling foods and liquids. The semi-trailers pioneered by Denmark can be plugged into deck installations to keep food refrigerated on the crossing between Esbjerg and Harwich or Copenhagen and Felixstowe.[28] Similar techniques can cope with the outsize units of 200–400 tons for new power stations, but loads of this size are frequently too large for existing lifting gear.[29]

There has been a remarkable growth compared with pre-1939 days, and even 1950, in petroleum's share of ocean cargo. In 1961, for the first time, more than half of total world freight carried was tanker cargo.

World Seaborne Trade — Weight of Cargo Carried[30]
(million metric tons)

Year	Tanker cargo	Dry cargo	Total
1937	105	375	480
1950	225	300	525
1955	350	450	800
1959	480	490	970
1960	530	540	1070
1961	590	550	1140
1962	660	570	1230
1963	710	620	1330
1964	800	680	1480

Just as companies have combined their sea and air business, in order to balance prospects in a changing world, so ocean passenger and freight lines have come together. In some parts of the world there have been long periods when trade has languished. Large sections of the merchant fleets have been laid up and cargo rates for those ships still in operation have been low. But the picture has not been wholly depressing. Critical events in the international field can serve to stimulate trade, and some countries, particularly the Soviet Union, have made very big efforts to increase trade and to build or buy a vastly augmented fleet to transport these goods. Shipping now carries a bigger proportion of total Soviet freight turnover (4·9 per cent in 1940; 5·6 per cent in 1950; 7 per cent in 1960) than it did a generation ago. The absolute figures for freight carried by

Transport

Soviet shipping were 39·7 milliard ton-km. in 1950, increasing to
106·3 in 1958, 115·7 in 1959, 131·5 in 1960, 159·1 in 1961, and 173·0
milliard ton-km. in 1962.[31] For a number of reasons the Russians
have been energetic in seeking to increase their merchant — and
fishing — fleets, and the areas of their operations. The speed of
advance has by all accounts been remarkable, even for the Soviet
Union. According to Soviet sources, two-thirds of her maritime
fleet came from the slipways in the eight or nine years prior to
1964.[32] According to the Americans, the Russians, in October 1963,
were building, or having built for them, merchant ships with an
aggregate cargo capacity of about 4 million tons.[33] This figure was
not far short of the combined total tonnage launched in 1963 by
the three leading shipbuilding nations: Japan, West Germany, and
Britain. 1965 figures for Soviet Russia showed an increase on those
of 1963, with 6·5 million tons of shipping on order. Targets for total
tonnages in 1970 stood at 10–11 million tons and, for 1980, 18–22
million tons,[34] the last figure comparing with the present American
and British fleets. However, even the Soviet goal is surpassed by the
Japanese, who are credited with plans to expand their merchant
fleet from the 1964 level of 10·8 million to 34 million gross tons in
1980.[35]

There is no necessary correspondence between tonnage launched
and the size of the national merchant fleets; and world tonnage by
flag has little relation to the trade of owner nations. The latter
discrepancy has arisen chiefly through the use of legal expedients.
Vessels, particularly tankers, have been registered under the flags
of minor States, especially Liberia, Panama, and Honduras. Some
British ships, for the sake of reduced taxation, use Bermuda as an
'accommodation address'.[36] Liberia has the largest tanker fleet in
the world — Russia, the sixth largest total tonnage.

World Tonnage by Flag — All Vessels[37]
('ooo gross tons)

Country	1961	1962	1963	1964	1965
U.K.	20,277	20,311	21,565	21,490	21,530
U.S.A.[38]	23,143	22,322	23,132	22,430	21,527
Liberia	10,408	10,560	11,391	14,550	17,539
Norway	11,775	12,459	13,669	14,477	15,641
Japan	7,257	8,111	9,977	10,813	11,971

World Tanker Tonnage[39]
(*'ooo gross tons*)

Country	1962	1963	1964	1965 (*prelim.*)
Liberia . .	6,792	7,042	8,619	10,623
Norway . .	6,701	7,064	7,664	8,345
U.K. . . .	7,466	7,792	8,002	7,939
U.S.A. . . .	5,230	4,647	4,595	4,516

NOTES

1. *Middle East* (Europa Publications, annually).
2. 'Canals: New Life for Hardening Arteries', *Financial Times*, 26 Sept. 1962.
3. British Railways Board.
4. D. L. Munby, 'The Future of British Railways', *The Times Review of Industry and Technology*, London and Cambridge Bulletin no. 49 (March 1964).
5. *Jane's World Railways, 1965–66*.
6. Including the Great Lakes.
7. F. C. Margetts, 'British Railways and the Future', *Railway Gazette*, 12 Oct. 1962.
8. British Railways Board, *The Reshaping of British Railways* (1963).
9. Ibid.
10. J. Kolbuszewski, 'Transportation Problems: New Thinking Needed', *Financial Times*, 15 Oct. 1962.
11. *Traffic in Towns* (H.M.S.O., 1963), p. 26.
12. Ibid., p. 26.
13. Ibid., p. 197.
14. A. B. B. Valentine, 'Lessons from the U.S. on City Traffic', *The Times*, 15 Jan. 1963. See also 'Mass Transport as a Traffic Solution', *The Times*, 12 Dec. 1963.
15. *Financial Times*, 18 Dec. 1962.
16. *Guardian*, 28 Feb. 1964.
17. H. G. Conway, *Financial Times*, 3 Sept. 1962.
18. Ibid.
19. *The World's Railways, 1963–64* (Sampson Low, 1965), p. 258.
20. Ibid., p. 344.
21. *Statistical Abstract of the United States*, 1965, p. 559.
22. F. H. Keenlyside, 'The Future of Passenger Shipping and Competition with Air', *Travel and Tourist Encyclopaedia* (Travel World, 1959), p. 285.
23. Ocean Travel Development.
24. Board of Trade.
25. Board of Trade.
26. Bengtson and Van Royen, *Fundamentals of Economic Geography*, p. 562.
27. Port of London Authority, *Annual Report*, 1965–66, p. 6.
28. *The Times*, 15 April 1965.

29. *The Times*, 13 Aug. 1965.

30. United Nations.

31. 'Russian Shipping Plans Big Expansion Drive', *The Times*, 2 Jan. 1964.

32. Ibid.

33. Ibid.

34. *The Times*, 4 Jan. 1965.

35. *The Times*, 13 April 1965.

36. *Financial Times*, 28 Nov. 1962.

37. *Lloyd's Register of Shipping:* Chamber of Commerce of the U.K., *Annual Report.*

38. Includes reserve fleet (9·5 million tons in 1965).

39. *Lloyd's Register of Shipping;* Chamber of Shipping of the U.K., *Annual Report.*

The simplest form of economy is usually primitive in the extreme, based upon local self-sufficiency where there is no recourse to trade. Wealth and progress depend upon a division of labour and upon the processes that this presupposes — namely, exchange and trade.

Exchange and Trade

In the simplest types of society, exchange is in the form of barter. No money transaction is involved and banking is not necessary; but such expedients are not confined to the peoples living near to the subsistence level. Barter has frequently been used in exchanges between different levels of civilization and between the Eastern and Western blocs. But the medium of most commerce is money.

Exchange and trade are expressions concerned with the same process: they are partly mathematical, partly social, involving an interchange between persons A and B and a movement between places X and Y. Trade proceeds by a limited number of given routes, mainly by road, rail, and water. The process involved may be complex. Not only does it require the use of money — expressed in as many denominations as there are members of the United Nations — but it commonly involves a great number of transactions. A buys from B, who pays out of the receipts obtained from C and D. A also trades with C and D, and all have dealings with E, F, and G. Exchanges may occur between individuals and groups, between regions and nations, but the decisive element in trade is that imparted by the national unit. It is still necessary to study the effects made on the pattern of trade by the decisions of statesmen who are motivated by commercial, political, patriotic, or even ideological considerations.

From the overwhelming reality of the very existence of independent nation-states arise the unwelcome facts of manipulation and interference with the 'natural' processes of trade. These last are presumed to approximate to the objective of a system of free exchange.

Trade

Free Trade and Protection

Ideally, free trade is suited to the concept of a perfect division of labour. By this, countries produce those items that they are suited best by nature to provide. Speaking purely geographically, one would need to substitute 'regions' for 'countries', but realism prompts us to accept the fact of political division.

Unfortunately, there are a multitude of reasons, commercial and political, to account for the reluctance, both of statesmen and their public, to admit the desirability of free trade in practice. Protectionist ideas have two main supports: the requirements of domestic producers and the strategic interests of the country as a whole. It may be argued that consumers, as against producers, are best served by freeing trade; but consumers are also producers, so that it is not always easy to be single-minded in interest and policy.

Protectionist devices have had many forms, the two main ones having been tariffs or import duties, and physical controls such as quotas. The quota can be a vehicle for commercial and political discrimination which, in its extreme form, leads to embargo. The opposite of discrimination is preference, the one being a negative deterrence to trade, the other a positive stimulus. For the past generation and a half, a main plank of British governmental policy has been Commonwealth preference, conferring large advantages upon exporters from countries such as Australia, New Zealand, and Canada.

Fluctuations in Trade

A great increase in production has in the past normally led to an increase in trade. The faulty elements in the economic process have occurred in the links joining producer to consumer. Production has often outrun demand, while at the consuming end of the process wants may have been extremely urgent but consumers too poor to satisfy them.

The 1930s represented the low-water mark in the recent history of international trade. Rescue came chiefly in the shape of rearmament and stockpiling against the threat of war. Similarly, successive crises have helped to promote trade since the end of the Second World War. The phenomenon of the 'trade cycle', with its alternation of boom and slump, was once considered inevitable — a fact of national as well as international life; but the recent appearance of giant trading blocs may well affect the pattern of future trade fluctuations.

304

Formerly, the economies of vast territories were ordered completely by the respective Imperial Powers: their trade was tailored to suit the special requirements of the mother country. Colonies were built originally upon the need to supply cheap raw materials in return for manufactured goods. There was no hard-and-fast rule: in British India, important native mercantile and manufacturing interests developed, but it is clear that the coming of independence and the end of Empire brought a greatly accelerated process of industrialization. This happened in India. The pattern of trade between Britain and Bombay has altered with the pattern of production. The example of Hong-Kong shows how a cohesive population can develop a commercial stature with important international implications.

For the past decade, there has been controversy over the role of the European Economic Community — the Common Market. Initially, the chief impact of E.E.C. was internal, consisting in an impressive increase in production and intra-Community trade. But the Common Market countries constitute a vast trading organization on an international scale. As such, they are a potent factor influencing the attitude of extra-Community Powers, such as the United States. Eventually, it may well be that we shall see a greatly enlarged Community, performing as an equal with the other trading blocs of North America and the Soviet sphere of influence.

From Colonies to Independent States

In commercial terms, Britain has a reputation as an exporter of industrial goods. She is also well known as a carrier. By means of the return from Britain's services to other countries, she is normally able to continue to pay her way, but this desirable position was not reached during 1964–66.

TRADE OF THE U.K.

Trade of the U.K.[1]
(£ million)

Year	Total imports	Exports of British produce	Export of foreign and colonial produce	Total
1961	4,395	3,684	159	3,840
1962	4,487	3,791	157	3,949
1963	4,820	4,081	154	4,235
1964	5,696	4,412	153	4,565
1965	5,763	4,724	173	4,879

L H.G.P.

Trade The list of leading imports is notable for the great significance of petroleum. In 1960, petroleum and products derived from it accounted for 10·6 per cent of all British purchases from abroad. In 1961, with slightly reduced total imports, the corresponding percentage had increased to 11·0. This is quite a recent trend. In 1920–30, petroleum took up barely 3 per cent of total imports; in 1931–35, only 4 per cent. Nevertheless, in examining the detailed list, one perceives that Class 'A' imports — the basic materials of manufacture, the metal ores, the rubber, fibres, raw fertilizers, and vegetable oils — are, in their aggregate, less significant than the total of imported manufactured goods.

When mineral fuels, especially oil, are added to the 'basic materials', we see that Britain's imports fall neatly into three almost equal categories:

1. *Class 'A'* — food, beverages, and tobacco.
   Value of imports of Class 'A' (£ million):

1962	1,569
1963	1,678
1964	1,771
1965	1,710

2. *Class 'B'* — basic materials.
   Class 'C' — mineral fuels and lubricants.
   Value of imports of Classes 'B' and 'C' (£ million):

1962	1,457
1963	1,553
1964	1,703
1965	1,728

3. *Class 'D'* — manufactured goods.
   Value of imports of Class 'D' (£ million):

1962	1,443
1963	1,569
1964	2,161
1965	2,253

4. The remaining *Class 'E'* is negligible as a portion of the total — this class comprises postal packages and live animals not intended for food.
   Imports of Class 'E' (£ million):

1962	17
1963	21
1964	62
1965	72

306

The items that perhaps occasion most surprise are the manufactured goods.

A number of items, in the manufacture of which Britain holds a world reputation, nevertheless form significant elements in our import trade. Examples are electrical machinery and apparatus, road vehicles, and aircraft. Traditional skills ensure that her clothing industry can still sell abroad. One of the most discriminating markets — that of the United States — takes large quantities of British ready-made and fashion goods; so do France and Italy. But for some years now Britain has been importing more clothing and footwear than she has exported.

In export figures, what is remarkable is the continued comparative (and absolute) advance of engineering products, especially machinery and cars. Successes have been gained in such highly competitive items as agricultural machinery. There has been a drastic fluctuation in sales of aircraft and aircraft components. Some lines have sold consistently well; many American-built planes, for instance, are powered by British engines, but the British aircraft industry as a whole was badly affected by a series of misfortunes, chief among which were the Comet disasters. It remains to be seen how the Concord project and Britain's entry into the supersonic race will affect her share of the market. The success of the National Plan, produced in 1965, depended partly upon a substantial growth in exports from the mechanical and electrical engineering industries. The decline of exports from the British shipbuilding industry continued, however, in the period 1958–63, with ships providing only 1 per cent of her exports in 1962–63.

Britain's chemical industry retains its status in production and exports, and this is one sphere in which trade may involve even larger items than the average cargo or passenger vessel; very large chemical plants are on order for the Soviet Union and Eastern Europe. A polyester fibre plant, sold in 1964, was worth £30 million. Chemicals are given a high rating in the prospects for 1964–70.

Britain's share of total world exports has fluctuated, but its general trend between 1913 and 1960 was decisively downwards. Central Office of Information statistics show Britain's percentage of world trade as having been 50 per cent lower in 1951 than in 1929. The C.O.I. annual figures are at variance with others issued by the International Monetary Fund, but the trend is agreed. In 1963, her

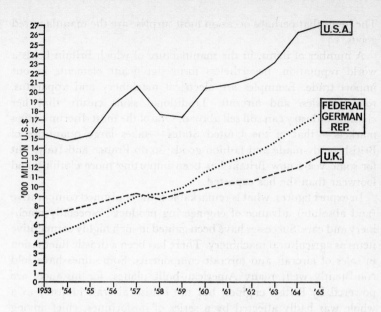

FIG. 21.1   Major trading nations — export trends
The U.S.A. is now by far the world's largest exporter. By 1958
West Germany had passed the U.K.

share of world trade was appreciably lower than that of West
Germany (Fig. 21.1).

A generation ago, Britain was still the world's leading importer,
though in exports she was being challenged by the U.S.A. By the
1960s, Britain had been left far behind by the Americans as an
exporter and had even been supplanted in second place by the

Comparison of Leading U.K. Exports[2]
(per cent of total exports)

	1955	1958	1960	1962	1963	1964
Machinery . . .	22·3	24·4	26·1	28·7	28·8	27·6
Road motor vehicles .	9·7	11·2	12·5	11·9	12·2	12·6
Aircraft, aircraft engines . .	2·1	4·5	3·8	2·8	2·7	2·5
Ships and boats .	1·9	2·0	1·5	1·0	1·0	0·7
Metals . . .	12·4	13·3	12·9	12·4	11·3	11·7
Textiles . . .	11·9	9·1	8·4	7·3	7·3	6·5
Chemicals . . .	8·2	8·3	9·0	9·1	9·0	9·7

Trade of
the U.K.

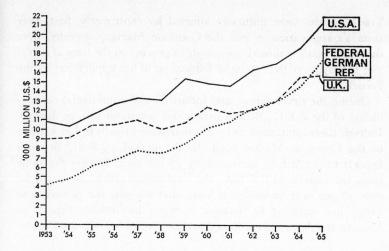

FIG. 21.2 Major trading nations — import trends

Britain's excessively high import bill was reduced by drastic
measures in 1964–66.

West Germans. As an importer, the United Kingdom had seen the
Americans draw ahead since 1955 in their selective purchases of raw
materials and manufactured goods. In their turn, the Americans,
having taken over Britain's former role as the world's greatest trader,
have learned some unpalatable facts about the responsibilities and
anxieties of this position. To export, as the United States does,
almost as much as the combined totals of her two chief rivals, is to
become dependent on other countries to an alarming degree. One
of the consequences of her commercial ties is to produce an American
involvement, even against her will, in the trading problems of the
rest of the world (Fig. 21.2).

The trading balance-sheet of the United States is rather different
from Britain's. The Americans, unlike the British, have a consistent
trade surplus. With Britain, her position is greatly eased by what
are termed 'invisible exports': that is, payment for the services we
perform as carrier and insurer for other nations. In the U.S.A., on
the other hand, there is actually a net financial loss because of
outgoings not shown on the normal import–export balance sheet:
'the total outflow of capital and of both military and economic
aid is sufficiently substantial to cause a massive overall payments
deficit'.[3]

L2 H.G.P.

309

Trade

Trade with
Common
Market and
Common-
wealth

Trade policies were naturally affected by controversy, first, over Britain's application to join the Common Market; secondly, over the terms that she should endeavour to procure at the time of entry; and thirdly, over the successful frustration of her application by the French.

During the development and industrial and commercial consolidation of the E.E.C., Britain's trade did not stand still, or decline. Indeed, there continued to be a remarkable growth in her exports to the Common Market itself. In the period 1958–61, Britain's exports to the E.E.C. increased by 47 per cent. During the same time, her exports to E.F.T.A., the rival organization, increased by only 38 per cent, showing, at least, that she was not powerless to better her standing in 'fortress Europe'; but British exports to Canada and Australia continued to exceed those to Italy and France.

E.E.C. Countries as Export Markets of the U.K.[4]
(export values in £ million)

Leading markets	1962	1963	1964
U.S.A. . . .	348	360	379
Australia . . .	231	238	252
Federal German Republic .	225	240	246
Rep. of South Africa .	148	198	225
Sweden . . .	158	174	204
France . . .	152	195	201
Netherlands . . .	158	176	200
Canada . . .	194	180	193
Italy . . .	148	176	140
India . . .	118	138	139

Important as the Commonwealth market is to Britain, the U.K. market has, in the past, been still more vital to Commonwealth members. But there are differences between individual countries. New Zealand leans very heavily on the commercial connection with Britain, but Canada's economic destinies are inevitably tied to those of North America in general, and the American market is also of growing significance to Australia. In Australia's export trade, Japan has assumed a greater role and, by 1964–65, a third of Australia's total exports were going to South-East Asia, considerably more than were going to Britain. In connection with the Common Market controversy one can, of course, add that, successful as Britain's trading was with the E.E.C. countries, it would surely be vastly more so with Britain as a full partner to the Six.

Britain's trade with the U.S.A. is of outstanding importance to her economy. Britain, and the other countries of Western Europe, are acutely sensitive to changes in America's trading policy. U.K. exports to the United States include such well-tried items as Scotch whisky, tweeds, and woollens. Engineering and chemicals are to the fore, and British tractor and cycle industries would have fared badly without the American market.

One possibility that has often been canvassed is a material increase in the volume and proportion of U.K. trade with the East, and with the Communist countries. In 1962, the total trade of Comecon countries (the Soviet Union and the East European States) with Britain amounted to £290 million. This was divided almost 50–50 between Russia and the smaller Communist States. Over the past few years, Britain's trade with Russia has been about equal to that with Belgium. Russia's volume of trade with the Six has been a little greater than that of her exchanges with Britain. In percentages, only 3–4 per cent of Britain's total trade has been with Russia; and less than 1 per cent of Russia's Gross National Product has gone into trade with the West. Clearly there is scope for trade expansion with a bloc of peoples that numbered some 350 million in 1965. In order for this to occur, there must be a positive attitude on both sides. Much of Britain's export trade to Russia has been in the form of large bulk orders. Examples from recent years have involved the furnishing of whole petro-chemical, synthetic-fibre, and sugar-beet factories.

The United Kingdom has for some years had an unfavourable balance of trade with the Soviet Union, and important restrictions have contributed to the curtailment of potential exchanges. British

Trade between U.K. and the Soviet Union
(£ million)

	1960	1961	1962	1963	1964
Exports from Britain of domestic produce .	37	43	42	55	38
Exports from Britain of foreign and colonial produce . . .	16	26	16	8	1·7
Imports into U.K. from Soviet Union . .	75	85	84	91	90

governments have not been willing to make trade agreements conditional upon the acceptance of Soviet oil. One simple, if short-term solution to difficulties such as the cereal deficiencies occurring throughout Eastern Europe since 1963 has been the trading of wheat — from the prairie lands of North America and Australia — for Siberian gold.

TRADE OF THE UNITED STATES

Today the United States has the largest national share of world trade. Since 1950 her percentage has been almost twice that of Britain. The details of America's trade illustrate the complexity of the cross-currents in modern national commercial balance sheets. There are almost no items wholly plus or minus in the table of imports and exports. One of the very few exceptions is wheat. This is an important export, but it is not listed as an import. On the other hand, the petroleum and automobile markets are notable for cross-trading, even though the United States is world-renowned as a source of both.

United States — Selected Imports (I) and Exports (E)[5]
(mill. U.S. dollars)

	1961		1962		1963		1964	
	I	E	I	E	I	E	I	E
Wheat, including flour		1,300		1,135		1,330		1,533
Petroleum and petroleum products	1,637	398	1,729	401	1,782	445	1,873	419
Chemicals	732	1,787	765	1,843	706	1,979	707	2,358
Metals and metal manufacturers	1,383	1,318	1,649	1,287	1,837	1,386	2,101	1,647
Iron and steelmill products	347	467	457	457	601	513	714	650
Copper (base metal)	188	270	280	222	296	206	384	225
Machinery and transport equipment	1,359	6,139	1,668	6,590	1,790	6,895	2,206	8,020
Transport equipment	573	1,651	719	1,719	756	1,784	902	2,023
Automobiles and parts	378	1,085	515	1,188	566	1,343	687	1,546

U.K. and U.S.A. Exports[6]

	Values ('000 mill. U.S. dollars)					Percentage of world total				
	1950–54	1955–59	1960	1961	1962	1950–54	1955–59	1960	1961	1962
U.S.A.	14·3	18·2	29·6	21·0	21·6	19·8	19·2	18·2	17·7	17·4
U.K.	7·4	9·2	10·3	10·8	11·1	10·2	9·7	9·1	9·1	8·9

America's attitude to trade with the rest of the world has not been without its doubts and contradictions and surviving isolationist attitudes have not helped. Opposed to the old traditions have been the interests, direct or indirect, of farm communities, in the disposal of huge surplus stocks of grain. In addition there has been the political aim of administrations in Washington to support friends and allies abroad by measures and agencies such as Lend-Lease, U.N.R.R.A., the Marshall Plan, and the Mutual Security Programme.[7]

Trade of the U.S.

U.S. Attitude to World Trade

America has been greatly interested, first in the developments leading to the creation of the E.E.C., and later in its abortive negotiations with Britain. Americans officially have welcomed the creation of a stronger and larger market in Europe, but this process has not been an unqualified blessing to U.S. industry. The Trade Expansion Act, passed by the U.S. Congress in October 1962, permitted the U.S. Government 'to halve tariffs on any goods in which more than half of the world's exports are provided by America and the E.E.C., and to scrap them altogether when the two trading groups account for more than 80 per cent'.[8]

There is no doubt of America's concern with the cumulative factors influencing the commercial life of the great nations and international consortia: her interest has been shown since the earliest days of the United Nations, but it has not been entirely positive or well orientated. The draft of an international trade charter — the Havana Charter — drawn up, during the crucial years 1946–48, by a Preparatory Committee of the United Nations Economic and Social Council, failed to obtain ratification by the United States. For the abortive Havana concord there was substituted the General Agreement on Tariffs and Trade, which came into force among the twenty-three signatories on January 1st 1948. It is this body, G.A.T.T., that is now the chief non-Communist international institution concerned with the regulation and ordering of commerce, and with attempts at major tariff reductions through agreement.

For example, in 1958, negotiations were commenced between G.A.T.T. and the E.E.C. which concerned world trade in some of the main tropical and subtropical commodities: tea, coffee, cocoa, tobacco, and sugar. Viewing the problem on a world basis, it is vitally necessary that G.A.T.T. should not acquire the flavour or reputation of a rich man's club. The underdeveloped nations must be assured of due consideration as political equals. The less developed

313

Trade

countries require, as their right, 'guaranteed markets at stable prices for their commodity exports, and outlets for their sheltered infant industries'.[9]

The Under-developed Countries and World Trade

The continuing economic crisis affecting the underdeveloped countries of the world has two main aspects: the dangerously increasing population pressure; and the growing difficulty of paying for necessary imports by the sale of primary products, some at least of which come into an already saturated market. There have been positive factors: demand has risen in the industrialized countries; there have been sudden stimuli — the Korean War, the Suez crisis of 1956, and the Vietnam war. There do exist potential (and actual) markets in the Soviet Union and China, which offer some promise, as industrialization takes hold on new regions in those nations. But there have also been depressive factors: 'various improvements in efficiency in the use of raw materials and an increasing use of synthetics — in part stimulated by the high price of natural products — meant that consumption of raw materials did not always keep pace with the growth of the economies of the highly industrialized countries.'[10] International trade cannot be a one-sided affair, with a permanent imbalance towards the more wealthy. Such a trend, if carried into the long term, can only impede general progress while hastening local crisis. Trade must grow and it must not be weighted against those who are most in need.

NOTES

1. *Statesman's Year-Book.*
2. *Board of Trade Journal*, vol. 186, no. 3489 (31 Jan. 1964).
3. Barclays Bank, *Intelligence Reports*, 13 Dec. 1963.
4. *Statesman's Year-Book.*
5. *Statesman's Year-Book.* Excluded from the list, for 'security reasons', military equipment, military vehicles and aircraft, and 'certain other apparatus'.
6. Bank of London and South America: International Monetary Fund.
7. See Sydney C. Reagan, *Export Programmes for Surplus Agricultural Commodities, 1954 to 1957* (Southern Methodist Univ. Press, Dallas, 1959), pp. 97–98.
8. *Sunday Times*, 27 Jan. 1963.
9. *Guardian*, 29 Jan. 1963.
10. Bank of London and South America, *Annual Review* (March 1964).

Bibliography

The Growth of World Industry. United Nations, 1963.

General

Bengtson, N. A., and Van Royen, W., *Fundamentals of Economic Geography.* 5th ed., Constable, 1964.

Birmingham, W., and Ford, A. G. (eds.), *Planning and Growth in Rich and Poor Countries.* Allen & Unwin, 1966.

Boesch, H., *A Geography of World Economy.* Van Nostrand, 1964.

Fryer, D. W., *World Economic Development.* McGraw-Hill, 1965.

Gregor, H. F., *Environment and Economic Life: An Economio and Social Geography.* Van Nostrand, 1963.

Hearst, S., *2,000 Million Poor.* Harrap, 1965.

Jones, C. F., and Darkenwald, C. G., *Economic Geography.* 3rd ed., Macmillan, New York, 1965.

Shonfield, A., *The Attack on World Poverty.* Chatto & Windus, 1960.

Stamp, Sir L. D., *Our Developing World.* Faber, 1960.

Thoman, R. S., *The Geography of Economic Activity: An Introductory World Survey.* McGraw-Hill, 1962.

Thomas, R. S., and Patton, D. J. (eds.), *Focus on Geographical Activities: A Collection of Original Studies.* McGraw-Hill, 1964.

Chapter 1

Commonwealth Economic Committee, Commodity Series (*Grain Crops; Plantation Crops; Dairy Produce*). H.M.S.O., annually.

Demographic Yearbook. United Nations.

F.A.O. Yearbook. Rome.

Beaujeu-Garnier, J., *Geography of Population.* Longmans, 1966.

Findlay, W. M., *Oats: Their Cultivation and Use from Ancient Times to the Present Day.* Oliver & Boyd, 1956.

Grist, D. H., *Rice.* 4th ed., Longmans, 1965.

Haarer, A. E., *Modern Coffee Production.* 2nd ed., Leonard Hill, 1964.

Harler, C. R., *The Culture and Marketing of Tea.* Oxford U.P., 1956.

P.E.P., *World Population and Resources.* Allen & Unwin, 1955.

Peterson, R. F., *Wheat.* Leonard Hill, 1966.

Bibliography
Russell, Sir E. J., *World Population and Food Supplies*. Allen & Unwin, 1954.

Thomas, W. L., Jr. (ed.), *Man's Role in Changing the Face of the Earth*. Chicago U.P., 1956.

Timoshenko, V. P., and Swerling, B. C., *The World's Sugar*. Oxford U.P., 1957.

Urquhart, D. H., *Cocoa*. 2nd ed., Longmans, 1961.

Van Royen, W., *Agricultural Resources of the World*. Prentice-Hall, 1954.

Woytinsky, W. S. and E. S., *World Population and Production*. Twentieth Century Fund, New York, 1953.

Zelinsky, W., *A Prologue to Population Geography*. Prentice-Hall, 1966.

Chapter 2
Agriculture in the World Economy. 2nd ed., United Nations, 1962.

Commonwealth Economic Committee, *Industrial Fibres*. H.M.S.O., 1965 (revised annually).

——, *Vegetable Oils and Oilseeds*. H.M.S.O., 1965 (revised annually).

F.A.O. Yearbook. Rome.

Barclays Bank, Intelligence Reports.

Brown, H. B., and Ware, J. O., *Cotton*. McGraw-Hill, 1958.

Hemy, G. W., *Cotton Growing in the Soviet Union*. Joseph Crosfield, Warrington, 1958.

Kirby, R. H., *Vegetable Fibres*. Leonard Hill, 1963.

Lock, G. W., *Sisal*. Longmans, 1962.

Matthews, J. M., and Mauersberger, H. R., *Textile Fibres*. Wiley, 1954.

Norman, A. G. (ed.), *The Soybean*. Academic Press, 1964.

Polhamus, L. G., *Rubber: Botany, Production and Utilization*. Leonard Hill, 1962.

Schidrowitz, P., *et al.*, *History of the Rubber Industry*. Heffer, 1952.

Chapter 3
Department of Scientific and Industrial Research, *A Handbook of Softwoods*. H.M.S.O., 1957.

Forestry Commission, *Annual Report*. H.M.S.O.

Handbook of Commerce and Industry. Ministry of Trade, Accra, Ghana (annually).

Herring Industry Board, *Annual Report*. H.M.S.O.

World Fisheries. United Nations (annually).

Morgan, R., *World Sea Fisheries*. Methuen, 1956.

Phillips, J.. *Development of Agriculture and Forestry in the Tropics*. Faber, 1961.

Singer, B., *Living Silver: An Impression of the British Fishing Industry*. Secker & Warburg, 1957.

Titmuss, F. H., *A Concise Encyclopedia of World Timbers*. 2nd ed., The Technical Press, 1959.

Wright, J. M., *Deep-Sea Fisheries*. Black, 1958.

F.A.O. Commodity Review. Rome (annually).

Government of India, *Report of the Plantation Enquiry Commission*: pt. i, *Tea*; pt. ii, *Coffee*; pt. iii, *Rubber*; Manager of Government Publications, New Delhi, 1956–57.

Yearbook of Agriculture, U.S. Department of Agriculture (annually).

Courtenay, P. P., *Plantation Agriculture*. Bell, 1965.

Gourou, P., *The Tropical World* (trans. Laborde, E. D.). 4th ed., Longmans, 1966.

Hopfen, J. H., *Farm Implements for Arid and Tropical Regions*. F.A.O., Rome, 1960.

Irvine, F. R., *A Textbook of West African Agriculture*. 2nd ed., Oxford U.P., 1953.

Jin-Bee, O., *Land, People and Economy in Malaya*. Longmans, 1963.

Ochse, J. J., *et al.*, *Tropical and Sub-Tropical Agriculture*. 2 vols., Macmillan, New York, 1961.

Tempany, Sir H., and Grist, D. H., *An Introduction to Tropical Agriculture*. Longmans, 1958.

Webster, C. C., and Wilson, P. N., *Agriculture in the Tropics*. Longmans, 1966.

Wrigley, G., *Tropical Agriculture: The Development of Production*. Batsford, 1961.

Chapter 4

F.A.O. Yearbook. Rome.

Fertilizers: Annual Review of World Production, Consumption and Trade. F.A.O., Rome.

President's Water Resources Policy Commission: A Water Policy for the American People. U.S. Government Printing Office, 1950.

Yearbook of Agriculture: Soil. U.S. Department of Agriculture, 1957.

Yearbook of Agriculture: Water. U.S. Department of Agriculture, 1955.

Chapter 5

Bibliography Coppock, J. T., *An Agricultural Atlas of England and Wales*. Faber, 1964.

Derry, T. K., and Williams, T. I., *A Short History of Technology*. Oxford U.P., 1960.

Digby, M., *Co-operative Land Use: The Challenge to Traditional Co-operation*. Blackwell, 1963.

Duckham, A. N., *Agricultural Synthesis: The Farming Year*. Chatto & Windus, 1963.

Filipchuk, A., *Agricultural Development in the U.S.S.R.* Soviet Booklet No. 98, London, 1962.

Haystead, L., and Fite, G. C., *The Agricultural Regions of the United States*. Methuen, 1955.

Hirsch, G. P., and Hunt, K. E., *British Agriculture: Its Structure and Organisation*. Evans, 1957.

Lee, N. E., *Harvests and Harvesting Through the Ages*. Cambridge U.P., 1960.

Meinig, D. W., *On the Margins of the Good Earth* [South Australia]. Murray, 1963.

Mighell, R. L., *American Agriculture: Its Structure and Place in the Economy*. Chapman & Hall, 1955.

Parson, R. L., *Conserving American Resources*. 2nd ed., Prentice-Hall, 1955.

Russell, Sir E. J., *The World of the Soil*. Collins, 1957.

Sanders, H. G., *An Outline of British Crop Husbandry*. Cambridge U.P., 1958.

Schad, T. M., *et al.*, *Western Resources Papers, 1960*. Colorado U.P., 1961.

Chapter 6 Belov, F., *The History of a Soviet Collective Farm*. Praeger, New York, 1956.

Chao Kuo-Chun, *Agrarian Politics of Mainland China, 1949–56*. Harvard U.P., 1956.

——, *Economic Planning and Organization in Mainland China*. Harvard U.P., 1959.

Crook, I. and D., *The First Years of Yangyi Commune*. Routledge, 1965.

Darin-Drabkin, H., *Patterns of Co-operative Agriculture in Israel*. Israel Institute for Books, Tel-Aviv, 1962.

Halperin, H., *Changing Patterns in Israel Agriculture*. Routledge, 1957.

Jasny, N., *The Socialized Agriculture of the U.S.S.R.: Plans and Performance*. Stanford U.P., 1949.

318

Orni, E., *Forms of Settlement*. Jewish National Fund, Jerusalem, 1963.
Walston, Lord, *Agriculture under Communism*. Bodley Head, 1962.

Quarterly Bulletin of Steel Statistics for Europe. United Nations.

British Iron and Steel Federation, *Structural Change in World Ore*. 1963.
Burn, D., *The Steel Industry 1939–1959*. Cambridge U.P., 1961.
Keeling, B. S., and Wright, A. E. G., *The Development of the Modern British Steel Industry*. Longmans, 1964.
McQuillan, A. D. and M. K., *Titanium*. Butterworth, 1956.
Pounds, N. J. G., *The Geography of Iron and Steel*, rev. ed. Hutchinson, 1966.
Sully, A. H., *Manganese*. Butterworth, 1955.
——, *Chromium*. Butterworth, 1954.
Voskuil, W. H., *Minerals in World Industry*. McGraw-Hill, 1955.

The Non-Ferrous Metals Industry, 1962. O.E.C.D., Paris, 1964.
U.S. Bureau of Metal Statistics, *Annual Report*.

Barclays Bank, Intelligence Reports.
Butts, A. (ed.), *Copper: The Science and Technology of the Metal, its Alloys and Complexes*. Reinhold, 1954.
Carlson, A. S. (ed.), *The Economic Geography of Industrial Materials*. Chapman & Hall, 1956.
Dennis, W. H., *Metallurgy of the Non-Ferrous Metals*. 2nd ed., Pitman, 1961.
Grainger, L., *Uranium and Thorium*. Newnes, 1958.
Hampel, C. A. (ed.), *Rare Metals Handbook*. Reinhold, 1954.
Lewis, W., *The Light Metals Industry*. Temple Press, 1949.
Mantell, C. L., *Tin: Its Mining, Production, Technology and Applications*. Reinhold, 1949.
Metal Statistics. Metallgesellschaft, Frankfurt-am-Main (annually).
Quin's Metal Handbook. Metal Information Bureau (annually).

Some Aspects of the Motor Vehicle Industry in the U.S.A. O.E.E.C., Paris, 1953.

Burn, D. (ed.), *The Structure of British Industry*. 2 vols., Cambridge U.P., 1958.

Bibliography   Cunningham, W. G., *The Aircraft Industry: A Study in Industrial Location.* Morrison, Ithaca, N.Y., 1951.

Dunning, J. H., and Thomas, C. J., *British Industry: Change and Development in the Twentieth Century.* 2nd ed., Hutchinson, 1963.

Estall, R. C., and Buchanan, R. O., *Industrial Activity and Economic Geography.* Hutchinson, 1961.

Jones, L., *Shipbuilding in Britain — Mainly Between the Two Wars.* Univ. of Wales Press, 1957.

Maxey, G., and Silberston, A., *The Motor Industry.* Allen & Unwin, 1959.

Nevins, A., and Hill, F. E., *Ford: Decline and Rebirth, 1932–1962.* Scribner's, 1963.

Rae, J. B., *American Automobile Manufacturers.* Temple Press, 1959.

Turner, G., *The Car Makers.* Eyre & Spottiswoode, 1963; Penguin Books, 1964.

Chapter 10   *Report of the Textile Enquiry Commission.* Ministry of Industries, Karachi, 1960.

Report of the Textile Enquiry Committee. Ministry of Commerce and Industry, New Delhi, 1958.

Airov, J., *The Location of the Synthetic Fibre Industry.* Wiley, 1959.

Allen, G. C., *British Industries and their Organization.* 4th ed., Longmans, 1959.

Burn, D. (ed.), *The Structure of British Industry.* 2 vols., Cambridge U.P., 1958.

Hague, D. C., *The Economics of Man-Made Fibres.* Duckworth, 1957.

Rainnie, G. F., ed., *The Woollen and Worsted Industries.* Oxford U.P., 1965.

Chapter 11   *The Chemical Industry, 1962–63.* O.E.C.D., Paris, 1964.

Allcott, A., *Plastics Today.* Oxford U.P., 1960.

Barron, H., *Modern Synthetic Rubbers.* Chapman & Hall, 1949.

Burn, D. (ed.), *Structure of British Industry.* 2 vols., Cambridge U.P., 1958.

Electronics in Japan, 1962–63. Electronics Association of Japan, Tokyo, 1963.

Hague, D. C., *Economics of Man-Made Fibres.* Duckworth, 1957.

Hardie, D. W., and Pratt, J. D., *A History of the Modern British Chemical Industry.* Pergamon Press, 1966.

Jewkes, J., *et al.*, *The Sources of Invention*. Macmillan, 1958.
Kaufman, M., *The First Century of Plastics: Celluloid and its Sequel*. Iliffe, 1963.
Robson, R., *The Man-made Fibres Industry*. Macmillan, 1958.
Whitby, G. S., *et al.*, *Synthetic Rubber*. Chapman & Hall, 1954.

Investigation of the Concentration of Economic Power: final report and recommendations of the Temporary National Economic Committee, transmitted to the Congress of the U.S. U.S. Government Printing Office, 1941.
Report on the Distribution of Industrial Population (Cmd. 6153). H.M.S.O., 1940.

Allen, G. C., *British Industries and their Organization*. 4th ed., Longmans, 1959.
Dunning, J. H., and Thomas, C. J., *British Industry: Change and Development in the Twentieth Century*. 2nd ed., Hutchinson, 1963.
Estall, R. C., and Buchanan, R. O., *Industrial Activity and Economic Geography*. Hutchinson, 1961.
Fuchs, V. R., *Changes in the Location of Manufacturing in the United States since 1929*. Economic Census Studies, No. 1, Yale U.P., 1962.
Hall, P. G., *The Industries of London since 1861*. Hutchinson, 1962.
Perloff, H. S., *et al.*, *Regions, Resources and Economic Growth*. Johns Hopkins Press, 1961.
Robertson, Sir D. H., *Control of Industry*. Cambridge Economic Handbooks, Nisbet, 1960.
Smith, W., *Economic Geography of Great Britain*. Methuen, 1953.
Thoman, R. S., *The Geography of Economic Activity: An Introductory World Survey*. McGraw-Hill, 1962.
Thompson, J. H., *Methods of Plant Site Selection Available to Small Manufacturing Firms*. West Virginia U.P., 1961.

Chapter 12

N.E.D.C., *Conditions Favourable to Faster Growth*. H.M.S.O., 1963.
——, *Growth of the U.K. Economy to 1966*. H.M.S.O., 1963.
Public Expenditure in 1963–64 and 1967–68 (Cmnd. 2235). H.M.S.O., 1963.

Bauchet, M., *Economic Planning: The French Experience*. Heinemann, 1964.

Chapter 13

Bibliography

Das, N., *The Public Sector in India*. 2nd ed., Asia Publishing House, Bombay, 1961.

Freeman, T. W., *Geography and Planning*. Hutchinson, 1958.

Hackett, J. and A.-M., *Economic Planning in France*. Allen & Unwin, 1963.

Hanson, A. H. (ed.), *Nationalization: A Book of Readings*. Allen & Unwin, 1963.

Peacock, A. T., and Wiseman, J., *The Growth of Public Expenditure in the United Kingdom*. Oxford U.P., 1961.

P.E.P., *Government and Industry: a survey of the relations between the Government and privately-owned industry*. 1952.

Robson, W. A. (ed.), *Nationalised Industry and Public Ownership*. Allen & Unwin, 1962.

Thomas, M., *Atomic Energy and Congress*. Oxford U.P., 1956.

Chapter 14

Annual Bulletin of Electrical Energy Statistics for Europe. United Nations Economic Commission for Europe, New York.

Atomic Energy Facts. U.S. Atomic Energy Commission, 1957.

Central Electricity Generating Board, *Annual Report*.

Oil Today (1964). O.E.C.D., Paris, 1964.

The Coal Situation in Europe in 1962–63 and Future Prospects. United Nations, 1964.

The Nuclear Energy Industry of the U.K. 2nd ed., U.K. Atomic Energy Authority, 1961.

Hemy, G. W., *The Chinese Coal Industry*. Joseph Crosfield, 1961.

Manners, G., *The Geography of Energy*. Hutchinson, 1964.

Modelski, G. A., *Atomic Energy in the Communist Bloc*. Melbourne U.P., 1959.

Netschert, B. C., *The Future Supply of Oil and Gas*. Johns Hopkins Press, 1958.

Neuner, E. J., *The Natural Gas Industry: Monopoly and Competition in Field Markets*. Oklahoma U.P., 1960.

Self, Sir H., and Watson, E. M., *Electricity Supply in Great Britain: Its Development and Organization*. Allen & Unwin, 1952.

Spangler, M. B., *New Technology and the Supply of Petroleum*. Chicago U.P., 1956.

Yuan-Li Wu, *Economic Development: The Use of Energy Resources in Communist China*. Praeger, 1963.

322

Minerals Yearbook of the United States. U.S. Bureau of Mines, Washington.

Statistical Abstract of the United States. Bureau of the Census, U.S. Department of Commerce (annually).

Yearbook of Agriculture. U.S. Department of Agriculture (annually).

Adams, W. (ed.), *The Structure of American Industry: Some Case Studies.* 3rd ed., Macmillan, New York, 1961.

—— and Gary, H. M., *Monopoly in America.* Macmillan, New York, 1955.

Alderfer, E. B., and Michl, H. E., *Economics of American Industry.* 3rd ed., McGraw-Hill, 1957.

Allen, E. L., *Economics of American Manufacturing.* Holt, 1952.

Estall, R. C., *New England: a Study in Industrial Adjustment.* Bell, 1966.

Frasché, D. F., *Mineral Resources: A Report to the Committee on Natural Resources.* U.S. National Academy of Sciences and National Research Council, Washington, 1962.

Gainsbrugh, M. R. (ed.), *American Enterprise: The Next Ten Years.* Macmillan, New York, 1961.

Glover, J. G., *et al.*, *The Development of American Industries.* 4th ed., Pitman, 1959.

Hubbert, M. K., *Energy Resources: A Report to the Committee on Natural Resources.* U.S. National Academy of Sciences and National Research Council, Washington, 1962.

Jones, C. F., and Darkenwald, G. G., *Economic Geography.* 3rd ed., Macmillan, New York, 1965.

Martin, R. C. (ed.), *T.V.A.: The First Twenty Years.* Tennessee U.P., 1956.

Mighell, R. L., *American Agriculture: Its Structure and Place in the Economy.* Wiley, 1955.

Schroeder, G., *The Growth of the Major Steel Companies, 1900–1950.* Johns Hopkins Press, 1953.

Schurr, S. H., and Netschert, B. C., *Energy in the American Economy, 1850–1975.* Oxford U.P., 1960.

Wilcox, W. W., *Economics of American Agriculture.* Prentice-Hall, 1960.

The Structure and Growth of Soviet Industry: A Comparison with the United States. Joint Economic Committee of Congress, Washington, 1959.

Baransky, N. N., *Economic Geography of the U.S.S.R.* Foreign Languages Publishing House, Moscow, 1956.

Bibliography   Campbell, R. W., *Soviet Economic Power: Its Organization, Growth and Challenge*. Sweet & Maxwell, 1960.

Cole, J. P., and German, F. C., *A Geography of the U.S.S.R.: The Background to a Planned Economy*. Butterworth, 1961.

Florinsky, M. T. (ed.), *McGraw-Hill Encyclopædia of Russia and the Soviet Union*. McGraw-Hill, 1961.

Hodgkins, J. A., *Soviet Power: Energy, Resources, Production and Potential*. Prentice-Hall, 1961.

Hooson, D. M. J., *A New Soviet Heartland*. Van Nostrand, 1964.

Hunter, H., *Soviet Transportation Policy*. Harvard U.P., 1957.

Khrushchev, N. S., *The Way to Further Economic Progress*. Foreign Languages Publishing House, Moscow, 1957.

Kish, G., *An Economic Atlas of the Soviet Union*. Ann Arbor, 1960.

Kramish, A., *Atomic Energy in the Soviet Union*. Oxford U.P., 1960.

Maksaryov, Y. (ed.), *Technical Progress in the U.S.S.R.* Foreign Languages Publishing House, Moscow, 1960.

Mikhailov, N., *Soviet Geography*. 2nd ed., Methuen, 1937.

Miller, J., and Schesinger, R. J. A. (eds.), *Soviet Studies — A Quarterly Review*. Blackwell, 1949 ff.

Nove, A., *The Soviet Economy: An Introduction*. Allen & Unwin, 1961.

—— and Donnelly, D., *Trade with Communist Countries*. Hutchinson, 1960.

Nutter, G. W., *The Growth of Industrial Production in the Soviet Union*. Princeton, U.P., 1962.

Taaffe, R. N., and Kingsbury, R. C., *An Atlas of Soviet Affairs*. Methuen, 1965.

Williams, E. W., Jr., *Freight Transportation in the Soviet Union*. Princeton U.P., 1962.

Chapter 17   *Economic Survey of Asia and the Far East*. United Nations Economic Commission for Asia and the Far East, New York (annually).

Agarwala, A. N., and Singh, S. P. (eds.), *The Economy of Underdevelopment*. Galaxy Books, Oxford U.P., 1963.

Bhagwati, J., *The Economics of Underdeveloped Countries*. World University Library, Weidenfield & Nicolson, 1966.

Campbell, R. D., *Pakistan: Emerging Democracy*. Van Nostrand, 1963.

Chandrasekhar, S., *American Aid and India's Economic Development*. Pall Mall Press, 1965.

Cowan, C. D., *The Economic Development of China and Japan*. Allen & Unwin, 1964.

Cutshall, A., *The Philippines: Nation of Islands*. Van Nostrand, 1964.

Das-Gupta, A. K., *Planning and Economic Growth*. Allen & Unwin, 1965.

Dobby, E. H. G., *Southeast Asia*. 7th ed., Univ. of London Press, 1960.

——, *Monsoon Asia*. Univ. of London Press, 1961.

Fisher, C. A., *South-East Asia*. 2nd ed., Methuen, 1966.

Hall, D. G. E., *Atlas of South-East Asia*. Macmillan, 1964.

——, *History of South-East Asia*. 2nd ed., Macmillan, 1964.

Hall, R. B., Jr., *Japan: Industrial Power of Asia*. Van Nostrand, 1963.

Schaaf, C. H., and Fiffeld, R. H., *The Lower Mekong: Challenge to Co-operation in Southeast Asia*. Van Nostrand, 1963.

Steel, R. W., and Prothero, R. M. (eds.), *Geographers and the Tropics*. Longmans, 1964.

U.N.E.S.C.O., *A Review of the Resources of the African Continent*. H.M.S.O., 1963.

Allan, W., *The African Husbandman*. Oliver & Boyd, 1965.

Boateng, E., *A Geography of Ghana*. Cambridge U.P., 1959.

Church, H. R. J., *Environment and Policies in Africa*. Van Nostrand, 1963.

Fordham, P., *The Geography of African Affairs*. Penguin, 1965.

Hill, P., *The Migrant Cocoa Farmers of Southern Ghana*. Cambridge U.P., 1964.

Jackson, I. C., *Advance in Africa*. Oxford U.P., 1956.

Kimble, G. H. T., *Tropical Africa*. 2 vols., Doubleday, 1962.

McArthur-Davis, A., *Atlas of Kenya*. Nairobi, 1959.

McIlroy, R. J., *An Introduction to Tropical Grassland Husbandry*. Oxford U.P., 1964.

Ochse, J. J., *et al.*, *Tropical and Sub-Tropical Agriculture*. 2 vols., Macmillan, New York, 1961.

Pedler, F. J., *Economic Geography of West Africa*. Longmans, 1955.

Tempany, Sir H., and Grist, D. H., *Tropical Africa*. Longmans, 1960.

Williamson, G., and Payne, W. J. A., *Animal Husbandry in the Tropics*. Longmans, 1959.

Wills, J. B. (ed.), *Agriculture and Land Use in Ghana*. Oxford U.P., 1962.

Bibliography

Chapter 19

Agrarian Reform in Latin America. Chatham House, 1962.
Brazil, 1960. Ministry of External Relations, Rio de Janeiro, 1960.
Economic Bulletin for Latin America. United Nations (twice yearly).
The Landless Farmer in South America. I.L.O., Geneva, 1957.

Adams, R. N., *et al.*, *Social Change in Latin America Today.* Vintage Books, New York, 1960.
Benham, F., and Holley, H. A., *A Short Introduction to the Economy of Latin America.* Oxford U.P., 1960.
Camacho, J. A., *Brazil: An Interim Assessment.* 2nd ed., Royal Institute of International Affairs, 1954.
Dreier, J. C. (ed.), *The Alliance for Progress: Problems and Perspectives.* Oxford U.P., 1963.
Ganzert, F. W., *et al.*, *Brazil.* Cambridge U.P., 1947.
Gordon, L., *A New Deal for Latin America: The Alliance for Progress.* Oxford U.P., 1963.
James, P. E., *Latin America.* rev. ed., Odyssey Press, New York, 1950.
Paul, G., and Butler, E., *South America.* Van Nostrand, 1960.
Rippy, F. J., *Latin America: A Modern History.* Michigan U.P., 1958.
Schurz, W. L., *Brazil: The Infinite Country.* Robert Hale, 1962.
Wagley, C., *An Introduction to Brazil.* Columbia U.P., 1963.
Worcester, D. E., and Schaeffer, W. G., *The Growth and Culture of Latin America.* Oxford U.P., 1956.

Chapter 20

British Railways Board, *The Reshaping of British Railways* (The Beeching Report). H.M.S.O., 1963.
Future of the Waterways. Interim Report of the British Waterways Board. H.M.S.O., 1964.
Ministry of Transport, *Public Road Passenger Transport in Great Britain, 1961–62.* H.M.S.O., 1963.
Traffic in Towns (The Buchanan Report). H.M.S.O., 1963.
Transport Needs of Great Britain in the Next Twenty Years: report of a group under the chairmanship of Sir Robert Hall. H.M.S.O., 1963.
U.S. Highway Research Board, Bulletin 293: *Urban Transportation Planning.* Washington, 1961.

Ackworth, W. M., *The Railways of England.* 5th ed., Ian Allan, 1963.
Appleton, J. H., *Geography of Communications in Britain.* Oxford U.P., 1962.
Bird, J., *Geography of the Port of London.* Hutchinson, 1957.
——, *The Major Seaports of the United Kingdom.* Hutchinson, 1963.

Calvert, R., *Inland Waterways of Europe*. Allen & Unwin, 1963.
——, *The Future of Britain's Railways*. Allen & Unwin, 1965.
Davies, E. (ed.), *Roads and their Traffic*. Blackie, 1960.
Jackman, W. T., *The Development of Transportation in Modern England*. Frank Cass, 1962.
Milne, A. M., *Economics of Inland Transport*. 2nd ed., Pitman, 1963.
Morgan, F. W., *Ports and Harbours* (rev. Bird, J.). Hutchinson, 1958.
Nock, O. S., *Continental Main Lines: Today and Yesterday*. Allen & Unwin, 1963.
Savage, C. I., *An Economic History of Transport*. 3rd ed., Hutchinson, 1960.
Sealy, K. R., *The Geography of Air Transport*. 2nd ed., Hutchinson, 1966.
Simmons, J., *Transport*. Vista Books, 1962.
Thornton, R. H., *British Shipping*. 2nd ed., Cambridge U.P., 1959.
Westwood, J. N., *Soviet Railways Today*. Ian Allan, 1963.
Williams, J. E. D., *The Operation of Airlines*. Hutchinson, 1964.
Wolfe, R. I., *Transportation and Politics*. Van Nostrand, 1964.

Accounts Relating to the Trade and Navigation of the United Kingdom. H.M.S.O. (annually).
Foreign Commerce Yearbook. Bureau of Foreign and Domestic Commerce, Washington.
Foreign Trade — Monthly Statistics. Statistical Office of the European Communities, Brussels.
International Trade. G.A.T.T., Geneva (annually).
New Directions for World Trade: Proceedings of a Chatham House Conference, Bellagio, September 1963. Oxford U.P., 1964.
Report on Overseas Trade. H.M.S.O. (monthly).

Allen, R. G. D., and Ely, J. E. (eds.), *International Trade Statistics*. Chapman & Hall, 1953.
Maizels, A., *Industrial Growth and World Trade*. Cambridge U.P., 1963.
Pryor, F. L., *The Communist Foreign Trade System*. Allen & Unwin, 1963.
Ullman, E. L., *American Commodity Flow*. Washington U.P., Seattle, 1957.
Woytinsky, W. S. and E. S., *World Commerce and Governments*. Twentieth Century Fund, New York. 1955.

Index

Numbers in heavy type refer to maps or diagrams

Index